A SAILING ODYSSEY

I0336954

NEVER DIE WONDERING II

ALISTAIR MACLEOD

Never Die Wondering II: A Sailing Odyssey
© Alistair Macleod 2024

Copyright ©2024 by Alistair John MacLeod

All rights reserved. No part of this publication may be reproduced, stored in a retrieval system, or transmitted in any form or by any means, electronic, mechanical, photocopying, recording, scanning or otherwise, without the prior written permission of the author.
The events and conversations in this book have been set down to the best of the author's ability, although some names and details have been changed to protect the privacy of individuals. While the author has used his best efforts in preparing this book, the advice and strategies contained herein may not be suitable for your situation. You should consult with a professional when appropriate. Neither the publisher nor the author shall be liable for any loss of profit or any other commercial damages, including but not limited to special, incidental, consequential, personal, or other.

ISBN: 978-0-6488065-3-0 (paperback)
        978-0-6488065-2-3 (eBook)

 A catalogue record for this book is available from the National Library of Australia

Published by Alistair Macleod and assisted by Ocean Reeve Publishing

This book is dedicated to my late mother, Edna MacLeod, for encouraging me to live my dreams, pursue an adventurous life, and to never conform to people's expectations of me.

Contents

CHAPTER ONE   1

    Introduction – From Hobble Chains to an Anchor Chain   1

    Western Port Bay   2

    Papua New Guinea – Expect the Unexpected   3

    The Highlands – Where Time Stood Still   6

    Asaro Mudmen – The Ghosts of Papua New Guinea   10

CHAPTER TWO   13

    Highlands to the Coast   13

    The Bismarck Sea Coastal Region   15

    Island of Kranket   16

    Manam Island Volcano   18

CHAPTER THREE   23

    Sepik River   23

    Out Post Angoram   26

    Islands of the Bismarck Sea   30

    The Sheiling   32

    India to Kathmandu   34

    Son of a Highlander   36

    Mekong River   38

    Crowther – SV Never Die Wondering   40

CHAPTER FOUR	**43**
Bass Strait	43
Twofold Bay	47
Old Tom the Whale	48
The Tasman Sea	49
Jervis Bay	51
CHAPTER FIVE	**54**
Shoalhaven River	54
Surfing to Port Hacking	55
Broken Bay	56
Fog and Shipping Containers	57
CHAPTER SIX	**61**
Yamba	61
The Coral Coast	64
Burial Site of Donald	65
Great Sandy Straits	68
The Sailing Ship Renfrewshire – Bundaberg	71
The Voyage of the Renfrewshire	71
Life at Sea	73
CHAPTER SEVEN	**76**
Town 1770	76
Pancake Creek	78
The Narrows	80
Percy Islands	81
Eulogy to My Mother	84
CHAPTER EIGHT	**89**
Whitsundays	89
Magnetic Island	92
Hinchinbrook Island	94

Contents

CHAPTER NINE — 99
- East Coast Cape York — 99
- Epic Captain Bligh's Survival — 102
- The Tip of Australia — 106
- West Cape York — 108

CHAPTER TEN — 111
- Restless — 111
- Paradise of the West Cape — 114
- Horn Island — 119
- Stranded in Cape York Paradise — 121
- VOYAGE — 126

CHAPTER ELEVEN — 139
- Torres Straits to Cairns — 139
- Head Hunters of the North — 141
- *Lagoon 410 SV Never Die Wondering II* — 146

CHAPTER TWELVE — 149
- Legal Pirates of the Sea — 149
- Voyage Back to the Torres Straits — 155
- Marooned Cabin Boy — 160

CHAPTER THIRTEEN — 164
- Crossing the Gulf of Carpentaria — 164
- Sailing Through the Hole in the Wall — 168
- Sailing Across the Top — 170
- Wet Season in Top End — 176
- An Old Salty Legend — 177

CHAPTER FOURTEEN — 179
- Crossing the Arafura Sea — 179
- Islands of Tual, Indonesia — 183
- Hazards of Coral Reefs — 187

CHAPTER FIFTEEN — 191
- The Spice Islands — 191
- Streets of Banda Neira — 193

CHAPTER SIXTEEN — 203
- Ambon to West Papua — 203
- The Moluccas Archipelago — 207
- West Papua — 212

CHAPTER SEVENTEEN — 216
- Sorong to the Philippines — 216
- Near Disaster on a Coral Reef — 219
- The Jewel of Raja Ampat — 223

CHAPTER EIGHTEEN — 228
- Islands of the Volcanoes — 228
- Crossing the Molucca Sea — 233
- Pirate Waters — 235

CHAPTER NINETEEN — 239
- Smashing Windward — 239
- Samal Island — 241
- Surf Coast of Mindanao — 244
- Enchanted River — 247
- Siargao Island — 249

CHAPTER TWENTY — 252
- Port Carmen — 252
- The Island of Giants – Islas de Gigantes — 254
- The South China Sea — 258

***If by* Rudyard Kipling** — 261
INSPIRING QUOTES FROM MY LIFE AT SEA — 263

CHAPTER ONE

Twenty years from now you will be more disappointed by the things that you didn't do than by the ones you did, so throw off the bowlines, sail away from the safe harbor, catch the trade wind in your sails, explore, dream, discover.

Mark Twain

Introduction – From Hobble Chains to an Anchor Chain

At present, I'm sitting on my yacht, *Never Die Wondering II*, in an estuary at Darwin, Northern Territory, Australia. It's the end of the wet season whereby late afternoon storm clouds bring the monsoonal rains, and lightning from the south creates a spectacular skyline, with the thunderous cracks echoing over vast distances. I'm now starting to write my third book, my memoirs since writing my first book, *Never Die Wondering*, published in 2009.

How my life has changed since then! Most of my life was spent in remote regions of Australia. For nearly twenty years, I had spent my life in the Snowy Mountains, following my dreams of developing cattle grazing properties, a timber mill, and developing and operating an adventure horse-trekking business. I lived and breathed the High Country.

Horses were my greatest passion. Exploring the mountains on horseback and leading a pack horse with one of my horses, Redgum—a palomino mare. She had taken me an estimated 5,000 km throughout the Alpine region. My world was far away from where I live now—on a yacht a 41-foot *Lagoon* catamaran, exploring unique and wonderful places by sea. Now, there are similarities to the lifestyle. The sense of freedom that you have when climbing up into the mountain ranges, you have a similar feeling when the power of wind is in your sails, taking you to your next destination. In the past, there was the smell of the peppermint eucalyptus trees at 1,100 meters above sea level when you climbed up into the mountain ranges carried by your horse. Now, there is the smell of the salt air which is powering you across the sea. There was horse tack gear like stirrup straps, reins, cruppers, and breast plates, while now there are halyards, sheets, etc. In the past, at night I would sit around the campfire, I would hobble my horses and rest comfortably in my swag while hearing the hobble chains peacefully making a clinking sound as the horses were content and not alarmed by Brumby stallions (wild horses). Now, it's the anchor chain, and I am comfortably resting in my cabin in calm weather, knowing that the anchor chain is sound and not dragging the anchor.

More importunately, the excitement is similar. Then, I planned a long pack horse adventure into the mountains to explore new areas where past inhabitants had left their mark by either a bush hut or a mountain trail. In contrast, now, I'm planning to sail into Indonesian waters and explore the likes of the Spice Islands where folklores tell stories of early sailors that could smell the aroma of the nutmeg miles offshore, where the spice was more valuable than gold by weight, and other exciting tales where fortunes favoured the bold.

I'm not really sure what was the main reason to take up sailing full time, it may have been the drought of 2006 where my 1,000-acre property ran out of water. The domestic tank and dam, as well as, the creek stopped flowing, and there was no feed (grass) so, I was forced to sell my entire 300 head of cattle. Therefore, this wanting to get close to the water, or maybe, I really needed to substitute the freedom I did have, not just owning the 1,000-acre freehold since it joined the 1.5 million acres of national estate creating a backyard where horseback riding and exploring was endless. That is why, sailing is the last real bastion of freedom where the water does more than connect all the continents on earth. Sailing enables one to explore exotic places by the power of the wind.

Western Port Bay

My son, Brandon, and I moved to Somers on western Port Bay, southeast of Melbourne in 2007. We rented a small, two-storey cottage, Brandon

CHAPTER ONE

attended high school, while I subdivided and marketed the properties in the Snowy Mountains along with other holdings I acquired in Victoria. Here, I started writing my memoir, *Never Die Wondering*, the bay was an incredibly inspiring place to write. After my morning walks, I would sit and look out onto Bass strait, smelling the sea, thinking of continuing my adventurous life, but this time, with the possibility of sailing. Unfortunately, staying here was short-lived as my mother had a major stroke, so Brandon and I moved to Melbourne to be closer to her in her time of need. In 2008, we decided to explore what many describe as the last frontier.

Papua New Guinea – Expect the Unexpected

Papua New Guinea (PNG) is a place I have always wanted to visit. It has been a place of intrigue for me ever since I heard the story of the two Australians who in search of gold cut their way through the jungles and climbed up into the cloud-covered mountains of the unexplored highlands, discovering unknown tribes believed to be an unknown population of a million people closed off from the rest of the world until then.

PNG has 800 distinct tribes with 800 language groups, ancient cultures with stories of tribal wars and cannibalism. It is a tropical island country with lush rainforests to high mountain ranges snow-capped at 4,884 metres. Compared to Australia's highest peak of 2,228 meters, it's more than twice the height. A country of which many parts are still unexplored, and many species of wildlife that are yet to be identified, a place where time has stood still.

In January 2009, my son, Brandon who had only just turned fourteen years of age, and I, flew into Port Moresby, the capital. Our plan was to work our way up into the Highlands, then down onto the coastal regions, and then travel along the mighty Sepik River in the far north. I had arranged that to eventually work our way to New Ireland in the Bismarck Sea, and from there, spend time sailing and exploring a little of the archipelago. We would eventually travel by several planes, two four-wheel-drive vehicles, twice riding on the back of trucks, several boats, dugout canoes, and finally, make it to New Ireland to sail on a catamaran. Along the way, we would meet tribal people from the

Highlands, and coastal tribes, to the Puk Puk (crocodile) people of the mighty Sepik River, and islanders of the archipelagos of New Ireland.

Discovering for ourselves this unique island of which many travellers have described as the last frontier, a natural paradise of 800 different tribes and ancient cultures. We travelled with a backpack each, waterproof jackets, mozzie netting, a methylated *Trangia* stove for cooking, a pocket size camera and a cam recorder.

The wet season was truly in full form with constant rainfall. Our first experience of accommodation at Port Moresby was a room with only a fan for cooling from the stifling humidity of the wet season. The accommodation was referred to as a compound, which was only a few rooms and guarded by security men, the perimeter had high walls topped with razor-sharp wire. I had just been drilled (questioned) by the PNG authorities when we arrived at the airport, regarding my travels. They continued to explain how dangerous their country was with *raskols* (criminal gangs) operating throughout the region, both on roads and the sea. I remembered reading literature on this that clearly stated if I was in a car that ran over someone then I should never stop to assist, for if I did, I could be killed in retribution.

To get a look at the city safely, we hired a taxi to drive us around. The place was now etched into my mind as the 'Murder Capital' due to a local headline in a paper. Our driver proudly told us that he had been a soldier and had fought in the Bougainville Civil War (1988-98), and with enthusiasm explained how he had personally killed six people during the war. Bougainville island lies in the east of PNG where a civil war had occurred that lasted ten years, ending in 1998. It is believed that the local Bougainville landowners opposed the mining of copper and gold in Panguna, as it imported mainlander Papuans to work there, and with 20% of the company owned by the PNG government, the locals believed that they were missing out on their own resources. As a result, a bloody civil war occurred and in total, the conflict claimed the lives of up to 20,000 people.

The driver showed us the water village where thousands of people lived on huts built on stilts out on the water. We were dropped off at the Boroko market next, and what a colourful place it was. Hundreds of people were there, mostly sitting on the ground, with all sorts of produce for sale, coconuts, bananas, sugar cane sticks, wads of tobacco and betel nut. Many other vegetables and fruits were on display of which I had no idea what they were. The sellers would be sitting in muddy wet conditions, some held an umbrella up while the rain soaked the surrounds, a newspaper stand with the papers laid out on a table, under a small iron roof for some protection from the rain. The headlines of *Post-Courier Highlands* read, 'Girl tied, burnt to death…killing barbaric, says Highland police chief'. Another paper, *The National*, had the headline, 'Murder Capital Port Moresby listed among the world's worse'.

As we were reading the headlines, commotion and yelling amongst the people started close by. We could see the police officers with shotguns arresting a person at gun point and kicking this person while directing him into the police wagon for what we believe was an attempted robbery. At that moment, I was thinking to myself, *Have I made the right decision to travel across PNG with my 14-year-old son? If this is the situation in the capital that has some sort of law and order, what about where we are planning to venture—regions where there is ancient tribal law, only it will most likely be with no law and order at all? We were the only white people at the market so we will be most likely be the only foreigners in the wild remote regions we are planning on visiting.*

A few years later, Port Moresby police were accused of arresting thirty people and walking them towards the police station, forcing them to lay on the ground whereby the police produced bush knives, and the officers chopped all the men's tendons.

One of the first things one notices throughout PNG in town situations, are the red-stained footpaths everywhere. Quickly, one becomes accustomed to the habitual betel-nut chewing. It seems most locals chew betel-nut, it gives them a slight high, and I have been told, it can assist in reducing hunger. The procedure is that the nut itself is broken open and the internal nut mixed with a mustard stick dipped in lime powder, this is chewed. It is known as *buai* which after chewing a while makes this concoction that stains their mouths red. Then, they spit out the red juice, hence, why there is red everywhere you walk that is not very pleasant to say the least.

While walking through the markets, an elderly gentlemen walked up to me speaking a little English. He was wearing a Victorian police shirt proudly showing me the Vic police badge on the shoulder. He had another type of identification around his neck, but I could not figure out if he was some sort of authority in the market.

Back at our accommodation (compound), we were joined at dinner by Raymond, a proud and friendly Highlander who was in Port Moresby for business. He was also running for a seat in the upcoming elections. Every election season in the Highlands, mayhem starts in the mountain region with tribal warring resulting in many deaths. Either by spears, bow and arrows, and now firearms, mostly shotguns. Recently, several deaths had occurred in the region I wanted to explore, and Raymond insisted on joining Brandon and I, to show us his country. He was flying back to the region anyway but changed a flight to Goroka with us, and I planned to hire a 4x4 vehicle to explore the region.

We caught an *Air New Guinea* twin engine plane into the Highlands, while flying up into this mountainous and partly cloud-covered region, I would think of the story of the Australian Lae brothers in the 1930s. Hacking their way through dense jungle for many weeks and climbing up into the high altitude on the quest to find gold, and discovering another nation, inhabited by over a million people, where time had stood still for tens of thousands of years. Primitive people who held onto their ancient customs and beliefs and who participated in cannibalism.

The Highlands – Where Time Stood Still

In the matter of an hour, in the comfort of a plane we landed at Goroka, the township in the capital of the Eastern Highlands Province of PNG with a population of 19,000 people. It is 1,600 meters above sea level. The PNG Island has a population of seven million people, more than 800 languages from the 800 distinct tribes, and most of the people lived a semi-subsistence lifestyle.

Being in the Highlands is like stepping back into time, with many highland tribes bringing their produce, fruit and vegetables to sell at the local market, along with artifacts like stone axes, head dresses adorned with Cassowary feathers, and the feathers of the unique Birds of Paradise. Woven baskets and bilum bags. Bilum bags are a woven bag that is carried by all tribes throughout PNG. Two elderly gentlemen with Cassowary and Bird of Paradise head dresses, started playing a bamboo flute, blowing through a hole at one end and placing a hand over the other end creating a fantastic musical sound. Another person produced a large fossil, a very heavy specimen of a sea creature. I would have liked to purchase it, but it would have been too heavy to cart around in our backpacks. Brandon was given a cane knife for free, the seller, the same person who had the fossil, refused money for it. There were bows and arrows, and spears for sale, full-face Asaro

CHAPTER ONE

Mudmen masks and even Boar jaws with large protruding tasks that many tribes use for jewellery.

I hired a 4x4 vehicle and Raymond showed us around the township, some parts of which I would describe as a ghetto. At one point, the air was thick with marijuana smoke and Raymond quickly asked us to get back into the car and drive away, as a few undesirables were gathering around us. Raymond was a very interesting and knowledgeable person who showed a great understanding of his country, he talked about the huge social problems of tribal warring and the country not going forward as a nation. He explained the *wantok* system which in the island's creole language called Tok Pisin (meaning one talk) referred to a social system whereby people are related to each other by a common language, ethnicity, and tribal boundaries. The system promotes favours between kin and community members. In a tribal based society, everything evolves around the relative welfare of the tribe and clan members as a whole, creating face to face relationships where intermarriage, kinship, and reciprocal exchange are paramount in creating strong ties to keep the tribes together.

We travelled into a valley that was once a cattle station developed by the Australian primary industries, all of which stopped once PNG became independent in 1975. As a result, the Australian government and private businesses pulled out of PNG, and one got the feeling that the entire country had gone back to tribal ways. Travelling through this scenic valley, we would stop at markets and eat the local produce of nuts and corn, etc. We visited a couple, Oliver and Nic, who had escaped tribal war where they had been living further into the mountains where many people they knew were murdered. They now lived on a ridge overlooking the once thriving cattle station of the primary industries.

"Adventure may hurt you, but monotony will kill you".

Oliver and Nic had a large vegetable garden and showed us all the produce they grew. It is believed that the Papuans maybe the oldest agriculturists on earth where their ancestral lineage can stretch back as far as 40,000 years. Oliver and Nic cooked us bananas and yams (potatoes) in the coals of their fire under a large thatched-roof hut that was made from Kuni grass which grew plentiful. Although PNG is an extremely violent country, I was to discover that they were also some of the friendliest people I have ever met, and I found that welcoming friendly nature throughout the entire county.

Raymond lived in the mountains near Kundiawa in the Simbu Province of west Highlands, an incredible drive from Goroka up into the mountain region passing many villages along the way. Daulo Pass has the most magnificent views looking 360 degrees around the valley of Goroka, from there one can look down to the countless huts with smoke billowing through the thatched roofs. At one of our stops, the village children appeared with an assortment of flower arrangements, either on long sticks or head bands made of bamboo and neatly threaded with a variety of colourful flowers. Obliged to buy, Brandon placed his purchase around his head, Raymond too placed his flower arrangement on his head as a head band. Raymond had an infectious laugh and when he started to laugh at himself with this flowery head dress, we all broke out in laughter along with the several children at his new attire.

Further along the rough road, the laughter quickly disappeared, and fear became the emotion of the moment, when we were stopped by armed men in some sort of police uniforms. Some of them were brandishing shotguns, all had police shirts with police badges and the flag of PNG on the front of their shirt. Some of them wore shredded banana-leaf hats, another a camouflage bandana, while some were barefoot. At this stage, I was not certain if they were police or *raskols*. They demanded our identification in a very aggressive manner, and I quickly produced my Australian driver's license. They were yelling at me and speaking in pidgin English which I could not understand. Finally, Raymond started speaking pidgin and they quickly changed their whole attitude. They immediately became friendly and seemed to apologise to Raymond whom they seemed to know or know of him. It then turned to be a friendly introduction followed by a photo shoot, with them proudly brandishing their guns for the photo. After that, we were quickly off again. During my travels through PNG, it became paramount that a known notable guide is a must. I wonder what would have happened if Raymond wasn't with us.

Raymond would point out the peaks of the mountain's valleys and rivers. The views along the road were spectacular. Mount Wilhelm was the highest mountain to the north of our travels and stood at 15,000 feet, twice the size of our Mount Kosciuszko. Many other spectacular mountain peaks were there that could be snow covered at times, incredible high altitude tropical zones where bananas grow. After spending twenty years in the High Country of Australia, living at a third of the altitude from where we were in now, I found this part of the world surreal.

CHAPTER ONE

We came onto a large river which Raymond called Warra Simba, *warra* meaning river. Children were swimming in the fast-flowing river with many people yelling out 'Whittie, Whittie!' as they noticed Brandon and me. Raymond became offended about this, but I wasn't bothered at all, it was not in any way disrespectful. In fact, we were white people and most of the places we were about to explore had rarely seen a white person since independence.

We asked Raymond about the practise of cannibalism as the Highlands of PNG were notorious for the eating of human flesh. Raymond explained when he was young, he had witnessed his father and grandfather cook and consume an entire person after he was killed in a tribal dispute. He told us how they even ate his shoes at which Brandon looked at me horrified while Raymond laughed. He explained that himself couldn't understand how they could or even why they ate the shoes, he added it was believed that eating the enemy gave them power and strength.

Raymond's wife and stepdaughter were there to meet him at Kundiawa. We had decided that with tribal conflict heating up due to the elections, it was a better idea to return to Goroka. As a part of our goodbyes, a prayer was given by Raymond for our safe travels.

We returned on the rough track and many kilometres later, while climbing up a rut in the road, the wheels of our vehicle started spinning. At that moment, two men brandishing an axe, and a machete showed up yelling at me excitedly, and running towards us. Due to the rut in the road driving up the hill, the wheels on one side fell into the deep pothole and I was not able to drive away. I found myself looking straight at these gentlemen holding an axe and a machete. My fear of a potential attack was quickly reduced, as these gentlemen were very friendly and just wanted to meet us. Another quick and difficult chat followed, as they only knew a little English while Brandon and I were quickly picking up a few pidgin English words.

Later, driving along, a magnificent mountainous peak on the southern side of the road could be seen and we were told it was called Anabelie. Many little huts were built on ridges with old men walking along the road with their pet pigs. A women stopped to talk to us while walking with her children and a baby suckling on her breast. Nearly all the people we passed would wave or want to stop and meet us. We stayed at the Bird of paradise hotel Goroka and somehow it didn't feel right, for we were the only people staying there that night. We had the pool to ourselves and several people catering for our needs while just outside this hotel compound over the barbed-wire fence, people lived a semi-subsistence life.

Asaro Mudmen – The Ghosts of Papua New Guinea

I wanted to meet the Asaro Mudmen, a tribe known throughout the Highlands as fierce warriors. Legend said that during a tribal conflict, the Asaro were outnumbered and were pushed into the shelter of a hill where a whitish wet clay fell from the walls covering the warriors. When they emerged from the side of the hill, the enemy fled thinking they were spirits, since sorcery and old ancient customs were prevalent. They continue with tribal laws and are still being practised.

I had arranged a guide who was a friend of some of the Asaro Mudmen. John had been working around the Highlands for quite some time. He drove our hired 4x4 vehicle and explained the dangers in some villages, how if we hit a pig, they would wait for our return and stop us. If we were unable to pay compensation, then we could be killed or raped. I got the first part, but the second part, rape, really was quite alarming. This was why I let John drive the car, after all, he was supposedly a friend of the tribe.

Most of the Asaro people live a primitive existence not far from Goroka, the population of the Asaro is believed to be 30,000 or more. We drove into a small village and left the car outside before following John who guided us to his friends' huts crossing vegetable gardens and wet gullies. We met Michael there; he was the son of the chief who had recently died, and his uncle had taken over the chieftain role. Michael could speak English and was a tall, extremely fit person. The other two Asaro Mudmen we met were Mathew and Cody who spoke little English. The Asaro speak a Dano dialect, part of the Kainantu Goroka language family.

Michael produced his bows and arrows and showed Brandon and I, how they fired the arrows at an enemy, then pulled the arrow out with its large arrowhead ensuring death to the enemy. They also discussed how in tribal wars the winner would obtain pigs and women from the spoils. I spent a considerable time being taught the use of the bow; their accuracy was outstanding.

Asaro homes were bamboo woven walls with Kuni grass thatched roofs. In the centre of the room was a fire hearth for cooking and

CHAPTER ONE

warmth, the smoke escaping through the thatched roof. I thought of my own ancestry as a MacLeod. My people had huts known as black houses with stone walls, a fire hearth on the floor, with the smoke escaping similarly through the thatched roof, hence, the black house name; really, no difference at all.

They showed us with pride their garden with a variety of vegetables, they even had coffee beans. Mathew cut down a bamboo pole and they all began to prepare a meal. They wrapped the chicken in banana leaves, and a mix of leafy vegetables from the garden, then placed them within the bamboo with both ends blocked up with a leafy type of plant, then placed it over the fire.

Michael's wife and baby along with many other Asaro people, all sat around the fire inside the hut. We also had the company of their pet dogs. The hut was a dirt floor and the family's Asaro mud masks were visible along the wall besides the bow and arrows. Their beds were a hessian type stretched by bamboo poles. Cody and Mathew left the hut only to return a short time later covered in the whitish mud and wearing their own distinctive Asaro Mudmen masks, a large clay type of helmet that covered their entire head and rested on their shoulders.

Asaro are also called Holosa translated meaning ghost, Incredibly, all the Mudmen have their own design of a ghoulish face with some having protruding pig tusks. They both were brandishing bow and arrows and pulling on the bow strings to create a thud-like sound as they came into the hut from the rain outside. I could just imagine thousands of such warriors attacking their enemy with their fierce-looking ghoulish image, no wonder the Asaro are feared.

Every year, nearby in Goroka, a hundred tribes from all over the Highlands gather for a 'Sing-Sing' event adorned in all their tribal head dresses. This is where the Asaro and other tribes come together without tribal warring. This event is regarded as the biggest mass tribal gathering in the world.

The meal cooked in the bamboo was tasty and steamed since it acted as a cooker, along with yams and bananas from the coals of the fire. Brandon commented about the dog as it looked hungry and I was reminded of what Raymond had explained at Kundiawa, 'How can we feed dogs when we find it difficult to feed ourselves?' There were a lot of pigs in the Asaro camp but rarely eaten since they were held for only special occasions. The Highlanders have been described as grass eaters, mostly vegetarian though they eat chicken when available.

Soon, elderly men came into Michael's camp with a variety of bows and arrows to show us. Still today, tribal conflict occurs whereby people are killed by bow and arrows. Unfortunately, shot guns were increasingly becoming the weapon of choice. We were told by the Asaro how many church organisations had come to their country with the promise of help, however, they had never received any help whatsoever. 'Not even a bar of soap,' Michael explained. They offered to show us around and we all climbed into the vehicle tray and went into areas where the church organisations were. Large fencers and buildings with new vehicles were there, and they all swore that they had been there for years though no assistance had been received of what was promised. It was along this track that we saw the largest spider web imaginable, it covered the entire track, you could park a bus inside it! The jungle has its little natural treasures.

Michael stated to me, 'We don't think you're a city person Al, you seem like us: a bushman? City persons don't seem to like our way of life.' I accepted this statement as a compliment and explained to them that I had lived most of my life in the bush with twenty years in the Snowy Mountains, not to mention living in a swag on the ground for three years while travelling. Michael then said, 'I knew you were like us.'

We then visited a rugby game, the muddiest situation imaginable, hard to tell which side was who since they all were covered in thick mud sliding from one end of the oval to the other. There would have been a couple of thousand people watching. A peace park was pointed out to us, and John explained that it was the area where tribal disputes were settled, sometimes with death.

Cody, at this point, requested that he would come travelling with Brandon and I to Madang on the coast to protect us. When I explained after thanking him that we would be alright, it seemed I really hurt his feelings as he really wanted to come along. We all said our goodbyes at last, and Brandon and I headed to the coast to Madang on the Bismark Sea by ourselves, no guide.

CHAPTER TWO

Fill your life with adventures, not things, have stories to tell, not stuff to show.

Highlands to the Coast

We arranged to drive by ourselves from the Highlands along the notorious road and drop the 4x4 off at Madang on the coast. Of late, no *raskols* had been heard committing highway robbery. There was no signage whatsoever along the way, so now and then we had to ask the locals. 'Madang, Madang?' we would say, and they would point us in the right direction.

We stayed in the hotel compound at Kainantu. *Kainantu Hotel* had seen better days, it had holes in floorboards and had the look of unkempt for quite some time, but the hospitality was great. It had a good bar and meals. Many locals wanted to talk with us, and at one stage the hospitality of Kainantu extended to the offer of a wife! I declined the offer, but this was to happen several times throughout our travel in PNG.

Driving through townships, there were large billboards everywhere with signs stating in pidgin English:

BOBI BILONG YU EM HAUS HOLI BILONG MI LUKAUTIM GUT LUKAUT LOU SIK AIDS

It was a warning to people about the dangers of Aids.

The road became increasingly worse and sometimes I had to get Brandon to stand outside the car and guide me over the gutters and ruts. We left the open valleys of the Highlands, and then drove down into the lush rainforest. The highway was in a terrible state, however, and at some places the vehicle had to crawl along due to the extensive potholes.

At one point, there were large boulders on the road with a diversion directing us to the left of the road. We were now heading along a narrow cutting with a sheer cliff drop to the side when suddenly, we came upon a truck parked on the steep side with the narrowest of margins for us to pass. As we slowly drove past the truck, a man appeared carrying a firearm strapped on his shoulder. I immediately thought the worse (*raskols*) but to our relief, we quickly realised that he was just an armed person protecting the broken-down truck as others were working on it. The frightening thought of just how easy it was to be attacked jarred me. Several years after we visited the Highlands, the news of about thirty women and nine children massacred as payback killing from warring clans, after an elderly mother of a tribal leader was killed during a raid, very disturbing event to say the least.

Along the way, we stopped to admire a large reservoir built prior to independence for irrigation downstream. There was a young boy at a guess around ten years old, carrying a bamboo fishing pole and some fish that he had caught in a basket which was strapped over his shoulder. We asked what the fish was called but he produced a knife and held it at us instead. We were not sure if he was afraid of us, but we made sure we didn't get any closer to him and travelled on.

In some places, the road became partly tar, but I found this more dangerous as there were enormous potholes now and then, with one hole in the middle of the road being more than four meters deep. We drove down into the Ramu valley, a fertile region where large scale palm oil plantations are grown. The Ramu river itself is spectacular and one of PNG's longest rivers at 720 km long, starting in the Highlands and flowing into the Bismarck Sea, where we were heading.

Along the way, entrepreneurial people had created their own fuel stations, these consisted of a forty-four-gallon drum and several five litre plastic containers on top of the drum. They would sell you petrol by the five-litre container if needed. The road was a hive of activity with people carrying their freshly caught fish. Villages were sometimes positioned with several huts on a ridge top with the others built close to the road. There were always people selling their produce, it was like a market after every few kilometres. We stopped by a riverbank for lunch, had the *Trangia* methyl stove out to brew some tea, Soon, we were approached by a person who lived close by, we offered him a cuppa and then before we knew it, his entire family was there. There was a dozen or more of them. They explained that they had returned from hunting Birds of Paradise and Cassowary since they eat the birds and make head dresses of the feathers to sell.

The Bismarck Sea Coastal Region

We arrived in Madang on the Bismarck Sea. This part of PNG was once ruled by Germany between 1886 – 1913 that finished during WW1. It was a great feeling to now be on the coast, and Madang was a picturesque town, the Highlands type vegetable produce markets had now been replaced with sea fish of all types and sizes. You could buy whole alive or dead fish, or in some cases, purchase cooked fish grilled over wire mesh on an open fire.

I had read in my *Lonely Planet* book that a small village on the water still carved large sea going canoes with outriggers. We went in search of these ancient craft along the way and found a local feller keen to take us to the said village. We couldn't cross the two-log bridge with the vehicle, so we walked into the village that was built right up to the high tide mark. To my surprise, there were dingoes loitering all over the village.

I have seen countless dingoes from the High Country to the outback of Australia. These were New Guinea singing dogs related to the Australian dingo. It is believed that the wild dog came to Australia 8,000 years ago, when Australia and New Guinea were joined before the sea rise, and the proof lies with the dogs here.

As for the long canoes, unfortunately, we were told that they have not built any large canoes for many years. Hence, we returned to Madang to drop off the 4WD vehicle, and our temporary guide requested us to be taken to the hospital since his wife had nearly died with a busted spleen. When I asked how it had happened, his reply was shocking to say the least.

"I hit her…I hit her, I am sorry now…I am sorry now," he explained.

Brandon looked at me horrified. Unfortunately, this wasn't going to be our last experiences of violent ways throughout PNG.

In Madang, we decided to get supplies as we had arranged to visit Kranket Island. Brandon was staying too long in the store for my liking. When he finally came out, I asked, "What did you buy in there?"

"Nothing," he replied.

I was not convinced, and he then showed me a knife, a flick type of blade that, he had bought for protection. I explained, "Brandon, if we get rolled and *raskols* get hold of that we could be killed, and by your own knife! We are better off in a foreign country to just lose all the possessions we have." We argued for a while and finally, I placed my son's new weapon down in my backpack.

Within minutes, we were walking pass a lane of sorts when several men, Highlanders who have a distinctive look, gathered around us. They were all talking to us, then became too close for comfort, and before I knew it, they were holding us. We were being mugged with one feller reaching his hand into my pocket. The others were trying to get into our backpacks. Brandon and I were pinned due to the backpacks and I could feel this feller's hand in my hip pocket, but that pocket was empty because my wallet was in a lower pocket of my trousers.

I somehow managed to grab most of his fingers in one hand while holding onto his wrist with the other. We all were now yelling at one another. I quickly was able to bend the feller's fingers back, and to my surprise, several of his fingers snapped as I deliberately bend them backwards. He was now screaming, and I was yelling at his face.

Brandon was yelling, "Dad, Dad!"

All the *raskols* started pulling away from us. The vendors in the market had heard the commotion of yelling and they came to our aid carrying machetes and clubs of wood. Brandon and I quickly walked away towards the jetty as there were many people chasing after the *raskols*.

Over the years. Brandon would often ask me what really happened to those muggers. I think, possibly, they were brutally punished by the mob of vendors if not fatally.

Island of Kranket

Kranket Island lies a short banana boat ride from Madang. It's a beautiful coral island with several lagoons within the island itself, that fill with water at every high tide. Many of the locals live a semi subsistence lifestyle, surviving on their vegetable gardens and fish caught form the nearby reefs. A traditional owner had given us the use of a hut, that was built on a tiny peninsula where, if you took a few steps on both sides of the hut, and you would be standing at the water's edge.

The hut was a great spot to spend a few days. It had a basic one room with a couple of beds – all we needed. It had no fan but relied

CHAPTER TWO

on a breeze off the water for some reprieve of the monsoonal heat. The island was well-inhabited with many families and large vegetable gardens. Many parts had waterways crossing them, passable through makeshift bridges of coconut tree logs placed in twos or threes as a walking bridge. The island was fairly treed with coconut and other palm type trees.

We had our mozzie nets over us at night and Brandon would say, "Dad, Dad, are you awake? These mozzies are huge!" Thank God, we had the mozzie nets but still, it was very difficult sleeping with the monstrous mosquitos buzzing around your head all night, along with the extreme humid heat and no breeze whatsoever.

We met a couple, David and Imelda, who had been living on the island for some time. David was a Sepik River man, and Imelda was a policeman's daughter from the Highlands. We spent a great deal of time fishing with them out on small reefs just a close swim away from the hut we were staying in, spearing many reef fish and cooking them whole in the coals of the open fire.

A local young feller quickly ran up a coconut tree, to retrieve coconuts for us along with getting some dry dead timber for the fire after rain. Brandon nearly spent a whole day in the water, so I asked Imelda how often sharks were seen. She explained that no shark had been seen for a while since the large saltwater crocodile moved in!

Fish were plentiful on these small reefs, but sadly, plastic bags were littered throughout the reef growing around the coral as a tangled plastic mess. While we were on the island, the local boys were being initiated by the so-called doctor. The doctor greeted us with a shake of hands and I noticed that they were bloody. He was performing circumcisions with a razor, and over the week, every boy would be circumcised for initiation. All the boys would wear a red band on their arm once initiated, we met a lot of them while they would climb trees for coconuts.

Brandon and I were forbidden to enter some spots of the island due to customary beliefs. I found it sensible to ask all questions and obtain permission before hand, as breaking tribal law could result in a lot more than offending someone.

This part of the world is close to the equator so only small tides appeared. Like all islands, the locals build dugout canoes with, outriggers for the swells of the Bismarck Sea. They would paddle out with traditional built paddles to the reefs and spend ages fishing these reefs to supplement fish with their vegetable and coconut diets.

We next planned to explore the mighty Sepik River. Our destination was Angoram which was a day's boat ride up-stream. We had to negotiate with the Watam tribe, a friendly coastal tribe that lived on the junction of the Sepik River and who would, for a fee, guide us by one of their boats up the mighty river. However, to get to the isolated Watam tribe, there was no road or air strip. So, we now had to find a trader boat at a tiny village at the end of the only track leading north, and that was going to be two trips riding in the back of a truck to reach a potential boat that could take us to the Watam tribe. On the way, we planned to visit an active volcano too.

Manam Island Volcano

Bogia is another coastal village north of Madang and about half a day's trip riding on the back of a truck. Before we left, Kranket islanders warned us to be careful as a fight had just happened with several people being killed. We were also informed that compensation had been paid so things should have calmed down. Apparently, Bogia village is on the mainland just off the live volcano of Manam Island that erupted in 1994. The islanders from Manam escaped to safety on Bogia, but only a few returned afterwards with the majority still staying at Bogia.

We obtained a lift from the only transport to Bogia, a truck. We rode in the back with the locals, along the way picking up more people at nearly every community. Within a short time, the truck was packed with people and all their belongings. At one community, several women were at the so-called truck stop and all of them were carrying several cooking pots on their heads each, well-balanced with only a head scarf for padding. Riding in the truck, you could see the mighty Manam Island with its still active volcano producing small amounts of smoke. It was a spectacular sight of the blue sea, steep pyramid volcano with a large cloud covering the top section, and the peak of the volcano breaking through the cloud while releasing puffs of smoke.

As we arrived in Bogia, there was a burial taking place near the road as we passed. They were lowering a body wrapped in a sheet into the grave by ropes. On the opposite side, there were the charcoal remains of several huts that had recently been burnt. We decided it to be in our best interest to not ask about the killing and the burial along with the burnt huts, since we were staying with the Manam islanders

CHAPTER TWO

on Bogia ground. We were to meet Charles who managed the accommodation at Bogia and the meals area. He gave us a room in the large Bogia building. This had an area where meals were cooked, and a large grass lawn out front, which during the night became the local cinema, a place where the local children would get to watch a movie.

The accommodation was built along the side of all the traditional homes along the coastal waterfront. I walked along meeting many of the community. Andrew Wannie who worked at the accommodation, was a Sepik River man, and this was the first time I would see the Puk Puk markings. It meant crocodile markings where scarred skin covered all the way down Andrew's back.

After getting to know several of the community, we were sitting outside during lunch talking about initiation. The coastal people explained that they have their penises pierced by a sharp bone as a boy, then they needed to drain the blood from the piercing. It was believed that the blood was their mothers' blood which they needed to remove. Once they had partially filled a coconut shell with blood, they were considered men. They said that there was hardly anything left of their penis as it shrunk to virtually nothing, but over time, they developed a large, deformed penis.

The Puk Puk tribesman explained that they only pierced their backs as boys for the same reason as the islanders, to rid them of their mother's blood. Then, they were placed in smoking huts where their backs festered and created a permanent scar on their backs, giving them the look of a crocodile's back.

When all this talk was happening, Brandon became quite alarmed as Andrew jokingly touched his clean white skin and said, "We make Puk Puk!" All the people present laughed at the serious concern in my son's facial expression.

Eventually, Charlie arranged a banana boat that was a fiberglass craft of twenty feet with an outboard motor on it. We were going to travel to Manam Island and climb part of the volcano.

Fuelling up in PNG is a very confusing situation. Most of the natives calculated how much fuel was needed, and then would fill up their fuel container to that amount only. It was very concerning to say the least because what if we happened to need more fuel either due to strong currents or to go a further distance. We travelled with Charles and two other islanders. We then sighted birds working fish on the water, so we headed for that spot with lures out on two handheld lines. Before we knew it, two large yellow fin tuna were brought into the boat, dinner for the night! One was for Charles, Brandon, and I, and the other two islanders had the second fish.

Approaching Manam Island was absolutely spectacular with the black volcanic sand we landed on, and the distinctive lava flowing from the peak of the still active volcano to the water's edge. We walked on the cooled lava along an edge of unburnt forest line that had escaped the burning flow. Charles pointed out that this was the spot where several huts were destroyed, and a couple of people had lost their lives.

We started climbing up the volcano along the cooled down stream of lava flow. The rumbling sound coming from the peak above and the smell of sulphur was overwhelming. The higher we climbed, the more alarming it became.

We were told that once a volcanologist who was studying the volcano went missing and was never found. Given the continuing rumbling and small blasts, one couldn't really blame the rest of the community for not returning to the island. It was 1994 when the volcano erupted, and the islanders were forced to cross the small band of water to Bogia for safety. While a small portion returned to the island where most of the buildings survived, the school and the Catholic mission were all abandoned.

We retreated to the boat after a while and made a short trip to the village of Charles, his former home at a small bay. Charles' relatives were there to greet us, and we were given fish cooked over a mesh grill. Along with it, there were coconuts for drinking, quickly husked, then hacked open at the top to drink.

We noticed that no one else was eating, just offering us the cooked fish. Peering eyes of at least twenty people were watching us. I mentioned to Brandon, "Make sure you eat all the fish, mate."

"I am, Dad," he said while pushing the fish into his mouth so as not to offend anyone and telling them it was good.

The island's water supply came from a dug well just above the high-water mark on the beach. The islanders explained that during king tides, the water supply could be swamped by sea water, thus, creating a desperate water shortage. The well, which was really a hand dug hole through the black volcanic soil, had water only a few feet down. They obtained their entire water supply in small containers retrieving this vital water source. The island would most likely not even support the original population now.

CHAPTER TWO

We sat eating fish and drinking coconut water in the shadow of the Manam volcano above us. It would often give a rumbling noise, and an odd puff of sulphur fumes would escape along with ash floating down on us. It would be an uneasy feeling living here. The thought that at any stage she would erupt again must be permanently etched into the minds of all who returned.

On our way back to Bogia village, the islanders took us snorkelling on some of the most picture-perfect tropical paradise imaginable. Naturally cleared hills coming down to the sea edge, thick coconut palm trees lining the water edge, abundant coral fringe reefs, and white sandy beaches with crystal clear water to snorkel. It was a real south Pacific scene.

Travelling along the coast, I noticed from the water just how populated the coast was with hut after hut. All traditionally built, with canoe outriggers everywhere one looks. I could also understand how disputes happened with the *wantok* system and with people, not traditionally from the area, moving into what others regarded as their country. With 800 different tribes throughout the island of Papua New Guinea, that meant 800 different nations and 800 different boundaries.

Charles arranged for a small truck to drive us to a small village at the end of the road. Once there, we had to negotiate with people who trade along the coast to get a lift to the isolated Watam village. One becomes used to the Melanesian time in the island, and this day was a typical Melanesian-time day. We were up before dawn as we were told it would be a several hours' drive. Then, we waited for what seemed like an eternity for our driver. When he finally arrived, there were many stops for betel nut *buai* along the way, or to have a smoke.

When we reached the end of the road, no boats were about. They had all left and no one knew when they would return. Charles had advised us, "If you cannot get a lift, please come back with the driver for safety reasons." That is exactly what we did. We returned to Bogia by nightfall, but along the way, our driver told us of a Japanese war plane. We had just seen a Japanese machine gun in one of the villages. They had mounted the heavy contraption at the front of their village, so we were keen to see this plane as well that was shot down by the allied forces after the Japanese had sunk thirty-five vessels in the Bismarck Sea.

We drove up a track to where several women were walking, carrying their belongings. The driver asked them where the plane was, and they pointed us in the right direction. What an incredible sight! Here was this Japanese plane, still intact, laying in the jungle. The driver believed the pilot survived the crash, but revenge happened by the natives. One can only imagine the Japanese pilot surrounded by angry natives who practised cannibalism.

Stories were still told of the cruel treatment that the natives received at the hands of the Japanese. One story was how the Japanese soldiers cut the breasts off mothers with babies! Horrendous despicable acts of cruelty. The Papuans talk about the invasion as if it was yesterday, and the overwhelming Australians are embraced by the people who refer to us as brothers for our contribution to pushing the Japanese forces out of PNG.

CHAPTER THREE

Life is not measured by the number of breaths we take, but those moments that take our breath away.

Maya Angelou

Sepik River

The next day was a repeat of the day before, waiting for the driver, stopping for beetle nut and smokes. However, this day we arrived in time to meet the boat man. He was trading goods from the mouth of the Sepik River along the coast.

There were four Highlanders in the boat as well. They had negotiated a trip to a village to trade for beetle nut, and they were going to bring back full bags of the nut to the Highlands. We arranged for a fee to be dropped off at the Watam village that was situated on a branch at the mouth of the Sepik. Finally, we were off, four Highlanders, the boatman, Brandon and me. I thought we would comfortably travel along the calm coastal beach to Watam, but to my surprise, we headed right out to sea many miles off the coast.

The further out to sea we went, the Highlanders became more nervous since they were not sea people, and so was I. Until then, all my guides had been highly recommended, the Watam Chieftain and community was highly recommended too, but this boatman was an unknown. The further we went, the further off the coast he was taking us. Suddenly, the waters became extremely muddy due to the mighty Sepik River. Then, the swells started. The boatman took out a piece of newspaper rolled his tobacco and other substances and lit it up. There were floating ambers every time this boatman took a puff, the Highlanders would point at him and then, to me with a very worried look. We were sitting on tarps that covered the items which this trader was taking to another village, it could have been anything as trading firearms and drugs are common business.

I could just see the coast in the far distance and the boatman was navigating the swells, I thought we would not even have a chance to swim if the boat capsized. It was too far of a distance and there were no life jackets, and the water was muddy. It was with great relief when we arrived on a muddy bank at Watam village to say the least. We paid the boatman with our agreed kina amount and walked into the Watam village carrying our backpacks. There were no roads, no air strip, no civilisation, we now were to explore a region where time had stood still for thousands of years, where tribal laws and sorcery were the norm. To be honest, I was in my element!

At the Watam boat landing spot, there were a couple of huts and a thatched roof under which several people were sitting. We made our introductions with one of the people there who was the Watam tribe's magistrate. He suggested that I meet their Chieftain Danny Watam, and he would arrange a boat to Angoram further upstream.

Walking into Watam village with all its traditional huts on stilts was like walking back in time. There was excited yelling from the community, as I got closer, many of the natives came out to greet me as well. Although they were renowned as friendly and helpful, it reminded me of those movies where a white person walking through an Indian native village had to withstand individual attacks like being hit with objects, as a sign of bravery. But these people were the opposite, peaceful and welcoming.

The councillor, Jim, was there to greet me. He then brought me to the Chieftain Danny and we sat down under the shade of a shelter along with dozens of others who gathered around us. Here, we discussed the price of fuel to Angoram and who in the tribe would escort us there. Once a price was agreed, they showed us their most loved possession – a dragon.

I could not believe what I was seeing. It was a huge, decorated dragon very similar to the Chinese dragon used in festivals that many people carry on poles. The face of this dragon was a carved ancient mask in the island's tradition. This dragon was paraded in their "Sing-Sing" event and had been used for centuries. One really wonders

CHAPTER THREE

where did dragon carrying originate from, was it the sea faring Chinese who may have explored this region in ancient times?

At my appreciation, the councillor who was the mask carver presented me with a smaller version of a mask carving as a gift. He also showed us an ancient drum that had incredible carvings. When the Japanese bombed their village, killing people by machine gun fire in the 40s, a bullet hole was lodged into the ancient drum too. We were also told that the population just a decade ago was close to 1,000 people but now, their numbers had been reduced to only 500 people due to the dreaded malaria disease. This was a world, where the population had a 50% fatality due to an illness that can be prevented with a malaria tablet and a mozzie net! Both of which Brandon and I were using.

The chieftain decided to allow eight people to escort us all the way to Angoram which was several hours up-stream. Again, the friendly Papuans gathered on the banks of the river to wave us goodbye. On a banana boat fitted with a large outboard motor (fibre glass open boat), away we went through the many tributaries making our way to the main river, the mighty Sepik. We passed many a dugout canoe all with their families and possessions aboard. What an incredible and ancient part of the world!

Only a few miles into our journey and we started having problems with the outboard and the guides decided to swap their boat over at a neighbouring camp. We slowly made our way through a partly vine-covered area, then came onto dozens of dugout canoes, all of them had the crocodile head carving at the front of the vessels. The Watam boys were calling out with the repose being heard of native drums, a pounding sound. They were all signalling to each other. We swapped banana boats and refuelled and went through the maze of waterways until we reached the entrance of the mighty Sepik River. The entrance was blocked by logs and vegetation. In fact, we had to lift and haul the boat over the debris and into the river. It is hard to explain the size of this magnificent river that is Papua New Guinea's longest river at 1,146 km long, with part of it flowing through West Papua which is controlled by Indonesia.

The river was running a strong current and I was glad we had swapped the boats to one with a more reliable outboard. Every few miles, had to lift the leg of the outboard as the propeller became clogged with water weeds that was abundantly flowing down-stream along with the occasional log of a tree.

Out Post Angoram

We arrived in Angoram just as the sun was setting. The first thing I noticed were the massive dugout canoes more than fifty feet in length, some having outboard motors on their stern. We walked up the small hill to *Angoram Hotel* and said our goodbyes to the Watam boys who were heading back in the dark to their village.

Josie Kenni was the owner of the hotel. Angoram had seen better days, and everything had fallen to rack and ruin since independence. The hotel had a pub with no beer, used candles for light, and a telephone service that the whole community seemed to use, that is, when it was working. All mail was also sent to the hotel. I found a fascinating collection of Sepik River carvings from masks to story boards to crocodiles in the hotel. Charles, the police commander, was also living at the hotel, besides him, there was a cook, Josie herself, and then Brandon and I were the only ones staying there. The meals were great local fish, freshwater prawns, rice, and plenty of chilli sauce that I have come to like, thanks to PNG.

Josie was a wonderful host. We would have our meals with her and Charles together. The cook liked Brandon's shoes so much that he kept asking if Brandon would give them up to him. The police commander, Charles, told us how the then Prime Minister, Michael Somari, had asked him to clean up the Sepik River of its *raskol* problems. Charles was given fire power and engaged a person from every community to be a policeman, hence, one of the Watam boys who had just travelled with us, wore a blue shirt proudly saying he was the Watam policeman.

During Charles' control, river pirates were not active. Josie told us the tale of a Canadian who had flown into Abunti, a small village up-stream, and planned to work his way down-stream to Angoram. The Canadian embassy contacted them since no one had seen him for many weeks. Both Charles and Josie went in search. After Charles' forceful persistence in some villages, they were shown a shallow grave and found the remains of the Canadian who had obviously chosen the wrong guide.

Josie had arranged a guide, Benny, to show us around the region in one of the large dugout canoes propelled by an outboard motor. Benny with his young son and a helmsman took Brandon and I, to a village called Kambaramba, a water village. What a fascinating place

CHAPTER THREE

this was! An entire village living in huts on stilts in the river. All the huts were traditionally built with only the church with a roof top of iron, and a crocodile farm with corrugated iron walls. The children of Kambaramba were swimming or paddling around in canoes with no fear of crocs. They were all naked with their pet birds and small piglets, sometimes riding in their canoes with them. Benny said that the population was about 3,000 people.

The huts had fires going, cooking meals on the hut platforms of logs, accompanied with pigs and dogs. All the homes were on stilts to escape from the wet season flooding. I was told that when their old people died, they left the bodies in the huts with all who lived in the homes. Gradually, they become mummified with the smoking to a degree, and once the dry season came and the water receded to its lowest level, it was then that they bury their dead. Seemed like a long time to have Grandma and Grandad hanging around sitting in the corner of the only room with the whole family for many months!

We travelled up a backwater tributary to the major rivers. The bird life was prolific with water birds galore. At one stage, we noticed we were heading off course and heading onto land. Benny screamed at the helmsman that stopped the potential landing quickly. The helmsman had fallen asleep.

We visited what Benny referred to as the second Kambaramba village which was partially on land. Here, we watched the process of sago making. The locals first cut down a sago palm tree, then with a sharp instrument pulverised the inner core, collected the matter and started the washing process on a dish-shaped surface. All the sago matter was then washed into a log where the sago particles washed out of the fibre and settled in the log beneath. Then, they scraped out the soaking wet glue type substance which was then made into breads. It was a very tasty bread that I enjoyed eating very much.

Benny told the people of the village that I was from Tumbarumba (a town in Australia). Still, some of them believed that we were the past dead come back to life, since we had white skin. The people mostly had a 100% subsistence life, living on hunting of birds and fish, and barter trading of goods as it had been for thousands of years. Many canoes with rafts and all their produce to barter frequented the villages. Wherever we went, meals were offered to us. Fish on the coals was more frequent than other food. We bought freshwater shrimp, the largest I had ever seen, from a woman who was attending to her many pot nets which were woven of cane and five feet tall. We brought the shrimp back to the hotel that night to eat along with the local produce and chilli sauce.

Josie told us about the custom houses where the storyboards were located. A storyboard was a carved board of timber which explained a timeline of stories of the river tribes. She spoke of the totem pole carvings of a half-crocodile and half-man, as the Sepik River people did not believe, that crocodiles take people or their children while swimming in the river. Rather, they believed the tales of sorcery of how someone had cursed the other tribe, and how a half-crocodile person was responsible for the ills, the Puk Puk man.

We decided to extend our stay and explore these regions, but staying longer meant I needed cash to buy fuel, etc. With no facilities at all in Angoram, I accepted a lift from Charles in the police van, as he was going to Wewak a town on the coast, to meet the Prime Minister. Brandon stayed back with Josie as she wanted to show him her extensive rubber and vanilla plantation along with the processing factory. She was related to the Prime Minister, Sir Michael Somari, who was a Sepik River man, so Josie and family would better be described as the upper echelon of the region.

Charles and I left for Wewak, it was going to be a several hour drive, starting in the black of the night so as to return the same day. The road, like all other roads in PNG was as rough as it got. Along the way, Charles knocked over the odd dog that decided to walk in front of the police vehicle. When he approached a truck with people just holding on to the back, he would blast the horn and order them to get inside the truck for safety. He had with him a waddy, a piece of heavy timber, that he used more often than a firearm.

We arrived in Wewak in time for breakfast. We went to Michael's place who was the harbour master, and the brother of Charles. On his way to attend the meeting with the Prime Minister, Charles took me to the bank. The bank in Wewak was an exciting place with guards and their vicious dogs at the front doors of the bank. Charles arranged a ride for me to return to Angoram in a truck. Those people were religious types who were freighting goods to communities. Charles had demanded they take me back as he was caught up in Wewak and I was given the front seat to travel.

Unfortunately, there was a problem at the wharf where the fuel container ship was having difficulty unloading due to the previous storm. As a result, the town had run out of fuel, and with the system

CHAPTER THREE

of only fuelling up what you need, we waited in a que with a hundred other vehicles for many hours to refuel.

We returned to the outpost which is what Angoram is sometimes referred to, just before dark. Along the way, we had to pick up people who were travelling to Angoram. At one stop, a women appeared with her arm broken in half, it was just hanging there! I assisted in getting her in the truck, while her husband was verbally abusing her. We discovered that he had broken her arm and now was angry that she needed medical assistance from a nurse in Angoram.

Such violent acts are unfortunately extremely common in PNG. Another disturbing reality that the driver and his assistant explained to me was that most of the girls escaping their tribal homes turned to prostitution when they arrived at Wewak. Bride price was another form of practice whereby women in some cases were used as a commodity apart from the dowry system present throughout the world in a lot of different cultures. Bride price is where the family of a groom must pay the bride's family at the start of the marriage. In the past, the price was rare seashells which still hold importance or pigs. Today kina (cash) is sometimes requested as a bride price.

We travelled to the villages of the custom houses or what the community called spiritual houses. This time in a fiberglass banana boat with an outboard motor, along the backwaters, whereby water birds in the hundreds would fly off from the reeds in fright as we whizzed through the waterways.

Along the way, we passed dugout canoes that had smoke coming from the centre of the dugouts. They had fires going to create smoke and reduce the mosquitoes that were prolific. These insects might be the largest mozzies on earth.

On entering the village, the first thing you notice is the enormous custom house on stilts with log timber floors and high thatched roof. It stood out among all the other huts and had a second large point in the roof, like a bow sprit on a sailing vessel. Below the point was a carved timber, large type of storyboard. Once we were invited to come into the cultural house, we quickly climbed up the rickety timber pole steps into the enormous room that had many ancient storyboards with intricate carvings.

These were timelines and stories passed down from generations ago, along with totem poles and life size carvings. One of the inner poles in the custom house had a larger-than-life carving of the half-crocodile and half-man. Some of the carvings were bizarre to say the least, with creatures that seemed to be partly human with huge eyes and erect penises, others were of pythons with dogs in their mouths, and numerous other masks.

Many of the women then came into the house with their bilum bags and placed them on the floor for Brandon to choose one for himself. He then carried it throughout the rest of our travels. He usually stored his sugar cane sticks in the bag to which he had taken a liking to. Out in the village, we watched the women weaving the bilum with a variety of different colours made from binding and dying natural fibres. Incredibly, a person was carving a plane, situated on a pole with a moving, carved propeller. Now and then, a plane would fly overhead, and that probably explained the fascination of carving what they had witnessed.

We visited several more villages and their custom houses. We also saw many women making woven matts from palm leaves that are used for walls of their huts to bedding needs. I noticed how most women had tribal markings scarred into their arms. We visited a village called Kambot which had two custom or spiritual houses. The poles of the custom houses were painted with spiritual creatures, and it was explained to us how there were eight clans that owned both the spiritual houses. We also met a feller named Max who was carving canoes with a distinctive crocodile head on the bow.

Once we were back at Angoram, Josie gave Brandon a beautiful large-scale mask. Unfortunately, it was far too big for us to take with us and would have been a nightmare getting through customs. It was time to move on with our travels, and we made arrangements to book a plane from Wewak to Kavieng from where we planned to sail a catamaran in the waters adjoining New Ireland. However, we were told that the plane to Madang was fully booked. So, Josie arranged for us to travel with her mother and sister to Wewak, where her mother had huge influence and would get us on a plane.

We travelled in a van with several others. Once we arrived in Wewak, Josie's mother just walked into the airport and demanded that Brandon and I be allowed on the plane that was fully booked. At first, we thought that we would be sitting in the cargo area but to our surprise, we had window seats!

Islands of the Bismarck Sea

We had to first fly back to Madang from Wewak. From there, we flew to Kavieng, the largest town on the island of New Ireland. Flying over the Sepik River while looking down from above at this magnificent river winding its way into the Bismarck Sea was, an incredible feeling. Especially, knowing how we had traversed this enormous winding river system to Angoram, meeting with the local inhabitants and exploring several tributaries of the Sepik while looking at it from the air gave us another aspect of just how remote and huge this river system was.

I found Kavieng to be a very peaceful and pleasant place, compared to the hustle and bustle of a lot of Papua New Guinea towns I had been to. The only exception was of walking down the street and having my feet splattered with someone spitting out the dreaded reddish betel nut.

We made our way to Nusa Island next, which was only a quick boat ride from Kavieng. And what a pleasant place to stay it was! The island had a retreat built by expats who had spent their lives in Bougainville and left due to the civil war. It was an ideal retreat. There were several huts with timber floors, bamboo walls, ceiling fans. and beds with mosquito netting. There was a bar that had a sand floor and a table tennis table where Brandon played many games with the local girls. A pet hornbill bird walked around like he owned the place, and large clam shells littered the beach along with a monstrous crocodile skull.

When snorkelling out in the front, looking at large clams, I could not stop thinking of the monstrous crocodile head wondering where he had been living or where his mates were. While sitting on the beach, I picked up what looked like a shell but to my amazement it was the top section of a human skull! Apparently, the spot was also a burial place.

I had arranged to go sailing on a catamaran that was owned by an Australian couple, Adam and Danni Smith. They had moved to New Ireland and operated a business of sailing around the archipelago. After a couple of months spent travelling throughout the wilds of Papua New Guinea, it was great to just relax while poking around these spectacular coral islands.

We set anchor next to a coral reef, then Brandon and I headed off for some snorkelling by swimming up-stream and allowing the current to carry us back to the catamaran. At that point, Brandon suggested, "Why don't you buy a catamaran, Dad? You could sail back to places like this?"

It was then that another goal was set in my mind and thirteen years later, I was going to find myself sailing my own catamaran near the same latitude where Brandon had suggested. I would end up sailing thousands of nautical miles and many years of living full time on my very own catamaran, named *Never Die Wondering*.

Adam, the skipper, made a loud sound by blowing on a large seashell that created a distinctive noise like a horn. The adjacent island people then returned a blow from their own seashells and within a few minutes, people would row out to the vessel in their dugout canoes with outriggers on the side, paddling with ancient timber paddles. I had bought lollies that I traded with them for coconuts (a fair exchange. I thought) and they paddled away happy with the trade.

We visited a small island where the inhabitants, a couple of families, were trying to sell half of their 500 x 200-meter island. It had beautiful coral reefs on one side, a magnificent beach lined with coconuts. and a fresh well with good tasting water. However, there were many horror stories of people in such transactions of land purchases who then had many clans claiming ownership.

The islands we visited had many relics form the second world war when Japan had occupied this archipelago of islands. There still remained many guns, bunkers, etc. and large holes where the allied forces had bombed the Japanese defences.

One island we explored guided by the local inhabitants had a large cave that seemed to me to be an ancient blow hole where the sea at one time had travelled through the underground area. It had dried eventually with huge palm trees growing within.

It was great to relax on the catamaran for a few days after our exploring of the Highlands and Sepik River region of Papua New Guinea. The travels we had, really exceeded my expectations of this unique part of the world, but it was time to return to Australia.

On our return journey, we made a very quick stop over at Rabaul on the island of New Britain. The Tavurvur volcano had recently exploded with many evacuating the area. The plane circled this massive active volcano and landed at the airport with volcanic ash covering the tarmac. As soon as we had landed, people boarded in a matter of minutes and away, we went. As the saying goes, in Papua New Guinea expect the unexpected.

The Sheiling

In Australia, I had formed a company, *AJ Macleod Property Pty Ltd*, to venture into residential properties as it had become very difficult

CHAPTER THREE

to obtain finance for rural holdings. For my holdings in New South Wales, I offered vendor terms. For instance, 10% down payment to take possession and an interest free period of twelve months, then an interest was payable. Some of the lots sold for cash while others had taken many years to settle.

I really did not plan to sell the entire 1,000 acres but to my shock when selling one of the properties, it was discovered that the state government had changed the zoning from "rural for timber production and grazing of livestock" to "Conversation 3". I was furious since as the owner, I was not consulted. Communism is where the government takes your land while socialism is where you still own the land, but the government controls it, so there was no point trying to continue any commercial operations on the Tumbarumba properties. Therefore, over time, I sold all the nine properties as lifestyle lots since that is what they had become.

Another dispute I had was with the road to the properties that had been destroyed by the state forest who were the managers of a global corporation and had planted a pine plantation on the western border that literally land locked my property and by way of planting the pine trees destroyed the existing road. I had taken the matter all the way to the state's minister because under the pine ACT, it clearly stated that it was the pine plantation's responsibility to maintain the road that is used by existing neighbours. This was ignored and fell on deaf ears, so I had truly had enough.

I bought a house on a large block of land at Bakery Hill, an inner-city suburb of Ballarat in Victoria, and obtained a development approval (DA) for another two houses. The bureaucracy of councils was becoming very hard to deal with. They wanted the environmental authority involved, even after the D.A was approved, and I had abided by the terms of the DA asking me to obtain soil samples signed off by the geo-technician the council itself recommended, stating that the site was not contaminated. Still, they seemed to change the goal posts, and I had to flip (sell) the property. I also purchased a small patch of land in Geelong that had a structure for billboard advertising for a small shopping precedent. Several properties I purchased and either development and or held and sold in time.

I was not at all happy living in Melbourne to say the least. I really did not like cities, never had. I was missing my freedom. I had taken sailing lessons in the Port Phillip Bay area, and even went out racing one evening but realised that I needed to get more experience. So, I purchased a trailer Sailer in 2012, it was an eighteen-foot long with a lead drop keel. This small craft's brand was *Ultimate* and it was built in the Mornington peninsula in the late 80s. It was canary yellow in colour and had an easy drop-down mast that enabled it to be trailable. It had a small two-stroke outboard motor on the back. Two sets of spinnaker kites, roll-up main on the boom, a genoa and jib, and a storm jib for the head sail.

My trailer sailer was named *Sheiling*. Incredibly, when I looked up the name, it was derived from the MacLeods of Skye Scotland and meant "shelter from a storm". How uncanny was that! At every available time, whenever the weather permitted, I was out in Port Phillip Bay, learning as much as I could, always bringing a friend along for assistance.

Meanwhile, I also became a member at a Melbourne horse racing club so that was as close to horses I could be, I even made a trip to Hong Kong with my old mate, Phill Daly from Tumbarumba. We visited the Sha Tin Racecourse for the Charter Cup along with the Happy Valley racetrack on the Island of Hong Kong.

India to Kathmandu

My son Brandon was now working as a carpenter, and he loved Melbourne. My mother was being looked after in an aged care facility. I was now on an extremely good financial wicket with the many sales of properties coming in and was fortunately able to cover the expensive aged care. Pensioners in high care are government covered but not low care ones, as was the case with my mother. The low care facilities were ridiculously expensive, being twice the cost of my own living expenses. So, I was grateful to finally be in a sound financial position. Still, Melbourne was destroying my soul, and I just yearned for my freedom.

I needed adventure, so I travelled solo to India, landing in New Delhi and making my way to Kathmandu in Nepal. I travelled by all types of transportation getting a lift in vehicles, *tuk-tuks* (motor bike fitted with a carriage), riding a crammed train, walking through the many slums, etc. I guess I really wanted to experience humanity in its pure form and India seemed to be the best place with a massive population of 1.4 billion people. It is the melting pot of so many diverse cultures and many religions like Hinduism, Buddhism, Muslim, etc.

CHAPTER THREE

While in Delhi, I was briefed at a Sikh temple called *Gurudwara Shri Bangla*, regarding the Sikhism religion, how it was formed in what now was Pakistan in 1400s! They condemned the caste system, the high caste being Brahmins and the lower caste being the untouchables where horrendous discrimination was experienced. I was then taken to what I would describe as an enormous basement under the temple. I found there what may be the largest soup kitchen on earth. Literally thousands of homeless people were being fed daily, the food was coming in from leftover meals, brought in by people who carry billy cans around the city collecting them as well as donated food from all over Delhi. They then, had the food prepared and cooked in large pots with fires constantly going, many people cooking for the hungry, and passing plates through to the masses who would sit and eat their meal with their hands, return the plates that were then quickly washed, and another meal prepared to feed the next person. Thousands were fed like this daily, it was a very humbling experience to say the least, witnessing this incredible generosity to others in need.

The oldest city in India is Varanasi at over 3,000 years old. I reached this ultimate pilgrimage location by a crowded train travelling overnight. I stayed in this ancient city that is regarded as one of the oldest townships in the world and has the mighty Ganges River flowing through. The cremation of millions of people takes place on what they call the *ghats*, steps to the Ganges. I was taken to an area where I was asked if I could pay for firewood to donate for some poor soul to be cremated. As I did so, I was shown how a certain amount of wood can burn a person. Another incredible and humbling experience!

All this was being done by the untouchables, the lower caste. I noticed they were panning the remains in the river once the body had been cremated. I discovered later that they were most likely trying to find any valuable items of the likes of gold teeth, etc. The person who was organising the cremation wanted to show me a view of the Ganges. I was taken into a small room that had an ancient floor of cobble stone and had people laying there. I asked, "What's happening here?"

The untouchable person started saying, "Die-die-die!"

I said, "They're not dead mate!" Some people were in a feeble position, others were just sitting against a wall, as the putrid smoke from the cremation blew into the room. Then, I quickly realised that all those poor souls were waiting to die, the ones with no one to pay for their cremation hoping someone like me donated. I was told that many old people were dropped off by their families in this way. The Hindus believe that the Ganges River is sacred, and souls are transported to heaven, and escape the cycle of rebirth if they have their ashes scattered in it.

Bathing in the Ganges is a purifying ritual that is believed to wash one's sins away and improve a person's karma. It was a cloudy wet morning, and the Ganges was running strong as a boatman took me along the banks. I watched massive numbers of people bathing while others were being cremated, to be honest, it was very disturbing at first, and it took a long time for me to appreciate my travels through India. That is why I went there to get an understanding of how other people exist and try to have an understanding of other cultures.

It was a relief once I reached Nepal, the air was clean, there were less people, and I spent a couple of weeks travelling through this unique country. I visited the birthplace of Siddhartha Gautama (Buddha)] and Chitwan, now a national park, that was renowned for tiger hunting during the British colonial era but now all protected. The park has an elephant breeding area and the entire park that borders India has many armed guards protecting the elephants from poachers. Local culture has it that the hair of the elephant brings good luck, but not so lucky to the unfortunate poor elephant being killed for a few hairs though.

I travelled up to Kathmandu, high in the mountains, along a slippery, wet, muddy road that has many fatalities every year. There are sheer cliffs right along the side of the road, very alarming to say the least. The day I travelled along the road, a police van slid off the road and everyone in the vehicle plummeted to their deaths. Kathmandu is a city in the clouds and has various temples, monasteries, and stupas. I stayed there for several days wandering through the narrow streets, admiring the incredible architecture of the old royal place built in Durbar square with incredible ancient timber work.

Son of a Highlander

The following year I travelled to Scotland, tracing my family's ancestral past. This resulted in the writing of my second book, *Son of a Highlander*. Here is the blurb:

Son of a Highlander is the true story of the author, a third-generation Australian of Scottish Highland descent discovering his ancestral history over eight generations, from father to son. This is a search for authenticity

CHAPTER THREE

of a verbal story handed down over a two-hundred-year period, along with a 1797 penny and a collection of photos and correspondence that are one hundred years old, which were from his late grandfather's old, tattered leather case. The author descended from the Clan MacLeod—Clan meaning "Children in Scottish Gaelic," Mac meaning "son in Gaelic," and the Leod derived from the Viking era; it basically means "children of the son of Leod." The family originated from a small two-acre semi subsistent existence on the Isle of Skye in far western Scotland. The Macleod Clan was once a warrior race that feuded with neighbouring clans in the bloodiest of warfare. A clan system of traditions and culture that lasted hundreds of years that eventually came to an end with the notorious Highland Clearance, whereby thousands of people were evicted from their lands and replaced by sheep. With the mass exodus of people, some forcibly left while others left in desperation. This book is the history of one Highland family who survived a dangerous sailing journey to Australia only to continue their struggle against adversity on foreign soil. A search for the whereabouts of a Gaelic-speaking great-great-grandfather to discover he was sent to an island off the Australian coast, where he eventually died and was buried in a pauper's grave along with 8,500 souls, whose only crime was that they were poor. This book is a must read for anyone wishing to trace their own ancestral history. It will inspire you and encourage you toward your own personal voyage of discovery.

During my travels to Scotland, I visited several other countries, such as the former battle fields of the western front in France and Belgium where my grandfather had fought in the 29th Battalion that I also wrote about in my book, *Son of a Highlander*. I also went to England, Wales, and Dubai, before returning to Melbourne frustrated that my trips away were really brief, only staying no more than two days in every place. I wanted to continue travelling, exploring and discovering new places, but at a slower pace where I could truly get an understanding of the places and its history, getting to know the people, absorbing the cultures. I did not like rushing through a place, I preferred taking my time to really breath the air, to truly get the feel of a place, not just eating their food but making the time to really taste the meal.

Back in Port Phillip Bay, Melbourne, I was trying to learn as much as I could sailing the little *Sheiling* trailer Sailer, but I was not getting as much time out on the water, that I needed to get my sailing skills and confidence to where I wanted it to be. So, I started trailing the little yacht to the Gippsland Lakes that was only 3.5 hours from Melbourne. They are inland lakes protected from the Bass Strait by sand dunes.

I was able to sail these waters solo, sleeping in the tiny cabin, and sailing the many locations throughout the lake system.

Over time, I decided to live there. I moved to this area as I would be able to sail weekly if I wished. I also tried to find a project with either water views or water frontage, so I rented a property at Metung and set up office selling all the properties I had acquired. Being near safe waters, I was able to sail whenever I wanted. I sailed from Lakes Entrance up to Lake Wellington only thirty odd miles in length and limited as most parts are very shallow. It was a terrific place for me to learn to sail properly and I would sometimes head out for many days and in all kinds of conditions to get my skills and confidence up. The goal in my mind was of getting a catamaran and sailing to New Guinea.

During this time, I purchased a 1.5-acre property that had water frontage with a jetty berth on Chinaman's Creek, Metung, on a very steep block. I had two buildings built in a factory and had these module type of buildings trucked to the site, crane lifted and placed on piers. This was to become *seafarer's Rest*, an accommodation property.

Mekong River

Prior to completing the property development, I made a trip to the Mekong River. At the Golden Triangle of Myanmar, Thailand and Laos. I travelled downstream on what is referred to as the "slow boat" with one helmsman navigating this mighty river. Through the jungle gorges in Laos, staying in a little village on the banks of the Mekong, watching working elephants come into the river with their handlers (Mahout), bathing in the cool waters of the Mekong. At Luang Prabang, Buddhist monks gathered every morning before dawn to walk along the streets to receive food from the devoted who offered food to them. People placed food into the monks' bags such as fruits, sticky pudding (a rice dish), even sweets, chocolates, etc. The monks did not say a word ever, it is called *Sai Bat* (morning alms).

As a traveller, you sometimes come away from places with more questions than you receive answers. The cope centre in Laos was one of those places, where they made artificial legs and arms for the victims of mine explosions, a legacy of the Vietnam War. Over 20,000 people, mostly children, have been victims of these bombs exploding forty years after the war. It is believed that 580,000 individual bombs

CHAPTER THREE

were dropped on Laos by the USA during the war when Laos was a neutral country. Another disgraceful act by a superpower and the question is why the USA hasn't returned to clean up their mess, God Bless America!

Over a few weeks, I made my way from Thailand, Laos, and Cambodia to Vietnam. I traversed these four countries on four planes, three trucks, three motor bikes, eleven buses, three cars, and nine boats, always trying to travel the road less travelled. It was great when I would be in a village being the only westerner as people are easier to meet and most are very friendly and welcoming to travellers especially the ones travelling solo.

In Cambodia, I walked through the killing fields where the Pol Pot massacred his people, nearly three million of them lost their lives to this murderous regime within four years. That is 25% of the Cambodian population, one in every four people murdered. I also met Chum Mey, one of the survivors of the genocide. He had written a book named, *Survivor: The Triumph of an Ordinary Man in the Khmer Rouge Genocide*, about being imprisoned in the notorious S-21 Tuol Sleng camp prison where he was tortured. They even pulled his toenails and finger nails out with pliers but he was one of the lucky ones, he survived. I believe if any person visiting this horrible killing fields where the largest massacres happened does not shed a tear, they could not be human.

On the Tonle Sap Lake, which is a back water of the Mekong, I met boat builders building ancient timber crafts chipping away with an adze (tool for working logs) creating the timber planks. I purchased two thirty-kilo bags of rice along with another traveller and delivered it to the floating schools for the children's meals. Many of the children lived in squalor conditions and lacked basic food. I had started writing newsletters of my travels, with photos and I wrote as follows:

So, you think you had a hard day at work? One in every 300 people are victims to mines exploding in Cambodia. Here are two great survivors, both have lost their legs, and they are not out begging but entrepreneurs selling books to feed themselves and families. Teng Dara is the man with the bicycle, and he has advanced himself, able to sell many different types of books due to carrying it on a stand on his bicycle. His opposition has not the luxury of a bike and relies on his hands wearing thongs dragging himself around selling only one book at a time. I bought one titled, First They Killed My Father, a survivor story of POL POT'S KHMER ROUGE. This is the face of Cambodia, I ask again, how hard was your day?

I stood in awe admiring the incredible temples of Angkor Wat build from the 9th to the 13th century. This area was once the largest city in the world with a population of a million people, when London's population was 50,000.

In Vietnam, I was privileged to meet and be fed by female Buddhist monks of a pagoda on the island of Cho Moi along the Mekong River delta. I was island hopping on the Mekong delta by motor bike where you cross the waters from island to island by ferries. Trying to travel the road less travelled. I stayed at Long Xuyen mixing with the locals, absorbing Vietnamese culture and hospitality. It was great to be in a region where I may have been the only westerner.

I ate the famed pho soup that has become one of my favourites. It was prepared for me on an open fire, under a rock shelter, high above the delta at Mount Sam. At the end of my Mekong River trip, I stayed on a floating vessel, the bed was comfortable but the odd rat running around was nothing to be desired. Outside in the water, the fishermen dragged their nets wearing their traditional *non la*, a circular leaf hat. The sound of the evening calls to prayers echoed over the waters of the river. The small island nearby was the home of the seafaring Cham people who are largely Muslim, an incredible moment to hear the middle east in an oriental environment. All the islands in the delta being either Christian, Buddhist, or Muslim seemed to get along together.

Crowther – SV Never Die Wondering

On my return to Australia, a vessel that had been on the market for quite some time in Paynesville, Gippsland Lakes, had the price lowered on the advertisement. I inquired about it; it was a catamaran of the *Lock Crowther* design considered by many to be the grandfather of catamaran design in Australia. The length of her was 10 metres and 5.1 meters wide, in the old language that is 32 feet 10 inches in length and the beam 16 feet 9 inches, called a *Eureka* design of a fiberglass construction. The owner had placed two *Honda* engines with 20HP powers on the back of the stern as opposed to what was an inbuilt one diesel engine, so manoeuvring was made easy. It had three open type cabins, two queen size beds in the fore section with a tiny cabin on the port quarter that was a single bed and a lee sheet to hold you in. The starboard quarter had a small bathroom, shower with hot water that

CHAPTER THREE

needed a generator to heat up. The saloon had a great circular seating where many people could sit around. Sails were good, both head and main, with a colourful spinnaker. It had been hardly used in the last few years. The trampoline at the front was in good condition too. The *Eureka* was similar to the *English Prout* in size as it was easier to lift out of the water up along the east coast and easy to fit into mono hull berths in marinas if needed by virtue of being only 5.1 meters wide. There was a single dagger board that was just fore of the mast that was used going windward that supposedly allowed you to point better but really was not that efficient.

I wanted this vessel to sail the length of Australia and although small in its category, it was huge compared to my trailer sailer. I gave them an offer and they accepted it. Finally, I was the proud owner of a vessel that was going to take me on an incredible voyage, but there was a lot of refitting to do. I also had enough of dealing with banks and with people in general, and just yearned for my freedom back, the freedom I had when riding up into the High Country, the freedom I had when travelling. Now, I had purchased this vessel to take me into the seas, a far cry from the protected sheltered waters of Gippsland Lakes which was really a puddle in comparison to the open waters. However, the biggest question was, *am I able to do this voyage and mostly by myself?*

For the next year, I sailed up and down the lakes on this vessel, I named it *SV Never Die Wondering*, after my first book. I upgraded all the electronics navigation gear to *Raymarine* chart plotter, depth sounder, wind instruments, radar, deck lights dry docked to antifoul, checked and replaced new through hull fittings and ensured the hull was sound. For my cooking, I placed a methylated stove, installed a 2KVA generator and had two *Engel* fridge and freezer too. I also installed an auto pilot, 2.8 metre PVC inflatable dingy, and bought a 3HP mercury outboard. I was to spend as much time as I could sailing the Gippsland Lakes from the entrance up to Lake Wellington and up the Latrobe River then return.

I kept the vessel on a swing mooring in Bancroft Bay near the property I developed, and started living there. I would walk down to the jetty and the little *Sheiling* would take me out to the *Crowther*. Unfortunately, I had a buster on a horse as I was asked to assist in getting the sting out of the problematic horse. I did that a few times, and my belief was, it had too many vices for my liking and suggested to get rid of it. Foolishly, I agreed to get the sting out another time, besides, not riding for several years, also didn't help, and I broke my shoulder needed surgery. Previously, I had all the bolts and plates removed from my leg after a broken *femur* hitting a tree at full gallop while chasing brumbies on my then property at Tumbarumba. All this was added along with many other breaks to my body and meant a delay in sailing up the east coast, but also meant plenty of time to have the vessel how I wanted it to be.

I removed the mast and had the wiring upgraded, it was an alloy mast and had steps as a climbing ladder that was great to get up the mast when solo. When the shoulder improved, I went out in all conditions that the lakes system had to offer. A real "shake down" for the vessel and myself, as I wanted whatever was to go wrong to go wrong in the lakes as opposed to out at sea and many miles from anywhere. The vessel had a *Muir* supreme anchor and 8mm chain of 70 meters, solar panels, lead acid batteries, and I bought many spares, tools charger, etc.

Many friends would come along during my sailing on the lakes and once I had branded and registered the name, *Never Die Wondering*, my lawyer mate from Melbourne, Gareth Benson, joined me on a sail. We went out into Bass Strait through the Lakes Entrance bar on a slack tide. With a bottle of whiskey, we did the traditional request to Neptune and Poseidon for fair winds, splashed the whiskey on the bow stern port and starboard, and swigged the remaining.

Although, I was ready for my voyage, to be truthful, there was a little hesitation, *was my vessel going to handle the swells of the Tasman Sea? More to the point, how would I handle it all, sailing sometimes in the dark of night, the freezing conditions of winter, far out at sea, alone?*

CHAPTER FOUR

When you follow the crowd, you will lose yourself, but when you follow your soul, you will lose the crowd. Eventually, your soul tribe will appear. But do not fear the process of solitude.

Bass Strait

The day to depart was here. All the preparations had been finalised the previous day, but with very little sleep. I was anxious and excited about what lay ahead – to sail the entire length of Australia from the south to the north. Alison, who I had being seeing for the last two years, decided to accompany me on the first leg to Eden (NSW) which was 150 nautical miles. In the last few days, Bass Strait had experienced gale force winds, but the front had passed, and the wind reduced. I, therefore, decided to head off on the tail of the weather system with the prediction of wind gust reducing dramatically to ten knots, a far cry from the forty knots of the preceding day.

I had the catamaran, *Never Die Wondering*, tied up to the jetty at the front of my property on Chinaman's Creek. All the provisions loaded, and the small jobs were completed, and as the first light of the day arrived, we were away.

Only six nautical miles to the bar at Lakes Entrance, and by the time we arrived there, the sun was up although the sky was overcast. I could see the conditions of Bass Strait and there were large swells, but the wind had reduced to a gentle breeze. Once you enter the bar, there is no turning back with the strong current from the Gippsland lakes ebbing, I knew then, it was now or never. I allowed the outgoing tide to drag us out into the sea.

Due to the bad weather of the past couple of weeks, this was going to be my only window of good weather as another low pressure was forming to the west. So, I really had only the next couple of days of the high-pressure system to make my way around Point Hicks to Eden. There were no bolt holes (safe anchorages) along the entire passage with a westerly wind, therefore, overnight sailing was necessary to make the 150 nautical miles.

Once we were over the bar, we saw a mono yacht outside in the big swells. I thought he was waiting for the tide to turn so that he could come into the lakes and was unfortunately, caught in the terrible swells on anchor. I wished him well and started my sailing logbook, hereafter.

Log: 27 April 2018; 0725 hours; Over the bar of Lakes Entrance; Swells 2-3 metres, Headed S/E toward the 40-meter mark depth, light westerly wind.

Bass Strait is a very shallow strait which divides mainland Australia from Tasmania. Although it was joined 6,000 years ago, it was not known if there was a passage from west to east from the early European mariners until George Bass and Mathew Flinders sailed a small skiff of twenty-feet length, through the strait in 1798 officially recording the passage. It had a terrible reputation as the "roaring 40s" meaning 40°S latitude is within the strait and the area had claimed the loss of over 600 vessels. So, picking your weather window is paramount. It must be noted that Flinders was also the first man to navigate to and name Australia.

I planned to sail along the coastline first, but due to the swells, I quickly headed to deeper waters for better sailing. I raised the main and head sail to full and was on a starboard tack due to the wind at 150 degrees. I was placing a preventer which is a line to the end of my boom tied to a cleat so as to stop the boom from quickly swinging the other way if gybing occurred.

The vessel was being lifted up into the air and down in the swells. It was all fine as there were only light winds, and the autopilot had the vessel facing the direction I needed to go. I was able to raise the main by hand at the mast, then quickly winch in at the cockpit. I had my lifeline on and was sweating profusely due to my waterproof clothing over the other warm layers as the weather had been cold and wet. However, I was soon hot due to the excitement and from working the lines.

When I came back into the cockpit, Alison quickly asked me for a bucket, I gave her one and she promptly vomited. I thought, *oh no, here we go, only a couple of miles out and she was already extremely ill!*

CHAPTER FOUR

I had to go back out of the cockpit to tighten the preventer line on the cleat. With the big swells, I found myself sort of bent over for a period of time, When I arrived back in the cockpit, Alison was continuing being sick. Seeing as she was having so much fun, I decided to join her sharing the same bucket!

Two miles out, and I had thrown up, but as soon as I had been sick, I felt terrific, *touch wood!* It turned out that I was never to throw up again for many thousands of nautical miles over many years. Unfortunately, Alison could not quickly recover like me. She went inside the saloon area and that is where she stayed for the majority of the passage.

Now, I was feeling ecstatic out there in the sea. All these years of planning and sailing inland waters of Port Phillip Bay and the Gippsland Lakes, and now at last, I was on my way, adventure bound. I was making good ground and was recording 6.4 speed over ground. In the afternoon though, the wind dropped off and I had to run one motor to keep consistency in speed. Also, I needed to make smoother sailing up over the Bass Strait swells.

After a while of sailing, you become accustomed to the Bass Strait swells that lift you up and suddenly bring you down. The wildlife is magnificent, seals and penguins are an incredible sight in their small family groups and seem so comfortable floating in the up and down on the large swells.

In the early days, Bass Strait region was a major fur seal hunting area. Sealers from around the world would hunt the seals for their fur, hence the name fur seals. They were mostly hunted along the coast and the islands of Bass Strait.

The penguins were fairy penguins which are Australia's smallest variety. They burrow into the sand dunes along the coast at night and feed out in Bass Strait during the day. I was able to have great views of both seals and penguins floating on the swells. As the dark set in, a full moon appeared in the east that gave Bass Strait a luminous glow over the water at night.

At 1850 hours, I passed Point Hicks where the first sighting of the Australian East coast was had by Captain Cook in April 1770. The headland point was named after Lieutenant Zachery Hicks who was the first to have sighted the mainland.

At 2155 hours, I passed Rams Head, another iconic landmark that was only three nautical miles to my port side. My paper chart was on the table along with my electronic plotter in the cockpit, my bearing would have taken me over the New Zealand Star Bank which was only twenty meters deep and breaks in heavy weather. I calculated the tides and it being low tide with still large swells, I decided to play safe. I planned to change course and sail between the New Zealand Star Bank and the Little Rams Head.

Little Rams Head was a known protruding rocky headland which would only be a little over two nautical miles to the rocky shore. Then, for some strange reason, my plotter went off, no power. I was not sure if I had leant over with my harness gear which had a heavy stainless-steel clip, and knocked the switch off, or if I had damaged It when it hit the screen in the swells.

In any case, this was not a time for my plotter to stop working. If I went off course by the southern westerly swells and wind, I could come to grief on the rocky coastline in the dark.

The autopilot I had installed was an *ACU 100 Raymarine* with an ST 4000-wheel control and it was working fine. Fortunately, the bearing I had plotted at 60 degrees would take me in between the Star Bank and the Little Rams Head.

I rushed to the paper chart with another GPS unit to quickly plot my position onto the paper chart, I could note exactly where I was and if I was sailing too far into danger, I would know. As long as I kept checking my position every ten minutes and kept to my plotted line on the paper chart, all should be fine, otherwise the worst could happen.

I was extremely worried and checked all my connections by pulling them out, reconnecting them, and then turning my plotter back on. Finally, the plotter started working and I could see that, I was heading in the right direction. The anxiety levels were high for those fifteen minutes.

On the VHF, there was a call by a yachtie asking for assistance stating that he was stuck on a sand bar. He was talking with the Mallacoota coast guard and also another authority at Gabo Island. They kept asking him for his position, "What is your latitude and longitude?" Yet, for whatever reason, he took a long time to communicate with the authorities. However, he did explain that he was not in any immediate danger though he had entered a river system that was sanded up and had landed on the sand bar at night.

Later on in the week, I discovered that it was the person with the mono hull I had seen at the Lakes Entrance bar. He had sailed along with me for some distance, but for reasons unknown, he decided to sail in the dark into Lake Mallacoota. It was unknown to him that the lake was not open to the sea because a large sand bar prevents entering, and he foolishly sailed onto the bar and became lodged. He was safe but the vessel required some major machinery to move it from the bar.

At 0340 hours, we had passed the NSW border at Cape Howe. The wind picked up at 0510 hours to a great fourteen knots and I was able to comfortably sail at six knots Speed Over Ground (SOG) with the change to port tack. The sun was now breaking through the horizon of the east, Alison had recovered from her sea sickness and came to the cockpit while we sailed north passing Green Cape and then turned into the magnificent Twofold Bay of Eden.

What a great feeling of accomplishment! It was a great sail, and we made the passage of 150 nautical miles in twenty-six hours, just averaging under six knots an hour.

Twofold Bay

We dropped anchor in the calm clear waters at the front of Ben Boyd homestead, with visiting dolphins swimming under the vessel. It was fantastic to be able to get some sleep at last since I had not slept at all on the passage. To say I was exhausted, would have been an understatement.

Ben Boyd homestead has been renamed *Sea Horse Inn* and is probably one of Australia's most picturesque hotels The homestead is fronting Twofold Bay and surrounded by timbered hills was built by the entrepreneur Ben Boyd, a Scotsman, in 1840. He had sailed from Scotland to Australia on his twenty-five-meter schooner named *Wanderer*. At forty-one years of age, he made Boydtown his base for his pastoral empire of which he had fourteen sheep stations in the Monaro district and two stations in the Riverina. At that time, he was most likely, Australia's largest sheep owner.

He was heavily involved in the whaling and shipping industry as well and had financed his sprawling dynasty by floating the Royal Bank of Australia. He was also involved in "blackbirding" whereby he would have natives kidnapped from New Caledonia and transported to Australia to work for him, since he had exhausted his convict and Aboriginal labour force. His bank was liquidated in 1846, therefore, sending Ben Boyd into bankruptcy. He sailed off back to sea on his schooner, *Wanderer*, and disappeared in the Solomon Islands, while out shooting birds.

The crew still aboard *Wanderer* were involved in a skirmish where muskets were used and many natives lost their lives. It was rumoured that Ben Boyd was still alive and held captive. In 1854, an expedition was sent to the Solomon Islands, and it was discovered that Ben Boyd had been murdered and his head was cut off and kept on display in a ceremonial house. The expedition leader was able to purchase Boyd's skull from the tribe and returned it to Sydney.

Alison returned to Lakes Entrance by bus, and I waited for a window in the weather to allow me to sail north. However, with another low pressure forming in the Tasman Sea and a possibility of an east coast low, it was going to be three weeks until I could depart. This meant plenty of time to explore Twofold Bay and its old whaling station and the tower, which was located in the bush, on the southern side of the bay.

Old Tom the Whale

I had visited Twofold Bay several times after hearing the story of a killer whale named Tom that had assisted the early whalers in the 1920s to harpoon the baleen whales. Legend had it that Tom was the leader of a pack of killer orca whales and would assist the whalers in surrounding the baleen whales like a pack of working dogs. Once the baleen whale was harpooned, he was known to even grab hold of the harpoon line and assist the whalers to bring the monstrous baleen whale to shore.

At the time of hearing the tale, I was convinced it was just a fabricated story, but it was indeed true. The local Aboriginal population have the killer orca whales assist them in bringing large pods of fish into the shore prior to the arrival of the Europeans.

When the whalers arrived in 1857, the orcas assisted the Davidson family. This was the family who established the whaling station on the southern side of the bay and would use Boyd's tower as a whale watch. Once a baleen whale was spotted, they would gallop a horse down to the whaling station and the whalers would row out to harpoon these enormous whales sometimes thirty meters in length, assisted by Old Tom and his orca mates.

Baleen whales or whalebone as they are sometimes referred to are not toothed and have a baleen plate which filters the krill (small ocean animals). The humpback, blue whale, and southern right whale are all baleens. Once the baleen whale was brought ashore, the orca whales were rewarded with the tongue and lips for their assistance.

It is believed that Old Tom assisted the Davidson family for three generations and died in 1930. His skeletal remains are on display in the Eden Museum with the distinctive worn teeth from the harpoon line that he had dragged in his mouth assisting the whalers.

For three weeks, I explored the abandoned whaling station and anchored in three areas of the bay due to the weather. I was becoming sleep deprived as the alarm for my anchor (dragging position) was hard to hear. Also, I would sleep with the mirror of my plotter on my tablet so I could see if I was moving at all while in my bed.

While anchored near the navy jetty due to a big blow from the southeast, I met an elderly American yachtie and his wife who had been sailing full time for thirty-five years. They were in the mid-eighties, and he put me onto an anchor app on my mobile phone that worked perfectly. I could hear the echoing alarm on my phone if I dragged so I was then able to get a goodnights sleep, and not waking or the time worrying of dragging.

Twofold Bay was an exciting place to wait out for a weather window. Dolphins and seals would frequent the bay along with a large fishing trawler that worked their catch right next to where I was anchored, dragging their nets with their smaller tenders. There catch was huge when the crane lifted up the enormous net full of salmon (Bay Trout). Large manta rays would also grace the sea floor of the bay and what an incredible sight that was.

I tendered into the Port of Eden for supplies. I collected food supplies with my backpack, and for the fuel, I paid a taxi to assist me in carting the jerry cans back to the tender on the beach.

The Tasman Sea

Log: Friday, 18 May 2018; 0600 hours; Departed Twofold Bay.

Once I sailed out of the bay, I was able to ride the southerly swells from the previous blow. The prediction was for westerly to south westerly, but more westerly to northerlies were experienced although it was light wind. Sailing was good as I spent the day close reached and sailing north. The swells were about a meter from behind, therefore, it made for very comfortable sailing and relaxing as I passed Tathra and Bermagui.

At 1400 hours, I sailed between a shoal and Montague Island then continued through the night. Due to the low tide, and approaching nighttime, I was not prepared to cross any bars on the outgoing tide. So, I decided to sail to Batemans Bay and anchor in the wide bay for the night.

At 2200 hours, the autopilot went off course. This was a little alarming since I had problems hand steering. I was not sure what the problem was, maybe I had hooked up a fishing net or maybe it was seaweed. As the swells were comfortably pushing me along, I was hand steering to the port side then to the starboard side trying to free whatever it was restricting my movement on the rudder. Then, all of a sudden, it was free. What a relief! I engaged the autopilot, and all was fine.

"Fear kills more dreams than failure ever will".

Mobile phone reception was terrific, and Doug Mathias convinced me to anchor in Batemans Bay as I was in good spirits and contemplating continuing to Jervis Bay as opposed to nighttime anchoring. However, Doug convinced me to trust my radar and navigation as being sleep deprived is a sure way of making errors. Doug was a long line fisherman from the days of commercial fishing in Port Phillip Bay. He did it alone, so he had a great understanding of the sea.

Nighttime sailing can give you false impressions. The swells seem more severe than what they really are, and the noises of the yacht are much louder than they are in the day light hours. As I was getting tired, I thought I could hear the noise of the whale cry on several occasions, since it was the migration season when humpbacks make their way from the southern waters to the northern waters to calve.

I thought I could hear the whale cry, but the autopilot wheel drive made another distinctive sound, so I was not sure if it was the autopilot, a whale's cry, or just my mind playing tricks. Then, I looked at my sounder and there was, only a few meters under neath my hull.

As soon as I noticed this, the sounder then showed deeper waters, was it a whale underneath or just seaweed, I thought next. Clearly, I was getting tired and I was glad I was making my way into Batemans Bay since the wind was up and the swells had become larger. Coming into Batemans Bay from the sea is fairly safe, you pick up the lead lights to enter into the large bay, without the treacherous bars that dominate southeastern Australia on most river entrances.

Batemans Bay has Black Rock and the Tollgate, both formidable rock monoliths at the entrance to the bay. In the dark of night, along with a southerly swell and a northerly wind, it creates a rise in the sea once you sail into this shallow water way. Not being able to see these rocky islets while only watching the radar, these large rocky monoliths look like passing a massive red blob, and then it becomes larger on the radar screen, it sure gets the anxiety level up.

Once I was passed the rocks, I turned north to find a spot to anchor at a spot called Chain Bay. I could hear the surf and dropped anchor at a safe distance from where the surf was breaking. In the vicinity, two other yachts were visible on my A.I.S *Automatic Identification System*. Once the anchor was set, and I secured, with the no dragging anchor alarm on, I fell asleep with all my safety harness and clothes on, utterly exhausted.

At dawn, I awoke to a perfect anchorage. I was very pleased with myself for navigating at night relying on the navigation gear. Thank God, I had bought a radar, and I decided to recoup and stay another night in this little bay.

The next morning, I departed at 0630 hours for my next destination of Jervis Bay. I motored out passing the Tollgate Islands from the opposite side of which I had come in the other night. What a sight! Huge, towering rocks only a few meters away from my vessel just two nights ago.

Then, I noticed large black buoys while passing the rocky islands, I quickly avoided hitting them as they were large nets drifting in the sea. How easy it would have been to get caught up at night in these dreaded nets. The weather conditions were similar from the other day, and I decided to sail out towards the continental shelve, the water distinctively changed colour here as the depth increased in the Tasman Sea.

Dolphins decided to travel along with my vessel keeping me company. Late in the afternoons, I was able to change tack and sail into Jervis Bay with Point Perpendicular, a sheer cliff wall, as my bearing.

Jervis Bay

The cliffs are stunning as you enter Jervis Bay. On the southern headland, it is the largest cliff in Australia, but to me, Point Perpendicular with its vertical cliff positioned at the entrance of the bay with the lighthouse above, was a sight to behold.

I passed this sheer cliff wall, turned to my port side, and sailed southwest to an area known as "the hole in the wall". Here, the sand type cliff ridge once had a hole through it, now had eroded away gradually. I was able to tie to a public mooring for the night. The next morning, I took the dingy to shore and walked to Cape St George. It was a ten km return bush walk and marvelled at the Tasman Sea from the passage I had just taken.

Back on *Never Die Wondering*, the night was uncomfortable with a beam swell rocking the vessel all night. So, as dawn approached, I was away to the town of Huskinson and grabbed a public mooring there. Jervis Bay has four areas that are "no fishing zones". They made up about 40% of the bay, it had a marine park and the fish within these areas were prolific.

It was going to be another three-week wait for the next weather window. Mick from the marine authority visited *Never Die Wondering* by marine craft and offered me another swing mooring in Currambene Creek. It was the marine authorities' mooring and was more sheltered given a blow was coming.

I accepted the offer and headed to the entrance of the creek. Within a few minutes of me releasing the lines of the mooring buoy and motoring to the entrance of the creek, the wind was up and strong, and waves formed at the small bar crossing as well. The local surfies on their surf boards were paddling out to just above the break sitting on their boards. Every minute, the wind was getting stronger, and the waves were becoming larger. I had placed myself in a position of no retreat as I needed to get into the creek as soon as possible.

As I lined up the best track into the creek, the surfies started cheering me on. I caught a wave and surfed into Currambene Creek, I was looking at my sounder worried that I could hit the bar itself since one metre showed up in the sounder, and my draft being .600 just. In all honesty, I would not have done it had the surf started prior to me being in a position of no return. Later that evening, the bar attendant from the R.S.L *Return Service League* who watched my entry said he had never seen swells like that before at the entrance of the creek.

The storm was big. It brought gale force winds along with torrential rain, a Taiwanese container ship had lost its load not far north from Where I was, with eighty-seven containers lost at sea. This became another worry, that I was going to have to endure, container dodging.

I had several visitors in my three weeks at Jervis Bay. On one occasion, another *Crowther* catamaran came calling, "You're Alistair?" he said, "You would be Stefan." It turned out that we both knew the same fellow yachties who had told him I would be visiting Jervis Bay on my way north.

Over the many years of sailing, meeting new people who know of you with equal friendships has become common. In in all honesty, it really is hard to become lonely in the sailing or cruising world. Even solo sailing, waiting for the right weather window is part of the journey, and you have to develop the mindset: of *letting time be your friend and patience be your ally.*

CHAPTER FIVE

It's impossible," said doubt. "It's dangerous," said fear. "It's pointless," said reason. "Give it a try," whispered the heart.

Shoalhaven River

There was a small window of opportunity to sail out of Jervis Bay and into the Shoalhaven River. So, on Saturday, 9 June, I departed Jervis Bay, sailed out past Point Perpendicular, and into the Tasman Sea again. It was a miserable morning, overcast with light rain, and I busted a shackle on my main at the tack point that had me sitting on the roof doing repairs.

It was only a five-hour sail into the Shoalhaven River, and I went straight onto a public mooring within the river. A local feller, who lived in the creek on his old steel mono vessel, came to assist me when I was tying up on the mooring.

"I am Captain Carnage," he stated by introducing himself. He was the unofficial Port Master, a friendly character. "I'll come back tomorrow night and pick you up. There's an all-you-can-eat at the local club for $15, its Chinese," he said.

I agreed. The next afternoon, Captain Carnage, true to his word, picked me up in his aluminium tender and we went in for Chinese.

Carnage was very eager to get a meal and in a real rush, "We have to be quick, so we don't miss out," he said.

"But we are the only ones here," I said.

He quickly went up to the smorgasbord and brought back an over filled plate and encouraged me to quickly get a feed. "I'm okay for now," I replied, as I was enjoying a beer. Suddenly, Carnage opened the backpack that he had brought in, and quickly scraped the whole

CHAPTER FIVE

contents of his plate into the bag! He then returned to the smorgasbord for another plate. When I eventually grabbed a meal, he was shocked that I had only got a partial plate. "That is all I need," I explained. I was not sure if the first serving that went inside his backpack was for a later meal for himself, or for his pet dog he had on board.

I stayed for a couple of days on the Shoalhaven River and one evening, made my way to the local pub for a beer. I sat next to an older feller who asked me several questions about my vessel and my plans. He told me that he had once bought a sailing vessel and planned to go cruising. However, his wife hated sailing, and he foolishly allowed her and other people in his life to convince him to sell his boat and not continue with his dream. He said, "I foolishly listened to others. Now, I am too old and regret my decision!"

It remined me of Mark Twain famous saying: *"Twenty years from now you will be more disappointed in the things you didn't do, not the things you did do"*.

Surfing to Port Hacking

Log: Monday, 11 June 2018; 0420 hours; Departed for destination Port Hacking, Sydney

I needed an early start to be able to sail into Port Hacking within daylight hours. However, leaving Shoalhaven River in the dark was a little daunting as there were many vessels on moorings in the river that I needed to avoid hitting, relying on my radar.

As soon as I was out of the protection of the river and into the open water, the swells were up to three meters. The day brought the light but also the wind at twenty knots from the southeast, and only with the head sail, I was flying. Later on in the day, I had the main out as well. At around midday, I received a call from Doug Mathias who was following me on marine traffic. He told me that he had seen me reach nine knots, "Not bad for a little 32-foot catamaran!"

Still, Doug was concerned that I was over doing it in the swells. But I was not surfing over the tip of the swells, just comfortably sailing on them since the swells and wind did not relinquish and after many hours, I became exhausted to say the least.

While passing Port Kembla, a humpback whale let out a blow and what a magnificent sight it was! I continued towards Port Hacking when the wind reduced to twelve knots giving me a little comfort, and yet the swells continued and seemed to get larger. It was difficult trying to guess how tall the swells were, but the *Crowther* handled it well. It was a relief coming into Port Hacking, rounding the area known as the Royal National Park. I was able to grab a courtesy mooring just southwest of Port Hacking itself.

Once the vessel was secured, I lay on the trampoline exhausted. It took a while to remove my harness along with my waterproof gear. I watched the yacht next to me where they were sipping wines in the quiet sheltered bay, oblivious to the fifty-nine nautical miles that I had just accomplished by literally surfing the whole passage.

I spent a couple of days exploring the Royal National Park with its incredible Aboriginal rock carvings. I also had a tame magpie flew onto my yacht and stay for a period of time. Meanwhile, the weather showed another cold front on its way, so, with the following day giving me a nice weather window, I decided to get into Broken Bay.

I was out of Port Hacking, and back up along the coast at dawn. With the full main and head sail being pushed by a westerly of fifteen knots, the sea was choppy but great sailing compared to the last passage. Whale after whale was seen, so many of them I encountered that I lost count. Trying to get a photo was difficult because as soon as one breached, it went down immediately. I had a small cam recorder, but I decided to place it away as I did not want to lose the moment spending my time on a video recorder. I decided on still camera use only.

When the sun came out, the wind dropped off enough for me to sit up on the foredeck near the trampoline. Trusting my autopilot, I enjoyed the view of the many whales, along with the sighting of the Sydney Opera House. This time I was able to take a photo.

Broken Bay

I sailed into Broken Bay, and it was magnificent with its tall sandstone cliff faces that seemed to encompass the bay. I arrived in a picture-perfect anchorage called Refuge Bay. It was another magnificent anchorage to wake up to. I took a dingy ashore and visited a waterfall. I was amazed by this massive bay that had hardly anyone there, only the one odd vessel called *Young Endeavour* motoring around.

The *Young Endeavor* was a so-called replica of the famous ship of Captain James Cook, *Endeavour*. This magnificent ship was a gift from the British Government to Australia for the bicentennial in 1988. The *Young Endeavor* is a sail training ship for youth development. It is a brigantine, meaning a two-mast ship, forty-four meters in length with a beam of 7.8 meter, and a displacement of 239 tonnes, that dwarfed *Never Die Wondering* being only ten meters in length. Ironically, Captain James Cook's *Endeavor* was a bark, meaning a three-mast ship, that was only thirty meters in length with a beam of 8.9 meters.

Dave Simmonds, whom I had known through a mutual friend over the years, drove to Brooklyn, a little town on the Hawksbury River as it entered the bay. David drove me to his home in Sydney for a BBQ with his family then assisted me in supplies, fuel, and a food run.

After a few days exploring the Jerusalem Bay, Cottage Point, and anchoring at Hallett Cove Beach, the weather predictions showed a great window to reach my next destination. I sailed out of Broken Bay from Hallett Cove Beach at 0710 hours, into a great comfortable Tasman Sea, with lighter swells and light winds. I experienced a great sail to Swansea. Here, I was able to tie to a courtesy mooring near the bridge which lifted to allow vessels into the Macquarie Lakes.

Fog and Shipping Containers

Log: Friday, 22 June 2018; Departed Swansea.

Almost 25% of my journey was now complete, going from Victoria to the Torres Strait. I decided not to explore the Macquarie lakes system although I wanted to. I had lost many weeks waiting for weather windows in Twofold Bay, Jervis Bay, and Broken. Bay. With good weather, calm conditions forecast, and sunny skies, I decided to continue. Some of the 87 shipping containers from the Taiwanese container ship had been washed up on the rocks just north of me. My plan was to keep watch on the bow in these light conditions. The weather being sunny and calm, it gave me more of a chance to see these dreaded containers to avoid disaster.

I was back out in the Tasman Sea sailing north this time. There was hardly any wind, so I was motor sailing. *At least, I can see any floating shipping containers*, I thought until only a couple of miles north of Swansea I saw this rolling cloud of fog coming in. In no time at all, the fog blocked out the sun and I could no longer see the water.

The weather became still in this eerie blanket of fog. My worry of hitting a container was now heightened but there was nothing I could do. In fact, hitting a ship was a far major concern and I quickly got the noise blower at hand, if needed.

I was sailing through the shipping lanes. For at least five hours, I sailed in the fog of Newcastle, and I dare say, it was not an enjoyable experience. That is, until a whale lifted its tail right near the starboard side of my vessel. Incredibly, the tail was white. Further along in the day, the fog had nearly lifted when another whale went under the vessel, or should I say I sailed over the top of this whale.

I arrived at Shoal Bay on the south side of Port Stephens at 1445 hours. I spent about four days at Port Stephens and anchored off Nelson Bay, arranging supplies. I even bought a new pair of binoculars.

While departing Nelson Bay, I sighted a motor cruiser anchored nearby. This was Brian Dorling with his wife Sandra, on their motor vessel, *Carmilita*. They had, both decided to sell up and move onto water cruising Australia. He told me of a great anchorage in Camden Haven River next to a great club which had meals and beer. We arranged to meet up there in a couple of days' time.

I headed to Forster next, a small town near the entrance of the Wallis Lakes. Along the way, I spotted several whales on their migration north. I wondered if I was seeing the same whales at times since we were all heading into the north direction. Once I had navigated through the Entrance, I again tied to a courtesy mooring. It was situated on the northern side of Forster, by a village called Tuncurry near the bridge.

The next morning, I was under way on a great beam reach which I had to reef in the main when the breeze become stronger. Along the way, I passed fishing trawlers which I gave a wide berth to in case of dragging nets. Not many fishing trawlers placed their AIS on, therefore, keeping secret their whereabouts from their competitors.

It's a nuisance to other mariners when boats do not show their AIS, as it clearly shows the direction and speed of the vessel, thereby reducing the dangers of collusion. It also reduces the need to call on VHF when in doubt, because sometimes other vessels cannot hear due to the working on deck.

Again, the whales, several of them, sailed along with me. This time, I was convinced there was a little camaraderie travelling together.

When I arrived in Camden Haven River, I was able to tie the bridal onto another courtesy mooring. It was two nautical miles up-stream

CHAPTER FIVE

near the Laurieton township. Brian and Sandra arrived as well, and we caught up for those beers and meal at the RSL. Over the years, I would catch up with Brian and Sandra in many places around Australia. Brian had gained his sea legs from serving in the Australian navy.

In the Camden Haven River, there was another catamaran occupied by Graham and Carolyn. They both remembered my vessel, *Never Die Wondering* from Metung. They had lived there for some time before selling up and moving onto the water.

I Departed Camden Haven River at 1000 hours on the rising tide. It was a warm day and the first since leaving Victoria, when I sailed wearing shorts and bare feet. Bare feet and shorts would be the norm for many years from then onwards.

Again, many whales were sighted but then came a radio call on the VHF warning mariners of a humpback whale caught in a net which was dragging a yellow buoy. I did sail past the unfortunate whale, but it had many authorities and other boats around it, most likely trying to remove the nets from this poor creature.

The sailing was getting better pushed along by the Tasman Sea south easterly swell, warm weather, and great gentle-to-light winds. By the afternoon, I had reached the mouth of the Hastings River and timed my estimated arrival window of entering over the bar on a rising tide. Once again, I was fortunate to secure to a courtesy mooring.

Port Macquarie was on the southern bank, and I spent a couple of days there. I even got the chance to watch the movie, *All Lost at Sea*, actor Robert Redfern at the local cinema. It was a movie about a yachtsman hitting a container that sank his yacht over a period of time. *Very appropriate*, I thought.

The water temperature was now up to 17°C and installing the latest electronic gear was all paying off – radar, plotter, autopilot, and the little luxury like temperature. The east Australian current runs north to south and is naturally warmer coming from the north, but it was a few miles off the coast. It was possible that if you were closer to the coast, you could miss the current. Therefore, increasing the speed, it runs at four knots, therefore, if there was a rapid increase in the temperature, then more than likely, I was in the current, but I found it difficult to determine by the temperature if I was indeed in the current or not as naturally, the further north I went the temperature was warmer.

I departed Port Macquarie on 0720 hours, 11 July 2018. With one reefed in main on a moderate westerly wind, I arrived at Trial Bay as the wind died off to calm anchorage and dropped anchor in this peaceful spot. The old gaol on Layers Point was close by from where I had anchored, and at night when it lit up, it was a fantastic sight.

At dawn, I was away again. By the afternoon, the temperature in the water was 20.4°C. I arrived in Coffs Harbour at 1350 hours and anchored just south of the jetty. The harbour is within two large break walls, creating a protective area. It was common knowledge that such anchorages were limited. And there are times due to no room and a yacht can be forced to raft up against fishing trawlers. It was all good at this time though, all courtesy moorings taken, but a couple of spots to anchor, it was about time I used my tackle gear.

Log: Friday, 13 July 2018; 0600 hours; Departed Coffs Harbour

At 1000 hours, the westerlies had increased, and I reefed in the head sail and main with 1–2-meter swells from the southeast. I was making good time with a comfortable SOG of 5.5 to six knots. Again, several whale sightings along the way.

At 1107 hours, the wind dropped so I removed the reef back to full main and head, but still had the never-ending southeasterly Tasman swells up. At 1225 hours, I sailed past the North Solitary Island watching the swells breaking against its rocky shore. At this point, I was officially in the Coral Sea. It was a self-achievement of sailing solo the length of the Tasman Sea from Bass Strait to the Coral Sea.

Winter had come over me, still, all I wanted was to just keep sailing into calmer waters. I had taken a photo of myself while in the Tasman Sea. I was in rugged up waterproof clothing, safety harness on, wearing a beanie, and supporting a beard. There were times in the light rain when it felt like ice particles hitting your face. I was so glad now to be in warmer waters.

CHAPTER SIX

Jobs may fill your pockets, but adventure will fill your soul.

Yamba

Jason Whyte who I had known from Tumbarumba rang me up asking when I was arriving. He had recently moved to Yamba in the Northern Rivers Region. He said, "I'll put the billy on?"

Incredibly, when I met Jason back in the 90s, we discovered that we had both Jackerooed with the same cattle sheep property. In fact, we had lived in the same quarters, a few years apart.

I negotiated the entrance into the Clarence River and dropped anchor not far off the beach where Jason was there to meet me. I stayed in Yamba for a few days, Jason assisting me with supplies and fuel.

Log: Monday, 16 July 2018; Departed Yamba.

With very calm conditions and light winds, I started motor sailing with only one motor and discovered a problem. The impeller was not pumping water, so I turned off the port engine and started the starboard one.

At 0900 hours, the davit holding my dingy collapsed into the water along with dingy and the outboard motor into the water. The steel piping had bent, and everything was laying in the sea. I quickly tied a couple of lines and winched the davit up, just enough to be out of the water and far enough to not hit my engines to allow me to be under way. If I had winched too much, I could have easily snapped the davit altogether. I had no option but to return to Yamba for repairs. Luckily, it happened in calm seas. Imagine what would have happened amidst the huge swells of the Tasman Sea and or at night?

I radioed the Yamba Coast Guard and reported my situation. They stated that they would come out and tow me back. I declined the offer saying I would sail back as it was great conditions for sailing. They kept on standby for my return, and I slowly sailed back over the bar with the Yamba Coast Guard reporting their observations of me coming back into the Calarence River. I thanked them and dropped anchor at Whiting Beach.

It was just getting dark, and I was preparing a meal, when suddenly, sirens and flashing lights came on right next to my vessel. An overzealous marine ranger started yelling at me, "Where is you mooring light?"

"For God's sake, my deck light is on! Also, lights in my cabin are on, what's the drama?" I responded.

He continued with this demanding demeanour, "No, no, no, can't have your anchor light off!"

I was not in the mood to listen to this idiot, so I switched all the deck lights on, but he went off like an obsessed control freak. "Your anchor light! Your anchor light! Do you not have an anchor light?"

So, I switched on my navigation lights just to be a smart arse, and then, I turned on my anchor light after which he finally left. *What a rude self-important type of person*, I thought, when a simple, polite, "Hey mate, can you turn you anchor light on as well?" would have sufficed.

For the next two weeks, I got my repairs done. I arranged for them at the marina, which is part owned by Kate Cotty, the first women to sail around the world solo. It was only a small sort of marina with a travel lift. I moored at the board walk at the front of the café- marina and waited for an availability to lift the vessel out as it was easier to work on the motors that way and too difficult on the water. I arranged metal fabricators to take back the davit and repair it in their workshop and to reinforce it with more solid tubing, the tubing was far too thin for being a davit.

During my time there, I met a couple of elderly sailors who had been in the marina for years. One in particular, Old Angus, would walk past my vessel every morning with his little dog and bid me good morning. I would return the greeting and then he would say, "Oh, if I were you, I would head to New Caledonia."

"Have you been there, Angus?" I asked him.

"Oh, no! I wish I had, I'm too old now," he replied.

He was a nice friendly character who had also written books, but time had taken its toll, and Old Angus was just at the end of his

CHAPTER SIX

hourglass. I was asked out for a meal and beers with the local shipwright workers, and they told me poor old Angus had fallen into the drink one night and they had to dive in and rescue him just in time. Meeting many old salty like Angus over the years, makes you so aware of living your life to the fullest now, because one day none of us will be able to sail or do what we desire.

Jason drove me up the Clarence River showing me this incredible river and countryside. We had a meal with his family in a bush local pub and while in there, a local feller was telling us about Aboriginal paintings he had on his property. He asked us both if we would like to see them, and we agreed eager to see these ancient paintings. We followed him in Jason's vehicle, a fair drive from the pub we were at. He shared the property with his father and brother. He brought out beers for us and showed us around his house and sheds with all kinds of bric-and-brac but no paintings.

We kept asking him where the paintings were, and slowly, he took us both walking down a track while he kept saying that they were a bit far. At first, we thought he was making excuses but then, we finally got to an area on his property, where he stopped and said, "They are here. But unfortunately, they have all been etched out, though their spirits are still here?"

It was obvious now that he just got Jason and I there for company. He then simply showed us a hole that he had dug by hand saying the spirits were in the hole and that he did not want to upset them. It was extremely hard not to laugh as we said our goodbyes and explained that we really had to get going.

Back at Yamba, I had *Never Die Wondering* lifted out onto the hard stand, both motors serviced, impellers replaced, repaired davit installed, and electrical work done. So, back into the water it went.

Log: Wednesday, 1 August 2018; 0700 hours; Departed Yamba, destination Byron Bay.

It was a fantastic day for sailing. The weather was warm with southerly wind and light southerly swells. Up went the spinnaker and the kite and the spinnaker stayed up most of the day. Dolphins followed the stern as well as riding the bow waves. I caught a large mackerel along the way on the lure, and then the Cape of Byron Bay was in full view. This was another great feeling of self-accomplishment having sailed past Australia's furthest, most easterly, point. I anchored at

Byron Bay within daylight hours, and the night was a great relaxing calm anchorage listening to the thumping bongo drums of Byron Bay echoing over the water.

The Coral Coast

Log: Thursday, 2 August 2018; Departed Byron Bay for destination Southport, Queensland.

The wind was a westerly with a slight southeasterly swell. I beamed and reached until 1030 hours then changed bearing and ran with the wind. I was able to goose wing both the main and the head sail out in different directions. With the wind behind, it looked like goose's wings out opposite directions and hence, the name. Along this passage, I had many whale sightings and this time, several of them were just slapping their tails.

At 1155 hours, I officially crossed over into the Queensland side of the border. Log: 28'09'827 / 153'36'811 Bearing 330 T

It was an incredible sight from the sea looking at the tall apartment towers of the Gold Coast. In the past passages, all the landmarks had been mountains and headlands named by the likes of Cook and Finders, now, I was looking at tall monstrous apartment buildings.

I crossed into the Gold Coast Seaway and into an area known as the Broadwater. Then, I sailed into a little inlet known as The Spit or Bum's Bay where I dropped anchor. Brian and Sandra from *MV Carmilita* were anchored there as well, and we socialised by having meals alternatively on each other's vessels. Many other yachties were there in this little inlet and there was only just enough room to swing while on anchor. What surprised us was the amount of people who come there to swim amongst the many yachts, oblivious to the knowledge where most of their head toilet waste was going. Maybe this was the reason for this inlet to be known as Bum's Bay!

After a few days of filling up water from the park and obtaining supplies by tender to Southport, as well as purchasing a new Nikon camera, that improved my photos, I was keen to get away from this crowded anchorage and the noise of the city. In addition, there were helicopters flying at the break of dawn, jet skis and small craft speeding around the place with no concern to others, I was glad to head north to North Stradbroke Island but as opposed to the sea, I sailed up through the enclosed waterways.

The enclosed waterways from the Gold Coast heading north meant sailing on the western side of south and North Stradbroke Island via Russell Islands. It passes the many small islands covered with Melaleuca tree or paperbarks. The area is fed by several rivers and creeks, and in places the sand dunes that are a barrier to the Coral Sea are an impressive sight of tall, steep, and sandy rises.

On one occasion, I came to a sudden stop due to sailing over a shallow area, but luckily, it was easy to reverse off. So, keeping to the main mark channel was a must since it was extremely shallow when not keeping to the main route. A wind warning alert was forecasted, and I anchored at a very sheltered part on the eastern side of Russell Island. The wind warning was cancelled, however, and the night was of an incredible calmness. A peaceful night on anchor, I could hear the distinctive night call of the common koel which also migrated to the Gippsland Lakes of Victoria.

Log: Tuesday, 7 August 2018.

I sailed from Russell Island to Dunwich on North Stradbroke Island and dropped anchor as close to the town jetty as possible near the green marker buoy. This was the place I wanted to see, as it was here that my great great grandfather, Donald MacLeod, spent his last years as an inmate and was buried in a pauper's grave along with 8,500 other poor souls.

Burial Site of Donald

In 2015, I had published my second book, *Son of a Highlander*, regarding my journey to find what happened to my great great grandfather, Donald MacLeod. This journey even took me back to my ancestral grounds on the Isle of Skye in Scotland, and I finally, was able to discover his journey. I was on Stradbroke Island where my great great grandfather was sent to in 1900. He had been on the wallaby (Australian term of travelling) for several years, a gold miner as well as a blacksmith during the depression years, he was hospitalised at Herberton in far North Queensland. He was sent to the Benevolent Dunwich Asylum for the infirmed Stradbroke Island because policy at the time was to be removed from the public eye if you did not have any money or assets.

I made my way to the Museum that was once a part of the asylum. The walk to the Museum took me over the cemetery which is a large green lawn with only one mark on a grave that read "Died 10 November 1908" erected by a few old friends. There was no name on this grave, but I had the records of Donald's death on 24 November 1908 which was only two weeks after this person was buried. So, it was highly possible that Donald was buried here, either to the left or to the right of the only visible grave of 8,500 other inmates.

It was so surreal to be standing there looking at the spot where my great great grandfather was laid to rest, and from there to be looking at *Never Die Wondering*, my thirty-three-foot yacht that brought me here, anchored in the bay.

My father and grandfather tried in vain in their lifetime to find out what had happened to Donald. All knowledge seemed lost from the point where he had left Bundaberg, Queensland in the 1880s. Yet, here I was, over 100 years later, his great great grandson. Although I had discovered and written a book about his burial, to be standing at his grave was an extremely emotional event.

At the museum, I introduced myself and was surprised that they knew me and had me on file regarding my research and my book a few years ago. They even had an A4 size picture of me in a suit. Considering I was wearing thongs, shorts, and a bandana on an unshaved face, they looked at me and at the photo quite a few times to be sure. I produced the book, *Son of a Highlander*, for their library and was shown around the Museum with much respect.

The Asylum had 21,000 inmates over its eighty-year history from 1865 to 1946. They had taken in the infirm, the blind, crippled, mentally deficient, terminally ill, cancerous, tuberculosis and leprosy patients. Of these, many were moved to Peel Island, very close to Stradbroke Island, in 1907.

I was given a small book, *A Brief Introduction to Dunwich Benevolent Asylum*, and it had a photo enlarged on one of the pages that said, "Some of the inmates, 1905". I have looked at the faces of those twenty-six elderly gentlemen many times. They all had long beards, and I look at their worn faces, are *any of these men Donald MacLeod*, I wonder as the photo was taken only three years before his death.

CHAPTER SIX

Log: Friday, 10 August 2018; Sailed from Stradbroke Island to Moreton Island with view of the city of Brisbane to the west.

It was a great sail, and I anchored close to the sunken ships that have been placed in a row. These were fifteen old steel vessels in total, placed in a north to south direction only a short distance of the beach, these acted as a great habitat for fish and created a fantastic diving place. I cannot say that the resort close to the Tangalooma Wrecks on Moreton Island is fantastic, quite the opposite, in fact. It was unfriendly and unwelcoming with a "no visitors allowed" policy.

The next morning, I was away at dawn for my subsequent destination, Mooloolaba. What a pleasant sail it was in the calm waters with the protection of Moreton Island! I lay on the trampoline and read the book, *Flinders: The Man Who Mapped Australia*, written by Rob Mundle. It was a brilliant account of this magnificent mariner. While lying on the trampoline reading the book on autopilot, a large P and O cruise ship passed by. I wondered what all these passengers thought of me laying on the trampoline reading and sailing solo. My sail was well-trimmed, and I had a relaxing sail over to Mooloolaba.

The Mooloolaba River has a narrow entrance compared to other rivers. Once past the break walls, one has to turn a somewhat 90-degree bend followed by another 90-degree bend to an anchorage area that is surrounded by what looks like an expensive area with mansion type of houses.

There was a mast protruding through the water, indicating that a sunken vessel lay there. Many times, I saw this occurring and I was always bewildered as to why these hazardous sunken yachts took a long period of time before they were removed. I have since then discovered the slow process of insurance companies. This was another reason why I always tried to anchor at a new location in daylight hours as it was impossible to see a protruding mast in the dark.

The next day, my friends, Geoff and Liz Blair, drove down from their home at Bauple to see me. We had lunch at a wharf café. I have known them for over thirty years, from back in the day when I was fruit picking, I worked for Geoff at Tumbarumba, as he owned an orchard, and later in life, we had worked together at the local timber mill. He even played the bagpipes, when I got married.

Log: Monday, 13 August 2018; yarn with another solo yachtie regarding potential anchorages on northerly passages; Departure 0900 hours.

Once out of the river, the wind angle had me sailing broad, reaching all the way to Double Island. The swells were up, pushing me along nicely. I had many whales and dolphin sightings in that one day. At 1830 hours, in the dark, I anchored at Wide Bay on Double Island Point. It was a bay which was exposed to the northeast but the light westerlies made it an ideal anchorage. I planned and timed the tide to cross the next morning into the Great Sandy Strait which separated Fraser Island from the mainland.

Great Sandy Straits

The following morning another solo sailor on a catamaran pulled up for a yarn. He along with another yacht had followed me into the bay, the previous night, and anchored nearby. He confirmed with me the tides as we were both anxious to cross at the right time and this bar can be treacherous if the wind is up.

The good rule is two hours prior to high tide, conditions must be calm with minimum swell of 1.5 meter. When all those points were covered, away I went. The other two yachts were both first timers to cross the bar as well and we spoke on the VHF regarding conditions, they both stayed back and watched me go first.

I picked what I thought to be the safest direction over the bar, and also lined up the Inskip Point leads. I positioned myself, and then slowly went forward. They were great conditions but the waves were breaking on both sides of *Never Die Wondering* although many meters safely away. You can imagine how many have come to grief here picking the crossing wrong. With my heart in my mouth, through the bar I went manually steering her through, with the other two yachts following. At last, I was safely in the Great Sandy Strait.

I anchored in Pelican Bay for lunch, then went up to Tin Can Bay anchorage where I anchored in amongst the many boats. I have been in the area before as several years ago, Brandon and I had taken our four-wheel drive to Fraser Island exploring the largest sand island in the world. It is 710 sq. miles or 1,840 sq. km. We reached the island by barge. So, I was excited to now explore the waterways that divided the island from the mainland.

CHAPTER SIX

Log: Friday, 17 August 2018; Departed Tin Can Bay, sailed north through the Great Sandy Straits.

Picking the favourable current, *Never Die Wondering* took me along this fantastic water way with Fraser Island on my starboard side. I was very close to the island's shore, perfect to experience this beautiful, timbered, sandy island along with the variety of bird life on the banks, the likes of ibis with their long beaks searching for a meal and oyster catchers working the mud flats.

I anchored at Yankee Jack's Anchorage, a well-known anchorage for boaties of all description. They were all anchored in a line running north to south. Sea eagles and ospreys would perch on nearby trees, watching you in their residential address. I awoke the following morning to a cloud of fog that literally blanketed all the waterway. It was an eerie feeling as I motored in the absence of winds through the straits. Soon, the fog lifted and the sun came out. Along the way, I passed a camping spot where Brandon and I had camped several years ago. We were nearly eaten alive by the mozzies that are renowned on the west side of the world's largest Sand Island.

Along the way, a dugong appeared with its large head. Dugongs are also called sea cows that seek their meals amongst sea grass. I arrived at Moon Point that opened into the large Hervey Bay where I dropped anchor southeast of the point.

In the anchorage, I met Ian and Carolyn again after our meeting at Tin Can Bay. They had built their mono yacht and had travelled to the Louisiade Archipelago in Papua New Guinea. We had had a meal together and socialised in Tin Can Bay and again at Moon Point with the hospitality of each of our vessels.

During the night, the howl of dingoes echoed across the water. I was fairly acquainted with the howl of the dingo during my past horseback riding days in the Snowy Mountains. I would hear many dingoes howl while I slept in my swag around a campfire, but this was the first time hearing the howl while I slept in a cabin of *Never Die Wondering*.

Log: Sunday, 19 August 2018.

Ian and Carolyn headed north while I stayed longer resting up. I had strained my back from carrying water containers in Tin Can Bay. The day was spent taking the dingy ashore where I was able to take some great photos and explore the tip of Fraser Island. The wind increased dramatically by late in the afternoon, and I had not checked the forecast as I had previously done daily. I was too relaxed in the safety of the Great Sandy Straits. The wind started picking up, and when I checked the weather on my mobile phone, to my surprise, there was a strong wind warning from the west.

Never Die Wondering was exposed to the weather, so, I had a very wet return to the vessel with waves coming into the dingy from the now strong winds. I quickly looked at the chart and decided to head for shelter on the leeward side of Woody Island that was in close proximity. However, as soon as the anchor was raised, I realised that the wind was so strong and the current against me, I was battling to get to Woody Island in daylight and unfortunately, darkness fell, I had to rely on my radar again and once in the shelter of the Island, I dropped anchor in reasonable depth as far off the shore as possible.

The next morning brought calmness to the day, a far cry from the previous night. The low tide exposed the area as very rocky, and I had dropped anchor in just the right spot safely away from the rocky reefs and extended rocky shoreline.

The day was spent bush bashing, exploring this small island. I found a well-kept grave that was engraved to the memory of Sarah May Hardie, who departed this life on 8 August 1883, aged just nineteen years.

I looked up the internet regarding Sarah and found that she was the daughter of Peter Hardie, the lighthouse keeper who had died from lung congestion. Apparently, there are nine burials on the island in total but the only marked grave was of Sarah.

That night I sat around a fire on the beach, cooked a meal, and enjoyed a beer thinking of the swells and passages so far. A feeling of contentment arose being in a warmer climate and now safer seas.

Log: Tuesday, 21 August 2018; Departed Woody Island for Bundaberg.

It was another great sailing day with the south westerly winds. Although the south westerly swells were choppy out in Hervey Bay; all had calmed down by the afternoon. Again, I had dolphins ride the bow waves, and I lay on the trampoline reading of shipwrecks along the coral coast.

CHAPTER SIX

The Sailing Ship Renfrewshire – Bundaberg

This passage to Bundaberg was a special moment for me, as I entered the river system and into the Port of Bundaberg. It was here that my family had arrived on the sailing vessel *Renfrewshire* from Scotland in 1882. On board was Donald Macleod along with his new wife, Christy, his son, Peter, and his two daughters, Flora and Maggie. His youngest daughter, Jess, refused to leave and at the last moment, ran down the walkway of the ship. Donald never saw his daughter, Jess, again.

They had joined the other Scottish Highlanders who were fleeing Scotland due to the notorious highland clearances where they had lost their tenant plots of land replaced by sheep. In desperation, they migrated to the new world but unfortunately, it was going to be one of continued hardship.

The Voyage of the Renfrewshire

This is an excerpt from my second book, *Son of a Highlander*.

In 1882, Donald left Portree and his island home where he and generations of MacLeods had lived for possibly hundreds of years.

The Isle of Skye's population had fallen from 25,000 people to 4,000 due to the Highland clearances and the potato famine.

The surviving Crofters, in some cases, had their rents increased by 30% in one year. Even though Donald was a master blacksmith, work would have been limited due to the exodus of the island people.

The Clyde steamboat was operating from Portree to Glasgow at this time, and more than likely this was the means with which the family reached Glasgow from where they would sail to Australia.

The "Renfrewshire" was one of the first iron-hull built sailing ships, a merchant ship, built in the Port of Glasgow by Henry Murray and Company in 1875 and owned by Thomas Law & Company. A fully rigged ship of three masts, square rigged. She was 202.5 feet long her beam was 33.1 feet. Her depth was 20 feet. She carried four boats, one only as a lifeboat. A pinnace with cork bags, and two other ordinary ship boats. She had at least three compasses, one in the pinnacle of which the vessel was steered. A standard compass on the fore deck and a tell-tale in the cabin skylight.

Donald and family boarded the "Renfrewshire" at the port at Lancaster, Glasgow, in June 1882. This dangerous voyage to Australia would take up to three months, a distance of up to 13,000 nautical miles, destination Bundaberg, Australia.

At the very last moment, his daughter, Jessie, refused to participate on the voyage. She was only sixteen years of age and may have stayed with her sister Anne in Glasgow. No information on the whereabouts of Donald's oldest daughter Mary, or whatever had happened to her is known. Australian Passenger records indicate that only three of Donald's children migrated with him:

Renfrewshire	*Arrival Bundaberg*
Donald McLeod	*14th September 1882*
Christy McLeod (wife)	"
Peter McLeod (son) *Flora McLeod (daughter)*	"
Maggie McLeod (daughter)	"

Another MacLeod had made the voyage with them, a Murdock who was about 26 years of age, he may have been related to Christy. This was going to be the last time Donald and his three children would see Jessie or Anne again.

In 1920, Jessie's son, John Paterson, migrated to Australia, staying with his cousin Peter's son, Jack MacLeod, in Melbourne. Family story tells of Jack's baby so, Harry, being wet nursed by Paterson's wife, Alice, who had the same age daughter. In the 1950s, Harry visited the Paterson's who then lived in Queensland tracing the family story, ironically Paterson's grandson, Ian Kindt, and I have made contact by both visiting Skye and visiting the same home as Donald, both share the same great great grandfather, hence the story unfolds regarding Jessie refusing to sail to Australia.,

Peter was sixteen years of age, his sisters, Flora and Maggie, were eleven and eight years of age. Deaths frequently occurred on these voyages, caused by dysentery in a lot of cases. Infants and young children were very vulnerable. As many as, one in five children, and one in sixty adults died on these voyages to Australia. For the burial, the body was sewn into a piece of canvas or placed in a rough coffin (often hastily knocked up by the ship's carpenter) and weighed down with pig iron or lead to help it sink.

The sailing route was known as the "Great Circle" or the Clipper route. This route from Glasgow caught the northeast trade winds of the Atlantic Ocean and take ships to the equator known as "the doldrums", where sailing vessels could be caught in a no wind situation causing them to lose up to three weeks of voyage time. Ships would continue south sailing past west of Africa reaching 40°S known as "the roaring forties". These strong prevailing winds that blew from the west would take sailing vessels passing far south of Cape of Good Hope in southern Africa across the wild seas of the Southern Ocean to Australian waters. Most captains preferred to sail around Tasmania than attempt to sail through Bass Strait, which was called "the eye of the needle". It was regarded as the most dangerous stretch of water in the world that became known as "the shipwreck coast" claiming hundreds of ships that tried to navigate the narrow path between King Island and the southern side of Victoria in Australian mainland. Hence, the term "eye of the needle". In good sailing, the distance of over 200 nautical miles could be achieved in one day.

Life at Sea

During 1882, life on a sailing vessel at sea was extremely difficult to say the least. In case of Donald MacLeod and his family, the voyage on the *Renfrewshire* in the Southern Ocean at the end of winter, the conditions would have been terrible. Wild seas generated by frequent storms led the sailing vessel to pitch and roll, waves rising above her, on both sides, occasionally crashing onto the ship's deck and water entering the cabins, soaking everything.

Lanterns and candles would go out leaving passengers in the dark, soaking wet and cold. Usually, ships had three classes. The steerage (the lowest deck and below the water line) was the cheapest and the most uncomfortable. Lack of ventilation and no port holes allowed neither views nor lighting. In the steerage, candles or lanterns were sometimes forbidden. Passengers would endure overcrowded and cramped conditions for ninety days or longer.

People in 1882 lacked simple hygiene, toilet paper had not been invented yet Rags were soaked in vinegar and hung on the back of the toilet door to be used by all. This led to the diseases like dysentery. Some ships had outbreaks of influenza and tuberculosis that had been brought aboard by other passengers undetected at medical checks.

Sailors would harpoon dolphins that followed the sailing vessel. Dolphin meat was known as sea hog, that supplemented their salted meat diet. Birds would be caught by fishing lines, albatross were a prized catch, their skins were sold in London to make muffins, the winged bones were used to make smoking pipes, and the webbed footing were used to make tobacco pouches.

On this none-stop voyage, passengers would entertain themselves by singing, card playing, reading, and church services were also held. Navigation of the *Renfrewshire* to Australia was a complex task that required great skill by the captain, with the use of various navigation tools. These included the telescope, compass, ship's log, and sextant. The captain needed to have knowledge of the position of the stars while sailing at night.

Donald MacLeod and his family arrived at Bundaberg Port, Queensland, Australia on the 14th of September 1882. The *Renfrewshire* continued making the same journey on the "Great Circle" for another six years. It was last seen on the 2 July 1888 by the steamer *Aconcagua* having left Glasgow to sail to Brisbane at latitude 17'S and longitude 38'W, it was never seen again, with the loss of eighteen people on board.

Log: 21 August 2018, 1400, hours; Reached the entrance of the Burnett River, and motored up-stream past the port of Bundaberg.

While tracing the route to the Port, I thought what must have gone through the minds of my Gaelic-speaking forefathers who had just survived the lengthy voyage to Australia. The climate would have been balmy in this strange tropical land, compared to the fresh cold climate of Scotland. *Were they frightened, did they regret boarding the Renfrewshire or did they wish they had all stayed with Jess?*

We know now that they landed on a foreign shore right here at the port area where I was passing through and continued a life of hardship in what was frontier land then. They tried to separate gold from clay on gold diggings, a life of adversity for many of those new Australians of the 1880s.

I made my way to the Bundaberg township itself. The unofficial Harbour Master [person living on a vessel in the river) warned me where the sunken ships were so as not to get my anchor tangled on the old wrecks. A lot of river anchorages had a salty (veteran sailor) who live permanently on their boats and are much useful for people coming into a new place to warn them of the hazards.

CHAPTER SIX

While in the Burnett River, I was invited for coffee on a junk, which is a classic Asian vessel of unknown origin, the sails are set square and are like a venetian blind that fold when lowered and are fully battened. The word "junk" is thought to be of Malay origin meaning large vessel. The crew consisted of four young fellers who were part of a Christian group. They planned to sail to Tully and purchase bamboo to create the spars, and then follow the winds. A great inspiring story of young fellers with a passion for adventure.

I spent the next couple of days obtaining provisions and even invested on a new Engel fridge. I was warned not to leave the dingy on the ramp at night as several had been stolen with one being set on fire by local hoons. After all the provisions were loaded, I went back down the river and anchored at a closer anchorage to the entrance so as to get an early start. Once anchored, I watched the full moon rise. At the same time, the sugar cane plantations were set on fire as part of the annual clean up, after harvest. What a spectacular sight this massive fire created! The entire sky glowed with the full moon adding to this fantastic event.

CHAPTER SEVEN

Who is a happier man, he who has braved the storm of life and lived or he who has stayed ashore securely and merely existed?

Hunter S. Thompson

Town 1770

Log: Tuesday, 28 August 2018; 0730 hours; Crossed the bar of the Burnett River destination 1770.

It was terrific sailing in the morning until I had wind against tides. I was able to broad reach then run with the wind from mid-day through the afternoon. Another whale sighting, Hervey Bay is renowned for having whales come into the bay during the migration.

The temperature was now 23°C in the water, and I arrived at the Round Hill point at 1530 hours. I rounded the protruding sharp point 180 degrees into Bustard Bay and headed south into 1770. Unfortunately, it was a low tide although 1.5 hours into a rising tide due to the previous full moon, I was caught on a shallow sandy part right in the marked channel.

I had another catamaran behind me who dropped his anchor knowing it was impossible to get through and I radioed a mono which was about to come into the channel and explained that it was too shallow at present, especially for their deep draft.

I opened a can of beer and just waited for the tide to rise. Unfortunately, it was dark by the time the rising tide lifted the vessel, and I carefully looked for an anchorage, passing another sunken vessel with only its mast protruding through the water. I was able to just see this hazard due to the glow of the moon. I could not get the radar working for whatever reason, but the great night glow from the moon light helped instead.

I awoke in the morning with my vessel on a huge lean. The tide had gone back into low and one of my hulls was left high and dry on the exposed sand with the other side in a trench in the water. Once the tide came in and I was floating, I lifted anchor and found a deeper spot not far from the marina. Locals told me that due to the sanding up of the inlet, many large, drafted vessels had not been able to get in or out of 1770.

The town of 1770 was named so due to Captain Cook's landing here on May 1770. It was the second landing in Australia after Botany Bay and due to this being the first landing of what was to become Queensland, the township claimed to be the birthplace of Queensland.

I visited the local bar in the afternoon, to contribute to the local community, and met lots of interesting people. Consequently, I stayed longer than planned and most likely had a few more ales than my quota. Hence, I was forced to return to *Never Die Wondering* by the dingy at night. I did not have my head torch that I usually use in such situations not just to see, but so that other boaties could see me.

I was motoring back to my vessel. I had turned the mast light on, and it was this distinctive candle glow shine that I was using as my bearing when I could hear voices on my port side. People in another boat were coming towards me and even they did not have a light on. I could not see them in the dark and they could not see me, but I knew the sound, it was like they were heading right towards me since it was getting louder. I yelled out, "Oh, Oh, Oh!" and the next thing I knew was this dingy, flew past my bow and just missed colliding. I made it a habit to always have a head lamp in my wet bag from then on. Within the week, a report came through of how this woman was seriously injured on a collision between dingys with no lights at night.

Log: Thursday, 30 August 2018; 1000 hours; Departed 1770 for destination Pancake Creek

Due to the low tide, it was a late get away and I scraped the sandy bottom on the way out again. The Christian fellers on the junk I had met at Bundaberg were trying to come through with their vessel which was a deeper draft. I explained to them that they would need to wait until the peak of the high tide to get in. So, they changed plans and headed to Pancake Creek as well. It was interesting sailing with the junk sail following.

I blew a block on the main halyard. While replacement was under way, all my display, autopilot, and my depth sounder stopped. Luckily, I had a second sounder on my old plotter as a redundancy.

Pancake Creek

I sailed into Pancake Creek that had the lighthouse on Clews Point as you sail into this safe anchorage. I discovered later on that a short on the wiring with a 5-amp fuse had melted. It took a quick repair, and all was good. Pancake Creek was safe anchorage. I spent a week here, catching up with several maintenance jobs and cleaning *Never Die Wondering*, which was a never-ending job, before exploring this wonderful natural environment.

An incredible place where the large goannas frequented the bush land. I was able to smoke fish on the beach that I caught, smoked in a handy stainless-steel smoker, I had owned for years. Turtles would come into the inlet as well. I walked up to the Bustard Head Lighthouse and was greeted by Ross and his wife who took care of it. I was shown the lighthouse and the cottages which had been restored.

Ross showed me the working of the lighthouse itself. Standing at the top and looking out to the water, watching humpback whales migrating, and looking down at *Never Die Wondering* on anchor in the creek. It was a different viewpoint, very surreal.

What was more fascinating than being on the tower were the bizarre events with a number of tragedies that haunted this unique lighthouse. This consisted of tales of shipwrecks that claimed many lives, drownings of people from the lighthouse who had come there to work, murders, abductions, and suicide.

Besides the three shipwrecks in the vicinity which was why the lighthouse was built, the cemetery had several people who had died at Bustard Head. The first was a worker constructing the lighthouse who was injured and died the next day. Then, forty-nine-year-old Kate Gibson, the lighthouse keeper's wife was tragically discovered the next day by her daughters with her throat cut. She had her arms on her chest with a razor blade from the Lighthouse cottage, and hence, it was ruled suicide. Niel Gibson, the lighthouse keeper, his daughter, Mary, aged twenty, along with the lighthouse assistant and his wife, John and Elizabeth Wilkinson, and the handyman, Alfred Power, were in a small sailing craft only 450 metres from shore when it capsized. All but Niel drowned.

Another family who resided as Lighthouse caretakers experienced tragedy when their infant son, born at the Lighthouse itself, died from being scalded by boiling water. Yet another Lighthouse caretaker's family had a teenager daughter who was rumoured to have been in a love triangle. She was being taken back to the Lighthouse by the local grazier's son when, he was shot but he was found while still alive. He told the people who had found him that the black bastard George had shot him and abducted the girl. George was a half-Chinese and half-Kanaka (Indigenous Pacific Islanders). Queensland's biggest manhunt of its time took place looking for the pair, but neither were ever found. One wonders, was it abduction or did the two of them run away to be with each other? No one will ever really know the truth.

Not being superstitious at all, I thought it was time to leave Pancake Creek. Besides the bizarre history, I was feeling terrible due to the sand flies who had taken a liking to my legs.

Log: Friday, 7 September 2018; Departed 1000 hours.

As I was under way, I had dolphins and a whale breach near me and with great winds I was able to broad reach to the entrance of the Boyne River. After that, due to low tide I dropped anchor out the front of the entrance, as the wind was up and the conditions were very ordinary to say the least. With my binoculars, I tried to figure out the safest way I could get in, but was unable to define the safe route. I rang the Gladstone Marine Rescue on the VHF to get local knowledge. They suggested to stay out for another hour to play it safe with my 0.6 draft. I then went into the Boyne River and dropped anchor at Tannum Sands township.

The next day at low tide, large bolder rocks in the water appeared where I was starting to drop anchor, then decided not. Now, that would have been a disaster to wake up to, a large yonnie under my hull. I got treatment for the terrible sand fly bites and rested for a couple of days and replenished supplies and, carted in water.

Log: Monday, 10 September 2018; 0600 hours; three hours into rising tide and caught on a bloody bar.

I followed my bread crumbs [*marker of previous route*] of way in and this time gave two hours more grace period for a higher tide, but to no avail, *Never Die Wondering* was caught on the sand bar. In some places, you only have to be a few metres off your track to get stuck. This was why rising tides for entering, and in this case, for leaving are a good idea. It was only a little wait until the tide lifted *Never Die Wondering*, and I was away.

The Narrows

Instead of continuing sailing along the Coral Coast. I decided to sail up The Narrows which is a very narrow stretch of water that divides Curtis Island from the mainland. It was only a twenty nautical mile waterway that follows north westerly from the large town of Gladstone to the open waters which is the mouth of the Fitzroy River at its furthest northern point.

It is mangrove lined with a cattle-crossing at one spot where cattle are run on Curtis Island and when mustered are brought across The Narrows at low tide when it has dried. Therefore, picking the tides are paramount because if you are wrong, you would become stuck high and dry until the next high tide.

Log: Monday, 10 September 2018; 0900 hours.

I caught the rising tide that took *Never Die Wondering* comfortably through The Narrows on the current. I passed Swan Island then hit the slack water, and distinctively saw the change of tide with murky water on the ebb. Dolphins that swam near me, seemed to be of a much lighter colour.

It was a great run as I only had thirty minutes with the tide against me and was able to get 7.5 knots SOG, when the tide became in my favour. The tide took me further north and then, out into the open waters with the extremely dark muddy water from the Fitzroy River. Although wind over tide made it rough seas, but with the full main and head sail I made it to Great Keppel Island arriving at 1645 hours, passing Middle Island on my port side and Great Kepple on my starboard side. I dropped anchor in a terrific anchorage on the north side of the island, at Leeks Beach.

The last time I had been here was in 1983, with Jeff Mullenger. We were only eighteen years of age at that time and in the 1980s it was a party island where you had a camping ground with a resort and a bar. The next day, I made my way by tender to the once popular resort, and walked the area, but there was no campground. It was not the place it was in its heydays.

CHAPTER SEVEN

Log: Wednesday, 12 September 2018; 0600 hours; Departed Great Keppel Island.

At twelve to fourteen knots of wind. I beam reached SOG of 6.2, and then 7.0 knots SOG. What a great sail! Two whales appeared as I sailed on the east side of the North Keppel Island. The swells were up but short and it seemed I was flying with only nine to ten knots of wind, having the current in my favour was a blessing.

More whales and dolphins were sighted, I was able to go onto the trampoline and get the full view of them swimming on my bow waves, wondering how on earth they did not hit the bow of *Never Die Wondering*.

At 1355 hours, I dropped anchor at the base of Flinders Mountain in the creek mouth, known as Port Clinton.

Log: Thursday, 13 September 2018.

I awoke with turtles around the vessel, and quickly started sailing as I could now run with the wind. I was able to get the spinnaker up, and had the pole out as well, and continued running with the wind with the kite up to nine knots of wind. I just got the kite down in the sock, and pole away when the winds freshened. You could notice the change of currents where I quickly had wind over tide, and rounded Cape Townsend dropping anchor near a big sign that said, "DANGER BOMB WARNING".

I was in the Shoalwater Bay Military Training Area, in another great anchorage between Townshend Island and Leicester Island. The military give warnings when any military explosive training is scheduled to happen over the VHF. Since there was no warning, I was fine, that is as long as my VHF was working.

I hooked a large shark here but lost it while bringing it in, as opposed to me cutting the line. I parted, this the potentially dangerous place, for Percy Islands.

Percy Islands

Log: Friday, 14 September 2018; 0815 hours; Departed for Percy Islands.

Against a strong current, not far into my sail, I was able to get a nice south easterly and broad reached the forty nautical miles to these incredible islands. They are on the southern side of the Whitsunday Islands that are the most visited island for yachties in Australia.

I had lost count of the whales I had seen by then but undoubtedly this day was going to be the record holder. Whale after whale I passed, and at one stage, I was certain one had died as it seemed to be just floating above the surface. That was until I passed fairly close to it and the enormous humpback just gave a flip of his wing, as if to say, I'm okay! After this encounter, on the port side close to my vessel at almost twenty meters, a huge whale came straight towards me, moving above the water line and making a dive into the water, like it was going to ram me. I quickly placed my hands on the cockpit roof to stop my head from smashing into the ceiling, as this enormous creature went right underneath *Never Die Wondering*. I waited anxiously with the palms of my hands still pushing the cockpit ceiling. Luckily, nothing happened, the whale did not even surface.

I anchored in West Bay, a very scenic place about which I had written in my log, *it was the BEST place so far*! It was quite exciting to be sailing into these hilly islands with native pines growing on some of the ridges, and a very scenic bay where I anchored on the west side of what is known as Middle Island.

On the beach was an open A-frame hut that had a line of coconut trees. The hills at the back were partially tree covered. This spot had become a type of pilgrimage for yachties. They visited this place and left somewhat of a tribute of their vessels in a way of sorts. In most cases, people wrote their names of their yachts on a piece of material like driftwood, old buoy, etc. I sprayed a wine bottle with my anchor chain marker, a spray paint that was an orange type of colour, then with black paint I wrote, *SV NEVER DIE WONDERING 2018*.

In September 1802, Mathew Flinders while mapping the Australian continent visited Percy Islands, the first known European to do so. He entered the little cove on West Bay on his rowing boat and he wrote:

> *I went to examine a little cove, or basin into which the height of the surrounding hills gave expectation of finding a run of fresh water. The entrance is little more than wide enough for the oars of a rowing boat, the Basin, within side is mostly dry at low water and the borders are overrun with the tiresome mangrove, but when the tide is in, it is one of the prettiest little places imaginable.*
>
> *Mathew Flinders, September 1802*

CHAPTER SEVEN

Mathew Flinders described the place well. I motored my tender into the lagoon with its narrow passage and explored the island. It had a handful of people living on the island. Several people had lived here on the island over the years and continued to do so. There was an additional hut on the beach which functioned as a book exchange. It had a sign saying, "swap or donate, take one leave one", along with an honesty box, jars of honey, and some of the produce from the island.

Prior to arriving on the island, I had been talking with Jason and Sharon Bon over the mobile phon. I had met them at Lakes Entrance Victoria in previous years when they sailed to the Gippsland Lakes on a couple of occasions. They were sailing south, so we planned to meet, However, no phone reception and with so many islands in the Whitsunday's (seventy-four in total), I was starting to think that it might not eventuate.

Then, I received a call by the VHF radio which is only good for a few nautical miles. They had taken a calculated guess that I would most likely sail to Middle Island first. They arrived with a Spanish mackerel for dinner, and we enjoyed several beers together before they quickly moved off at dawn due to a good weather window.

One day, the *Young Endeavor* arrived at the A-frame, that I had passed near Sydney in Broken Bay. She was anchored, the crew came ashore, and among them was Brad Lancaster who had taken me through the marine radio test at Lakes Entrance just prior to my departure. He assisted in training the development of the participants. While speaking with the crew, two humpback whales swam around the *Young Endeavor*, splashing their fins and tails, and putting on an incredible show for all to admire. What a sight to behold!

The skipper of the *Young Endeavor*, Adam, got me the latest weather print out. I decided to stay and socialised with many other yachties who visited. All the while, the whales continued to come into this unique little bay.

Log: Tuesday, 18 September 2018; Middle Island.

I walked up to the high part of the hill where I could get phone reception. My son, Brandon, was trying to reach me, since my mother had been taken to hospital. The doctor had informed Brandon that she might only last for twenty-four hours. I was able to have a conversation with Mum, and then, quickly made my way back down the hill. The next destination was Melbourne.

Luckily, the Mackay Marina was just a day's sail away. The next morning, I lifted anchor, and with sail up and both motors running, I went straight to Mackay Marina. I got in touch with the Marina by mobile phone when in range of reception and arranged a berth for my vessel and flight tickets for myself.

I took a taxi to the airport, then a flight to Brisbane followed by another flight to Melbourne. Brandon picked me up at the airport and we went straight to the hospital to see my mother before she left this world.

I was concerned that I would not make it, while I was in the taxi in Mackay. The driver said to me, "She will, mate. They seem to hang on to say their goodbyes." He was right, although Mum had been given twenty-four hours to live, by then it was well over that time period.

When I got to her, she apologised to me for becoming ill, "Sorry, Al. But I am okay now." In fact, she said, "I feel better, I can come back with you and Brandon sailing. I would love to come with you both. Can I come sailing in the Whitsundays with you?"

Even in her last moments of life, Mum was still positive and supportive of me, wanting to join in the sailing adventure. The next day, Friday, 21 September 2018 at 5.20 pm, my mother passed away with both Brandon and I, by her side.

Eulogy to My Mother

My mother was a glamour princess, the most well-dressed, stylish woman I have known. A person who never suffered fools, was free spirited, mentally strong, with a positive mind that lasted even in the final moments of her life.

She was a woman who seemed to always get her own way.

Mum was born on the 5th September 1929, in a little rented cottage in Footscray, and grew up in another rented home in Walter Street Footscray. She was the middle child of Alby and Laurie Hamid, she had an older brother, Alby Junior, and a younger sister, Pat. Her father, Alby, was a boxer who originally supported his family with the earnings received from the boxing ring. Later, he became a jeweller, a trade he learnt from his father, Casim Abdul Hamid. This was my mother's grandfather, who came to Australia from Ceylon as a teenager, an Asian, black man who was a Muslim. My mother was extremely close to her grandfather. She wrote in her diary about him and I quote:

CHAPTER SEVEN

"I loved my grandfather so very much. He was so Generous to all us grandchildren, the most lovable Human being I have ever known".

Without doubt, the close relationship that my mother had with her grandfather forged her strong, outspoken beliefs against racism, and her acceptance of all people. She had a great sense of social justice and become furious if she heard anyone speak in a racist way. She did not tolerate ignorance, nor people who showed no empathy or understanding of others.

Mum attended the Hyde St state school in the 1930s and then went onto the *Footscray Girls School*. The school in its day was called, *Domestic Arts School for Young Ladies*, so you can see where the foundations of a glamour princess started. Mum studied there for the length of the second world war, 1939 to 1945.

She once told me a story of how her father had bought her a pair of shoes during the war years. When she tried them on, she complained to him about how they were silly shoes as they did not fit probably. Later on, in the day, her father presented her with a second pair of shoes which fitted perfectly. So, Mum got her own way again. During family dinner that night, her mother questioned her father as to what had happened to the clock that was now missing from the wall. It turned out that her father had hocked the family clock, so that his daughter had shoes that fitted.

Mum entered the work force as an apprentice hairdresser, and once qualified would work as a beautician come hairdresser stylist. Her work led her to train other women in hair styling, and she spent several years travelling and working in Sydney as well as Melbourne and managing a hair dressing saloon in Footscray.

She became engaged to a feller at nineteen years of age, whereby her father held her a nineteenth birthday party along with an engagement party. Mum told me, "That first engagement quickly ended when I met your father!" So, that was the end of the engagement.

My father, Harry Bliss MacLeod, was ten years older than my mother and introduced her to a world she was not accustomed to – bush and camping life. Still, that was not the end of Mum's glamour and princess days. She went on to become the most stylish and well-dressed woman, probably in the history of the Australian bush. She never left the tent unless she had her perfect attire and make-up on. Dad would be fishing before the break of day and. my mother, on the other hand, saw no reason to be out of bed at that time. You could probably count all the sun rises on one hand she had witnessed in her eighty-one years.

One morning, Mum was in the tent, zipped up in the sleeping bag, while Dad went fishing. When the sun was up and beating down on the canvas tent, Mum tried to get out of the sleeping bag but the zip was stuck. She nearly perished by the time Dad returned to assist her escape from the torture chamber. You can only imagine the earful Dad got but that didn't dampen her camping spirits at all.

Dad purchased a house in 17 Archer Avenue, Ascot Vale, an inner-city suburb in Melbourne in the late 50s, and this became the home for Mum for the next twenty-five years. I came into the world in 1965 in this home which was also hair dressing salon that Mum operated in a back room.

There was a constant flow of women, coming and going with funny looking hair styles. Today, you would call them Marge Simpson lookalikes. I remember Mum placing all these women under funny looking dome heaters. Hair styling while non-stop talking, always up for a conversation.

My parents had an incredible relationship, two opposites that supported and encouraged each other. Mum would always motivate my father to continue his bush pursuits. She came along on most camping trips, once camping for three months in a tent on a riverbank.

Dad stepped up in the world and purchased a foldout camper trailer where Mum could cook inside, away from the flies. One time, Dad asked Mum to guide him while he was reversing. She started yelling at Dad. and Dad started yelling back at her as to why was she yelling at him. A little later, he realised that he had driven over her feet, and they were trapped under the tyres!

She would attend the Flemington racetrack all glamoured up, of course. She attended social events like the gown of the year, and in her later years, prior to the stroke, Mum was renowned for having her second home in the Crown Casino, returning home at 3 am in the morning.

Mum was involved with everything I did, from the school canteen to, school council, cubs, and then scouts. My mother taught me not to put up with stressful situations, if they were unnecessary, not to conform to other people's expectations that differed from what I wanted to do in my life. She refused to put up with people's trivial dramas. An extremely positive woman, this positive attitude was put to the test when I introduced my mother to a world she was not accustomed to.

In 1994, I faced a lengthy prison term when I shot a known criminal in self-defence during a home invasion. My mother started learning about the so-called legal system, attending all the lengthy court cases, driving interstate while emotionally supporting me. Her no nonsense attitude and support, for me during that horrendous time cannot be justified in words. However, the stress she must have endured while watching her only child, face the prospect of a long prison term, must have been a terrible strain on her. Still, not once did she show any negative attitude towards that situation, just 100% support.

My mum stood by me, where I felt like others had not. That was just the start of my mother's learning about the injustices of our legal system. Unfortunately, my bad choices in relationships led my mother back into many courtrooms. Either to the family law court when she was legally required to give evidence of how she was given shares in a grazing property, or the emotional legal battle with obtaining full custody of my son. Mum was there with me riding the whole emotional roller coaster, again with 100% positive support and an attitude that said, "You will win my son." And win, we did.

Mum was dragged into court for the last time, regarding a dodgy solicitor who had billed mum for services that she did not request. In refusing to pay, she was forced to attend a local matter in Victoria. So, Mum was representing herself and now I was there supporting her. Mum's glamourous attire got a new look, like a smart looking barrister. I mentioned to this solicitor before we went in how there was no evidence that she had employed him, and that the professional standards would be notified.

Then, the boxer's daughter came out in Mum, and she told this dodgy solicitor just what she thought of him. He quickly signed a "no contest" and stormed out of the court. Mum now was enjoying the legal system. "We fixed him," she said. I think Mum's glamourous barrister attire did assist again; she got her own way.

In 2007, Mum's smoking took its toll and she suffered from a major stroke. Again, she kept the positive attitude. "I will be alright. I will get out of bed," despite every doctor saying she would not. I was also told by the so-called medical experts, that I must commit her to a high care facility. Mum just said, "That's bullshit! I'll just need physio." So, despite the medical opinions we got a physiotherapist and Mum worked very hard to get herself to a standard that where no high care was needed. She was able to go to an aged care facility of her choice. Again, Mum got her own way.

Over eleven years, she had the quality of life where she first lived at Corandirk House, then Mount Alexander Lodge and made great friendships. That positive mindset again. She never ever played the victim card, saying. "I'm not a stroke victim, I'm a stroke survivor!"

When I first purchased a live-aboard yacht, Mum again glamoured up wearing a sailor's attire. We sailed for five days on local waters with her, along with Brandon and Jeff Mullenger. She wanted to be involved with all the sailing tasks. When the wind picked up a bit, Brandon quickly handed Mum a rope. "Quick Grandma, hold this tight and whatever you do, don't let go!"

A couple of hours later, we get back to Metung and I tried to take the rope that Mum was holding. She said, "I can't let this go, I have to hold it! Brandon said so…." She was holding a three-metre piece of rope that didn't do anything. Mum had insisted on coming sailing and being useful. So again, Mum got her own way.

The last property project I did was building a house in a factory and transporting it to a steep waterfront block. There were cranes and semi-trailers, people running around lowering this dwelling onto stumps. Mum was there, involved with the process. I looked across when Mum got out of the car and I told her to sit and wait inside, not to get out due to it being a dangerous site. Nevertheless, she managed with her walking stick to walk to the crane operator and all the workmen, congratulating them on positioning the dwelling, shaking all their hands. Again, Mum got her own way.

In that last week. I was on an isolated island in the Coral Sea. Brandon was to fly into Mackay, and we were both supposed to be sailing back to Papua New Guinea. I climbed a hill on the island to get reception to talk to Brandon when he told me, "Dad, you've got to get back. I don't think she's going to last."

Getting back was a day sailing trip along with a couple of plane trips. Still, she wasn't happy that I had come to Melbourne, saying she was sorry she had got ill and I had to come back. She then added that since I was there, she believed she was good enough to sail with Brandon and I. "Just help me get out of bed, and I'm coming. I want to come sailing…," she said.

So, this free-spirit, proud woman, who taught me to be a free spirit, like her, gets her own way again. Mum will come sailing in the Coral Sea with her son and grandson in the next few days, only in a different form.

CHAPTER EIGHT

The distance between your dreams and reality is called action.

Whitsundays

Brandon and I wasted no time after Mum left us. We quickly returned to *Never Die Wondering* in Mackay, hired the marina courtesy car, arranged supplies and fuel, and away we went.

Log: Friday, 5 October 2018; 1300 hours; Departed Mackay Marina for destination Brampton Island.

Not the best of sailing conditions with a northerly, therefore, we went windward through the short passage, in any case, we were extremely keen to be on our way. I decided to end the relationship I had been in for over two years, for many reasons. Mostly because all I needed now, was for my son and I, to have some peace with no dramas.

Sometimes you have to break your heart, in order to save your soul.

We arrived on the western side of Brampton Island in a sheltered bay protected from the northerlies. The next day we went exploring the island and walked along the foreshore among rocky boulders. It once had a railway that brought supplies from the jetty to the now abandoned Brampton Resort, an eerie place considering it would have been a thriving hotel in its heyday. The air strip on the eastern side of the resort had planes still landing, only for a quick visit though. The resort was a thriving tourist destination up until 2010, when two brothers behind *United Petroleum* bought the resort and closed it in 2011 to redevelop. However, that never eventuated, and the place had been left to rot since. There was a caretaker and a security guard who made sure that no visitors entered the severely damaged buildings.

We walked back to our vessel through the middle of the island, and had to negotiate the tender through a coral reef. It had clams and was full of black tip sharks as well as a couple of large green turtles.

Brandon was keen to operate his recently acquired drone, so we went to a large part of the beach at low tide to fly this contraption. When Brandon had this drone buzzing up in the air, he started yelling as it seemed the contraption had a mind of its own and it flew straight towards the water. Well, into the drink it went, and that was the end of the drone.

Log: Sunday, 7 October 2018; 0755 hours; Departed West Bay Brampton Island for destination White Bay, Haslewood Island.

Another great day of sailing although gentle northeasterly winds were there but we still made good ground. It was terrific to be exploring the Whitsundays with my boy, the area is well protected by virtue of the many islands and the Great Barrier Reef protects you from the Coral Sea. We sailed between Mandela and Shaw islands arriving at White Bay at 1610 hours and noticed a yacht further closer to the beach.

Consequently, I thought it was safe to head in that direction as it was a mono with a longer draft and one would presume mine being 0.6 of a meter should have clearance as well. We slowly entered the bay looking at a turtle and watching out for bommies (submerged offshore reefs) since it was low tide. As luck would have it, we came close to the bommies and realised it was impossible to get into the bay further. The other yacht must have entered on the high tide. One of the bommies resembled a turtle, the type that would not get out of the way!

Log: Monday, 8 October 2018; 0725 hours; Departed for Whitehaven Beach

We started against the tide at only 1.5 SOG and struggled against wind and tide to reach our destination. However, once we went around the islands and out of the current and wind on the nose, we came into the picture-perfect Whitehaven Beach that many describe as Australia's best scenic beach. We dropped anchor in the turquoise water and walked along the incredible white sandy beach and swam in the warm crystal-clear waters.

It was an ideal spot, and we decided it would be a nice place to scatter Mum's ashes, as she loved the beach and was able to get her dying wish of sailing with Brandon and I, although in a different form. So, at Latitude 2'17,176 and Longitude 149'02,803, we scattered my mother's ashes.

We sailed further north to Butterfly Bay on Hook Island and was able to grab one of the protection moorings. These are used as preference to the anchor to protect the coral. We could hear the sounds of goats on the island coming from high up in the rocky hills. Brandon went climbing up the hills to see the goats, while I stayed on board watching the event. He climbed and climbed while this goat appeared and seemed to sneak past him. It then made its way down the hill and stood out on a rocky ledge on the foreshore, and just bleated, like saying, "Ha…ha, I have outsmarted you!"

Log: Tuesday, 9 October 2018; 0745 hours; Depart Butterfly Bay for Gloucester Passage.

As soon as we left the bay, the wind was on our stern. Therefore, we raised the spinnaker and had a great run with the kite, until the autopilot stopped working. Since this was a mechanism failure, it was hand steering from then on.

The passage is between the mainland of Cape Gloucester and Gloucester Island. We arrived at Cape Gloucester Resort to the south of the passage at 1515 hours and tied onto the one of many moorings. What a fantastic place this was with, free mooring use as long as we had meals there. We did so along with consumption of beverage in the bar and playing pool.

The autopilot obviously needed replacement parts, so we decided to go into the Bowen Marina and sailed the short passage the next day. In two days, we had hired a car, drove to Airlie Beach, purchased the replacement part for the autopilot, obtained supplies and fuel, and again, enjoyed beverages in the *Bowen Island Yacht Club*.

Log: Friday, 12 October 2018; Destination Upstart Bay.

We were only a couple of hours out when we noticed a hazy smoke conditions in the vessel. We quickly started looking and discovered that it was an electrical fire as one of the wires had been exposed to water over time. We quickly pulled out the burning wire and later found out the leak was from the deck, being fresh water, during this ordeal, so we caught a nice mackerel for dinner.

Anchored in Upstart Bay, we used live bait and burly for fishing during the night. What a scene it was with sharks of all sizes in frenzy! We had to cut lines as they were too large to pull in. This was all happening with a lightening display and a small shower of rain.

Magnetic Island

Log: Friday, 13 October 2018; 0945 hours; Departed Cape Upstart for destination Cape Bowling Green.

It was an overcast day and the threat of thunderstorms loomed large. We were sailing windward at 60 degrees and dropped the centre board, but in all honesty, all the times that I have used this device, I could not find a great deal of benefit. *Never Die Wondering* has ¾ length keels although only a 0.6 metre draft, it really sufficed, and it was difficult to bring the centre board up if needed when the wind shifted. So, I rarely used it, especially solo.

We rounded the sand spit of Cape Bowling Green and dropped anchor just inside the bay where the sand spit had a bay within a bay. A great stop with the now calm conditions in our favour.

Log: Sunday, 14 October 2018; Depart 0700 hours; Destination Magnetic Island.

The light winds picked up from the south enabling us to be able to fly the kite. It was a great sail with the power of the wind pushing us from behind. Brandon was on the helm, and I was sitting up on the trampoline when all of a sudden, we went off course. Brandon yelled, "Dad, we are in trouble. All the steering has gone!"

After a quick inspection, it was evident that the cable steering had broken and therefore, we were without control. We opened the floor to try to repair the cable, any temporary fix would suffice for trying to tie extra lines, etc. to the broken cable. We were a fair distance from the shore so in no danger. The mono that was sailing behind us called to offer assistance, and in good faith, stayed nearby as we tried to repair the damage.

CHAPTER EIGHT

We were using clamps and when we thought we had the cable repaired it would give way again. The mono, *SV Celantro*, offered us clamps, so, I lowered the tender and rowed over to their vessel to get them, then rowed back. Brandon and I worked frantically to repair using all sorts of means trying to tie the broken wire by attaching another piece of wire with clamps. When we thought it was done, we motored away only to have the wire give way again. In the frantic work environment, we managed to have the tether line to the tender get caught in the prop and snap it. I quickly jumped into the water and swam to the getaway tender. I was swimming amongst a large school of mackerel wondering what might be chasing them.

Back on board, we managed to join the wires in a spot where they would not break being clear of other parts, but we were only able to turn 15 degrees at the most. It was still alright for a temporary fix, and away we went to Magnetic Island, knowing quite well we had been lucky. If that had happened close to a rocky cape, or God forbid, at nighttime along the Bass Strait or Tasman Coast, it could have been fatal.

We contacted the marina at Magnetic Island, explaining that we could hardly turn, and they were there to assist us coming in at 1445 hours.

Magnetic Island is only a few miles off the coast from Townsville and is a very picturesque place with large granite boulders dominating the landscape. The hilly terrain protected coves and fringing coral reef. The island had eucalyptus and hoop pine, and even a koala population. We were able to get all the new wiring, and several other jobs completed and hired a car and explored this wonderful place that had a reasonable population of 2,300 people. The entire island was less than 13,000 acres.

Log: Tuesday, 14 October 2018; 0850 hours; Departed Magnetic Island.

We sailed on the west side of Magnetic Island and noticed James and Sandra from *SV Celantro* who had waited for us when we were in trouble. They were heading south, so, we radioed them, and then Brandon rowed out with the tender and gave them a bottle of wine in appreciation. They were heading to Townsville to repair their gear box problems.

We sailed north passing Acheron Island, then sailed along the western side of Great Palm Island that has an Aboriginal settlement with a population of 3,000. We also passed another magnificent looking island with its tall hills although only 554-metre peaks from sea level, it really looked mountainous.

We continued to Juno Bay which lays between Orpheus Island and Fantome Island where we anchored on the Orpheus side. What a magical place with coral fringe reef where turtles swam around. Unfortunately, there were many huge shells of clams littered that people had destroyed to get the clam meat. Terrible to see as they can live up to 100 years only to be destroyed for someone's greed. Australia has had many illegal fishermen come in from southeast Asia and illegally fish our waters and dive for the clam meat, killing many of these creatures. Although these would have been destroyed most likely by locals, they were protected in Australia and many other countries under the convention on international trade in endangered species of wild fauna and flora appendices.

On the beach, we cooked a BBQ and sat around the fire at night. I fell asleep on the sand tired but feeling privileged to be able to sail from one island to another in the most scenic of places. We spent our time snorkelling in the fringe coral reefs and Brandon climbed a coconut tree to harvest several coconuts. We enjoyed drinking the juice and eating the flesh of this diverse fruit.

Hinchinbrook Island

Log: Wednesday, 17 October 2018; 1200 hours; Departed Orpheus Island for Hinchinbrook Islan.

This was a short passage, and the now hilly type of islands made room for mountainous type islands with Hinchinbrook's peaks. At the highest was Mount Bowen 1142 metre and several others near the 1,000-metre mark.

We planned to sail through the Hinchinbrook Channel that separated the island from the mainland. Once you entered the channel, the fresh smell of the rainforest was evident, a very strong inviting smell. The clouds formed a misty shroud covering the high points of the mountain ranges where you got to see glimpses of the peaks, an incredible sight and smell.

CHAPTER EIGHT

We anchored at Haycock Island, what I would call a postage stamp island, in the middle of the channel. We took the tender through the mangroves exploring and dropping the crab pots.

Log: Thursday, 18 October 2018; Departed Haycock Island.

We cooked and ate a large mud crab while sailing up the channel. We dropped anchor at a place called Scraggy Point on the northwest side of Hinchinbrook. We went ashore on the little beach and cooked some mackerel by way of smoking it. There was an inlet with a narrow creek that had the distinctive crocodile tracks along the sand. We walked up the creek where the fresh water was, we watched out if any reptiles were about before safely taking our fresh baths. During the night, around the fire on the beach we could hear crocs in the creek inlet.

Log: Friday, 19 October 2018; 0800 hours; Departed Scraggy Point for destination Dunk Island

The tide was ebbing in our favour and with a nice easterly we managed a comfortable sail and made great timing with a constant six knots SOG. With dolphins riding the starboard bow waves, we both spent the day reading on the trampoline, arriving at Dunk Island at 1245 hours. There were several other yachts anchored, adjacent to the abandoned Dunk Island resort.

In 2006, Cyclone Larry made its mark on Dunk Island. Unfortunately, only five years later in 2011, Cyclone Yasi further damaged the resort. It was rumoured that insurance being impossible to obtain was the reason this once popular resort never reopened.

Brandon and I explored the island, and the abandoned resort with its once popular swimming pool. It had the trademark of a Ulysses butterfly on the floor of the pool, now left to deteriorate further. We climbed the hills to get a brilliant view of the area looking down at *Never Die Wondering* from the high hill, that was once used as a military look out in second world war.

The next day, we were underway taking advantage of the great weather condition and departed at 0530 hours for Fitzroy Island, beam reached as the wind was a gentle easterly and caught spotty mackerel for our dinner. We passed the picturesque Russell Island and were tempted to drop anchor but given the great sailing, we pressed on.

At Fitzroy Island we anchored out the front of the resort on the island's western side, protected from the south easterlies.

We went ashore by dingy; the beach was covered in broken coral. We visited *Foxy's Bar*, it was a great open-air type of bar where Brandon and I enjoyed meals and many beverages, and met many people that came across in boats from Cairns as it was only a short passage.

I received a call from Graham Tuppen who was living in Cairns. We had first met while playing against him at football under-12s at Parkside in Footscray. Later, we went to tech school together. I had not seen Tuppen for more than thirty years. We sailed to Cairns up the Cairns River, passing the city with several high-rises, a far cry from how I remembered the place back in 1986. We anchored in the river and tendered over to the yacht club. Tuppens had a car for us, to get supplies and we enjoyed the thirty-year catch-up over a few beers on *Never Die Wondering*. We exchanged stories, of the likes of Papua New Guinea where he was working as a fly in-fly out worker.

We put the crab pots out to be checked at night. Then, Brandon took me for a joy ride up the little creek tributary, lined with mangroves, on the falling tide and in the dark with the spotlight. There was a concern of getting caught in the mud. It would not be ideal as the dingy was just an inflatable PVC and would be easy for the crocs to use as a teething ring.

Log: Tuesday, 23 October 2018; 0800 hours, Destination Snapper Island.

We left after filling up fuel and water in Cairns Marlin Marina. We motored out into Trinity Bay since there was no wind whatsoever. During the day, we decided to veto Snapper Island and head for Low Isles. Along the way, the vessel clicked up 2,000 nautical miles since entering into Bass Strait six months ago.

At Low Isles, we anchored between two islands on the northern part of the large fringe reef. It was here that the first study of coral on the barrier reef was conducted. The small islet on the western side of the reef, had a lighthouse, established in 1878. We waked around the isle meeting the caretakers and witnessing thousands of imperial pigeons coming into the little isle to nest at night. This white bird migrated from Papua New Guinea every year. I found dozens of islands throughout the north into the Torres Straits that are home to these migratory bird for a large part of the year.

CHAPTER EIGHT

We snorkelled amongst the coral and the many black tip sharks that frequented the fringe reef. The next morning, we were away again, this time sailing close to the magnificent rainforest of what is known as Daintree. We passed steep mountainous terrain at one place, the distinctive land slide that had created a large scar on the environment.

Log: Wednesday, 24 October 2018; 0945 hours; Passed Cape Tribulation.

Brandon and I had been to, this protruding cape several years before as we explored Cape York in a 4x4 but exploring through the sea is by far a greater experience.

Here is how the log was written in my diary. It enabled me to remember events by log, photos, and paper charts.

> Lat. 16'12.629 N Long. 145'31.255 E Bearing 347 T
>
> Distinctive land slide/steep mountains
>
> 0835 EES 4.7 Knots wind SOG 5.2 Full sails
>
> 0945: Passing Cape Tribulation Turtles x 2
>
> 16'04.099 N / 145'29.212 E, B = 346 T
>
> 11.30: Passing Bloomfield River entrance, passing Toll Ferry starboard TOLL Firefly
>
> 1225: 15'54.696 N/ 145'26.766 E, B = 343 T
>
> 1300 passing Hope Island Reef on Starboard side dolphins x 2
>
> 1400: Passing Newcastle Bay, Cargo ship
>
> 1445: 10 knots wind S/E GREAT SAILING SOG 5.0 Broad reach
>
> 1555: Passing Dawson reef on starboard side
>
> 1730: Anchored Endeavor River opposite ramp.
>
> To date 2,081 nm today 60 NM

I had first come to Cooktown in 1986 and lived on the beach at Quarantine Bay with my then girlfriend, Carmel. I had visited several years ago with Brandon as well. I could clearly make out the camp site sailing past, due to the tall coconut tree on the beach. It's great to sail into places where you have stayed at before, it gave an entirely different aspect to the region.

We spent a couple of days in Cooktown enjoying pub meals and visiting the two great Museums of the town. The modern one had a great collection and information of Cooks landing and the near loss of the *Endeavor* that hit the reef, hence, the name Endeavor Reef. There Cook was able to throw overboard heavy weighted objects of the likes of cannons, etc. to be able to move the *Endeavor* off the reef. Luckily, it had a beach where they were able to do repairs. The town was named after this great mariner.

CHAPTER NINE

At sea I have learned how little a person needs, not how much a person needs.

East Coast Cape York

Log: Saturday, 27 October 2018; 0740 hours; Departed Cooktown.

We waited for the tide to lift *Never Die Wondering* as it was caught on the sand. Once the tide lifted the vessel, we sailed north with very light winds, so, we were forced to have one motor running. At 0930 hours. with ten knots of wind from the southeast and full sails, we sailed slowly at four knots SOG. The distinctive Cape Bedford resembled a tabletop with a horizontal layer of rock on its steep sides. The white silicon sand dunes are another scenic attraction along this coastline that seemed to go on for many miles. We watched the back of the stern amazed, as a shark followed for a while.

We were able to raise the kite and had a spinnaker run for a couple of hours but had to drop the kite passing Cape Bedford. We had to resort back to full main and genoa until Cape Flattery, passing a police boat, and then a fishing boat with its several tenders being dragged behind the fishing vessel. We anchored at Cape Flattery at 1720 hours.

Cape York peninsula is the largest wilderness area in northern Australia, it is uninhabited in most parts, with no substantial towns on the eastern Coast. It is roughly 400 nautical miles until we get to Seisia, a small settlement on the western tip of Australia or Thursday Island in the Torres Strait.

This enormous peninsula has a population of 7,500 people, the majority being Aboriginal and Torres Strait Islanders. It is

1,37,000 sq. km in size with the east coast being the Coral Sea in the north, bordered to the Torres Strait and the Gulf of Carpentaria to the west. With its countless rivers and creek systems, mangrove forests, flood out swamp country, and massive savanna eucalyptus bushland, it truly is a wilderness region.

Log: Sunday 28 October; 2018, Depart 0600 hours; from Cape Flattery Bay for destination Ninian Bay

We caught a great spotty mackerel only a short sail away from the bay. With a nice southerly, we had the kite up, peacefully sailing along. I was able to take a photo of Brandon siting up at the bow looking out towards the sea within view of Noble Island which was clearly visible resembling a cone like rocky beacon with the spinnaker flying. That photo would later be used as an advertisement board at the front of the Metung property for accommodation that would be named "Seafarers Rest".

As we admired this endless sailing voyage, I remember Brandon saying, "How can you return to the Gippsland Lakes now, Dad, after sailing here?"

> *"The cost of not following your heart is spending the rest of your life wishing you had".*

Another great sized mackerel was caught, and Brandon even pulled in a large shark that was released. The freezer was now full of mackerel fish steaks.

The mountain ranges ran along the coastline and are magnificent with rocky outcrops. Some had timbered areas, other parts had open forest type and sandy beaches that seemed to go on forever, and hardly anyone in sight. In some cases, the rocky cliffs dropped straight to the sea. We anchored in Ninian Bay at 1810 hours and feasted on mackerel. What a great day!

The next morning, we sailed a short passage of thirty-two nautical miles to the Flinders Island group and passed Cape Melville to sail into these remarkable rocky islands. We had a magnificent place for anchoring at Frederick Point which was just off the west side of the main Flinders Island bordering Owens Channel. We explored Flinders Island by climbing the hill for a great look towards the many coral reefs and the several islands.

There was a large mushroom style rock that had a cave like entrance. We crawled underneath to discover many Aboriginal paintings of hands that were distinctive but other paintings that seemed to be of tools. There was also an ancient water well, that the local inhabitants had chipped away in the rock to fashion a deep well for their water source.

We dinged across the Channel to Stanley Island and walked a trail to a shelter where the Aboriginal paintings were of great quality and had stood the test of time. There were paintings of animals like a fruit bat and one that resembled a dugong. The red ochre was used along with a white ochre to paint along the border. For instance, a boomerang in red ochre and a fine white ochre fine line along the outside of it. There were fish with similar white enhancing look.

The most magnificent painting was of, what is believed to be, pearl luggers, several of them with masts and bow sprits, crocodiles, and sea snakes, and other paintings that can only be described as some sort of mythical creatures with splayed out hands.

Log: Tuesday, 30 October 2018; 0500 hours; Departed Flinders Island

We needed the radar as we headed out in the darkness of the morning, as early as possible to be able to reach Morris Island in daylight hours. There was a stormy look in the weather, coming in from the southeast. Booby birds were prolific, flying about the vessel, turtles and dolphins too, Cape York had it all. This area had two distinctive passages through the barrier reef system, the inner route which was closer to the coast, and the Lads Passage further out to the east. We chose the first route and by late afternoon Morris Island came into view with its only distinctive tall tree, a coconut palm, on this little sandy island which acted as a beacon.

We anchored on the northern side of the island that had an enormous coral reef on the island's southern and easterly side. This broke the southeast swells and allowed for a comfortable anchorage.

The island itself was extremely small, only a few acres, with literally thousands of pigeons coming to nest at the island. It was incredible walking amongst the small trees with nearly every tree having a nest from where the constant noise of the pigeons came, alarmed at our presence. It would be an ideal spot for crocodiles to obtain a meal.

We walked towards the tall coconut palm tree. At the base of it, there was a grave believed to be of a sailor. As the sisal palm throngs were in abundance, they were planted to knock down the coconuts by early sailors on pearl luggers. The grave itself had a fashioned cross from driftwood with shells and the odd bottle within a rope circle.

Log: Wednesday, 31 October 2018; 0905 hours; Departed for Night Island.

We slept in due to strong winds over the night and decided to sail a short passage to another small island, only twenty-three nautical miles away. This would allow us to shorten the sail to Portland Roads on the mainland, the next day. We only used the head sail that pushed us along nicely with winds under twenty knots throughout the day, arriving at Night Island in a delightful anchorage with the striking blue water up to the beach. Again, thousands of imperial pigeons were nesting there.

We ventured ashore and the place we landed had distinctive crocodile marking leading from the water to the vegetation within the island. We followed the tracks and saw the entire belly of the reptile showing incredible markings and the size of its feet. This was in a spot with pigeon nests and feathers scattered around, obviously had a meal. On the eastern side of the island, amongst the debris washed up from the prevailing south easterly swells, it seemed to resemble a crocodile's nest. So, we decided not to hang around the eastern side. We had a great fire on the beach, burned and cleaned up the rubbish that unfortunately washes up.

Log: Thursday, 1 November 2018; 0650 hours; Departed Night Island for Portland Roads.

The wind was up twenty knots along with large swell. We had one reef in the main and furled the head sail in 20% and we had a constant six knots SOG, flying along passing Ashton Reef and Cape Direction, and then Restoration Island was in view.

Epic Captain Bligh's Survival

Restoration Island got its name for being the island where Captain Bligh stopped to rest, on what is arguably, the greatest survival open boat voyage in maritime history.

On the 28 April 1789, Master Mate Fletcher Christian led a successful mutiny by seizing the British naval vessel *HMS Bounty* at Tofua,

CHAPTER NINE

north of Tonga in the South Pacific. The *Bounty* was commissioned to transport breadfruit saplings from Tahiti for planting in the British colonies of the Caribbean. The voyage had been extremely difficult, but most of the sailors had enjoyed the paradise of the Tahiti islands along with relationships with the exotic local women. What may have contributed to the mutiny was sailors preferring the exotic islands than returning on a dangerous voyage to the English cold.

Captain Bligh was forced into the *Bounty* launch that was only twenty-three feet long, open wood two-masted boat, along with eighteen loyal sailors, no chart, and very little provisions. The launch had a fifteen-person capacity, so it was five men over weighted and the free board was only the length of a hand which made for constant bailing.

Incredibly, Bligh was able to navigate his way from Tofua to Timor, 3,618 nautical miles within an incredible forty-seven days. All of them had survived, on some of the world's most remote and unforgiving seas. Avoiding islands that he believed to have cannibals living and reaching this small island just off the mainland of Australia where they caught and ate Booby birds to survive. Hence, the name Restoration Island.

We anchored at Portland Roads, a small settlement, for a couple of days while waiting for the strong winds to reduce in strength. We enjoyed the renowned prawn rolls served at the only store there. We met French yachties who did not venture off their yacht as they were concerned about the large crocodile they had seen swimming past their vessel. They also were waiting for a break in the strong winds.

While returning to *Never Die Wondering*, we unfortunately hit the propeller on the outboard in the shallows and therefore, spent hours repairing the pin in the shaft. We had to make that by cutting a coat hanger and filing the wire while in the cockpit which became the makeshift workshop.

Log: Saturday, 3 November 2018; 0700 hours; Departed Portland Roads for destination Margaret Bay.

Wind gusts were up to twenty-two knots, and we were running with the wind. We only had the head sail, sailing across Weymouth Bay and the entrance to Pascoe River. The swells were high from behind that created a great momentum, pushing us forward. We kept to the shipping route and passed a couple of ships during the day.

At 1520 hours, we dropped anchor at a perfect anchorage Margaret Bay, after rounding Cape Melville. This spot has great protection from the south easterly trade winds and had a large flat sand area exposed at low tide. Another catamaran was taking advantage of the spot, careening their vessel. On the southern side of Cape Melville is Indian Bay, a fantastic anchorage when there is a northerly.

Strong winds had increased, and we were glad to be in this nice spot, tender to the eastern section where we climbed up onto a rocky ridge and watched turtles and sharks swimming below us in the clear blue water.

Log: Sunday 4th November 2018, 0450 Hours depart Margerat Bay destination Escape River we needed an early start so we could make it into Escape River to anchor in the day light hours the only other anchorages was not ideal being small coral islets not ideal, when the winds were up.

The day was overcast and stayed like that throughout the day. We had dolphins ride the bow waves that seemed to be a smaller and darker type. We had both full sails and making a comfortable six knots SOG. We arrived at the mouth of Australia's most northerly river with plenty of daylight hours. The area is known for pearl rafts, so I was adamant on arriving in daylight. We made our way up into the entrance of the Escape River when the chart plotter played up. We could not move the chart, it had frozen. The water temperature had been recorded at 40°C, so that was an indication that things were not working. We were glad to be in daylight hours as we anchored on the southern side of the mangrove lined river.

When I was a boy, I read the tragic story of the explorer Edmund Kennedy. The book at the time had an illustration of Kennedy being speared that was still vivid in my memory. In May 1848, Kennedy set out from Rockingham Bay, which was now called Cardwell, to explore the east side of Cape York and then met up with a supply ship at two occasions. The plan was to explore the Cape. At the time, the only port in Northern Australia was Port Essington, north of Darwin, and the government of the day needed a suitable port and area to develop on the trade route from Singapore to Sydney.

Kennedy set off with twelve men, horses, carts, and sheep for their rations. After only twelve miles of walking, they abandoned the carts and pushed on into the wilderness in a foreign hostile landscape

CHAPTER NINE

crossing swamps, lagoons, and rivers. They travelled vast distances around mangrove forests and slashed their way through thick rainforest. The first rendezvous was to be at Princess Charlotte Bay in August, but Kennedy's expedition was two months late. The men were exhausted and frail, and by the time they arrived at Weymouth Bay. Portland Roads in November, Kennedy had no choice but to leave behind eight of his men as they were too weak to continue.

Kennedy and the four others kept going towards the tip of Australia where the second rendezvous was planned, and the ship *Ariel* hopefully would be there. Then, near Sherborne Bay, not far from Margaret Bay, one of Kennedy's men, Costigan, accidentally shot himself while tending his horse and could not continue. Thus, two others, Luff and Dunn, were forced to stay behind to care for Costigan, and these three men were never seen again.

So, Kennedy and his Aboriginal tracker, Jackey Jackey, continued over land trying to reach the tip of Australia for the rendezvous. Then, while at the Escape River in December, Kennedy was speared several times by the local inhabitants and died in the arms of Jackey Jackey.

Jackey Jackey was an Aboriginal from a different nation of the Sydney region. He spent, ten days alluding the attackers and made his way from the Escape River to the tip of Australia, and finally, made it to the supply ship, *Ariel*. Following the directions of Jackey Jackey, the ship returned to Shelborne Bay but there was no sign of the three men left behind. They then sailed back to Weymouth Bay but only two of the eight men had survived.

Jackey Jackey was obviously the hero of this tragic story. If it was not for his brilliant bush survival skills, the other two men would have not survived, and no one would have known of this incredible story.

Log: Monday, 5 November 2018; 0845 hours; Departed Escape River for destination Somerset Bay.

We calculated the tides as we needed to sail through the Albany Passage and needed the tide on our side. Hence, the late departure, when the wind was a nice fourteen knots. The swells were challenging once we got near the pass and the chart plotter was working fine but still very confused about the cross seas with the tide against the wind. It was exciting to know that we were nearly at the tip of Australia, and we passed familiar places which Brandon and I had explored several years ago in our 4x4.

We sailed into the Albany Pass and into calm waters, a tremendous feeling. It was like a natural gateway to the top of Australia. We decided to drop anchor at Somerset Bay for lunch and have a walk around to see the graves of the likes of Frank Jardine. A legendary figure who pioneered the Cape York region. He and his brother, Alick, completed an epic cattle droving trip from central Queensland through the unexplored Cape York to Somerset. He operated pearl luggers and developed Somerset Homestead. Legend has it that he found Spanish coins from a wreck in the Torres Strait, melted the coins down for cutlery when he entertained guests marrying a Samoan princess and raising a family. He had become a controversial character. An elder of the Wik Wik people informed me a year later that many of his people believed he was responsible for many Aboriginal deaths.

Joshua Slocum anchored here in 1897 on the sailing sloop vessel named the *Spray*. He was the first man to sail single handed around the world. He was entertained by the Jardine family in the Somerset Homestead.

> *Mine was not the sort of life to make one long to coil up one's ropes on land, the customs and ways of which I had almost forgotten...I was born in the breezes, and I had studied the sea.*
>
> Joshua Sloccum

The Tip of Australia

We weighed anchor as the tide was turning against us and quickly sailed through the rest of the Albany Pass and headed northwest and around Eborac Island and York Islands which lay above the tip of Australia. What a feeling of accomplishment it was to sail from the southern point of the Australian mainland. Point Hicks, where Captain Cook had sighted it, to the far most northern part of the mainland. We turned south and anchored as close to the tip as possible and dinged ashore to stand and walk to the tip where we had been years before and had camped. However, to stand on the tip of Australia after sailing there with my son was by far a greater moment.

The next day, we anchored only a short distance west of the tip at a place called Punsand Bay. We were told of a horse race as it was the first Tuesday of November of which meant Melbourne Cup Day. What a great event it was, literally hundreds turn up from all over the

Cape York and even the gulf and surrounding islands along with the many 4x4 travellers.

Rob, the owner of the Punsand Bay, had horsemen from one of the local Aboriginal settlements to train horses that are sometimes brumby. They are caught and enter this race, an event that is held along the beach at low tide. A Calcutta is also held whereby horse by horse are auctioned and the highest bidder got ownership of the horse for the day, and all proceeds of the auction went into a pool and a percentage of the winnings went to that day's owner of the horse.

What a great day we had. The beer flowed constantly, and we met many people. Brandon and I put in a nine-hour session before returning to *Never Die Wondering*.

Log: Wednesday, 7 November 2018; Departed Punsand Bay for destination Thursday Island.

The tides in the Torres Straits are legendary due to the narrow water way and shallow waters between the mainland and Papua New Guinea where the Pacific Ocean on the east powers the water to the Indian ocean to the west during tidal change. Many vessels have come to grief at this place, and for the last few decades, it has been compulsory for all international ships to be accompanied by local pilots.

As we were sailing, we had hardly any wind at all and loosened all sails and were being pulled along at ten knots. Passing Possession Island. *This was the island Captain Cook raised the British flag and claimed the land from here, to Point Hicks near Bass Strait for the Crown of England.* Hence the name Possession Island.

After passing Possession Island, we had to motor towards Thursday Island along with full sail. Now the tide was turning against us, and from an incredible ten knot SOG, it kept dropping to six, five, four, and three; We started both engines and then SOG dropped to two and then one 1 knot. We had both engines going at maximum revs, I had no idea just how strong these currents were, and it was a battle working my way to Thursday Island. Passing the large island called Prince of Wales we were out of the strong current and temporally and anchored at the front of Thursday Island to the west of the jetty. It was not the best anchorage as the tide was extremely strong, and although the anchor held well, it was not ideal, so after a trip into the township for meals and beers, we were weighing anchor and headed over to Horn Island where it was a great safe anchorage.

West Cape York

The next day Brandon jumped on a flight back to Melbourne for work. Jeff Mullenger, an old school mate, was planning to arrive on Horn Island by flight in nine days to sail the next passage wherever that was supposed to be. As the odd north westerly wind occurred showing the start of the monsoonal season, I decided it was time to head for a bolt hole (safe anchorage). The islands of the Torres Straits did not have any ideal places, so I decided to head to Weipa on the west side of Cape York in the gulf of Carpentaria. I arranged to have *Never Die Wondering* moored on a cyclone mooring in a mangrove lined creek for the wet season.

Log: Sunday, 18 November 2018; 0800 hours; Departed Horn Island for Seisia.

Jeff had arrived the previous day eager to sail. He had in the past visited Thursday Island, so we wasted no time and were underway and back into the strong currents on the Torres Straits. However, this time winds were in our favour and, we were flying at ten knots. We also witnessed an enormous shark working the waters. Arriving at the anchorage of Seisia at midday. My son and I had spent the new year here several years ago after exploring the region by 4x4. The village Seisia along with the nearby town of Bamaga inhabitants were originally from Saibai and nearby islands situated only eight km south of the mainland of Papua New Guinea. They had settled on Cape York after the second world war.

During the night, Jeff and I would watch a large crocodile swim very close to the yacht. The eyes are easily picked up when you shine a spotlight. Seisia is named after the first letters of the names Sagaukaz, Elu, Isua, Sunai, Ibuai, Aken they were the sons of one of the Torres Strait Islanders. They also named the pearling boat S.E.S.I.A which migrated to the mainland due to their coral island being inundated with the sea.

The passage to Weipa was only about 150 nautical miles with the protection of the west side of Cape York from the south easterly trade winds that had dropped off significantly due to the transition period towards the monsoonal. The Gulf of Carpentaria is a massive gulf covering an area of 3,00,000 sq. km with only a handful of settlements along its expansive coastline. Roughly, 350 nautical miles east to west and over 400 nautical miles north to south. It was here in 1606 that the first known landing of Europeans occurred when the Dutch explorer, Williem Janszoon, landed on the western side of Cape York on a vessel named the *Duyfken*.

Log: Tuesday, 20 November 2018; 0845 hours.

The border force called via aircraft VHF requesting details of departure and where we were heading. It was a common occurrence for the checking of the border force patrolling this vast area of Northern Australia. Along the way, the fishing did not let us down with the catching of Spanish mackerel and then Jeff hooked a monster Wahoo. We had this enormous creature up onto the sugar scope with its hypodermic needle teeth that could do serious damage. This was a catch and release due to its size and quickly after the release we caught another one that was easier to handle.

At 1630 hours, we dropped anchor between Doughboy and Macdonald River. This entire length of coastline has a bauxite reef and being on the lee side made anchoring very easy. The crocodiles were a common sight along the coast, and during the sunset and the dawn we would watch the magnificent brolgas that were nesting in waterways adjacent to the sand dunes. The brolga bird is part of the crane family, a large bird that made a honking sound and is truly a sight to behold with the mass numbers in the air forming a distinctive flight shape. On the ground, they are renowned to give an extraordinary dance routine which the Aboriginal culture had assigned as a creature totem to some of their clan, along with a traditional brolga dance.

The next morning, we watched two crocodiles close by as we weighed the anchor and headed to Port Musgrave with a pod of dolphin's riding the bow along the way. Port Musgrave is a huge bay that is nearly enclosed, its river source is the Ducie and Wenlock rivers along with many other creek tributaries. Coming into this bay, dugongs could be seen swimming nearby. We dropped anchor just within the port itself near a campground that had been built by the local Aboriginal community. It had a water tank where fresh water was pumped for the campers. We met a couple of locals who were fishing, and they explained to us that a few of the old fellers out hunting with spears would now and then pierce the poly pipe to obtain water, therefore, creating a headache for the repair. We placed a couple of crab pots out only to have one being dragged away quickly by what we thought was robbing by one of the local reptiles.

Log: Friday, 23 November 2018; 0645 hours; Storm conditions building

We sailed back out to the gulf and caught beautiful winds and were able to cover our passage to Albatross Bay Weipa in good time as we could get six knots SOG.

Following the markers into Weipa, a large tanker radioed and we pulled over at a marker pole to allow the tanker to pass. Then we arrived at Weipa and anchored up close to a beach near the lighthouse. It was only stone's throw to the beach where many locals would fish and spend time. We watched an elderly man with spear wade in the water spearing fish, and late at night listened to many Aboriginal women singing their tribal songs as they gathered on the beach.

Weipa was a large mining town where they extracted the bauxite which was then shipped overseas to make aluminium. The township had many nice homes and nearly all had fishing boats. We frequented the local pub and clubs.

I had arranged to place my vessel in Robert's Creek that was on the southern side of Weipa while I returned south for the wet season. The creek was mangrove lined and a perfect bolt hole during a cyclone, also home to many crocs. Jeff jumped on a plane back to Melbourne and I stayed another week preparing the yacht on a mooring for the wet season. I planned to be back once the storm season was over and then haul it out for maintenance, anti-foul, etc. After the vessel was secured, I jumped on a plane to Melbourne.

CHAPTER TEN

Not all who wander are lost.

JRR Tolkien

Restless

Flying back to southern Australia was an incredible feeling. I took a flight to Cairns, then to Melbourne. On occasions, I looked at the vast seas which I had travelled in a small catamaran. Two plane trips within the day and I had returned; a far cry from the seven-month sailing voyage.

I returned to Metung, but it was not long, before I became very restless. All I could think about was the fantastic journey I had experienced, the people I had met, the places I had explored, and the sailing—both the highs and the lows, it was a little overwhelming being back and thinking of the journey. All I wanted to do was continue sailing, exploring and discovering new places. Moreover, there was a desire to upgrade to a larger catamaran, one that would be more comfortable and safer to cross seas and ride out bad weather. Not to mention spacious and more comfortable especially, when caught for periods of time on board in the likes of mosquito mangrove creeks.

There was an advert for a larger, 44-foot *Crowther* at Darwin. I inquired about the vessel and flew in to inspect. It was owned by a former senator of the Territory Government and was well looked after. The cockpit area was extremely larger than what was needed. For instance, the helm position was at a high point, therefore, making it a long step down or up into the seat. In addition, the visibility from the cockpit floor would make it difficult although not impossible to sail solo. It handled extremely well, but I would still need extensive work to bring the floor area up to create a manageable single-handed operation. In hindsight, I am glad that the owner knocked back my offer, for it allowed me to later get the vessel I needed.

There were a few other vessels in the meantime to consider. Soon, another vessel hit the market, a 40-foot *Seawind*, and the person selling it was due to come back to Sydney within a couple of weeks. I had the surveyor report sent and arranged to inspect the vessel. I drove to Melbourne and was about to fly to Sydney when I was told that they had increased the price substantially. The following day, it was sold to another person.

Over the three months, I caught up with many people and did road trips back to the High Country. I even went out west in my 4x4 wheel and swag to Lake Mungo where the oldest evidence of mankind had been discovered from 50,000 years ago. In March, Cyclone Trevor passed over Cape York east to west and went over the top from where my vessel was moored in Robert's Creek. I thought the worse but was informed the next day that it was alright. It worked out to be a great safe spot, and another two tropical storms went over near the same path that season.

I turned Metung into an accommodation unit by having Brandon place up a wall dividing the office area from the two bedrooms. I named the place, *Seafarers Rest* and placed a large billboard at the front of the premises with a large photo of Brandon sitting on the bow while sailing in Cape York with the colourful spinnaker. I gave management rights of the premises to a management team. The fully furnished place was quickly booked out for a nice little return on weekends.

During this time, my firearms that were in a safe at my cousin's property were stolen and one was cut down and used in an armed robbery, so, I had to identify the firearm. So much for gun registration as professional criminals know exactly which properties have firearms. In my case, they used jack hammers to break the safe lose from a concrete floor and what is believed to be a crane to lift the heavy safe onto a vehicle. No other item was stolen, so these were purely professional criminals, obtaining arms for the black market. I lost seven firearms of which three were from earlier generations of my forefathers.

The sea was calling me, and I returned to Weipa on 25 April 2019 on Anzac Day. I stayed at a local pub for the night. Nearby the Club which was alive with a game of two-up that is traditionally played across the county on Anzac Day. The next day, I was taken by a boat back to my vessel. My first task was to assess if any damage was wrought from

CHAPTER TEN

the cyclone along with any weather damage, because keeping a yacht locked up for months in humid wet weather is not ideal.

Just jumping on board was a terrific feeling, *I'm back and no signs of damage at all!* However, once I opened the door, the smell of mould was evident. The walls were covered in mould, though there was no water inside with the exception of a small area from a hatch leak. Overall, I was impressed.

It was not long until the large saltwater croc showed himself and for the next few days, I would see the croc laying on the muddy embankment in low tide only a few meters from the vessel. On a spring tide, the vessel would be caught in the mud. I often talk to the croc, called him "Snarly" since he would open his mouth as large as he could, and swim under the vessel. At night, when I lay in my cabin, I could hear him brushing up against the side of the hull as he made his way under the vessel in the shallow water.

I had a three-week wait to be able to get my vessel out of the water and onto the hard, because boats needed to come out to make space for the yacht. Steve Rehn, the owner of the boatyard, had a trailer. We had to place a large timber beam horizontally across the trailer to be able to fit both keels on. Then, we positioned it in the high tide and slowly pulled the vessel and trailer across the road to his yard. There I spent three weeks, anti-fouling, replacing hatches, servicing engines, and repainting the inside bathroom along with many other jobs.

Finally, the vessel was back in the water on 5 May, ready for sale and advertised on all the boat and yacht selling sites. I thought it would sell quickly, and that anyone serious about purchasing the vessel would not have a problem flying into Weipa. In the worst-case scenario, I would take the vessel to the east coast and place it in the hands of an agent, as the priority was to continue the sailing odyssey. Little did I know then that this procedure was going to take a lot longer than I planned.

Another *Seawind* catamaran became available in Fremantle, Perth. It was a Tony Grainger design, and Jeff Mullenger had been on a tour on it several years ago when he was in Broome. Jeff told me it was in very good condition, although that was several years ago. The agent had it advertised as beautifully presented, well-equipped, and ready to cross an ocean. *How could I go wrong, surely, the agent would not lie?*

After two plane trips, I arrived in Perth and while staying at a local hotel, I inspected the boat. What a disgrace it was! It had been terribly neglected compared to the days Jeff had sailed on it. There had been a lot of rain in the Perth Region that weighed in my favour to inspect, as the vessel was leaking at most of the windows and a lot of water had filled the bilges. Most of the electronic navigation gear, including wind instruments, were not working, dodger and boom bag were nothing but shredded cloth, a strong smell of sulphur, and the batteries were all flat. To add, it had ripped saloon seats, gunnel rail damaged, the motors shuddering when we finally got the engine going after charging. On the sea trial, no water was cycling through one of the engines, overheating, I thought the mould was bad in my vessel after leaving it in Robert's Creek for the wet season, but it was way better compared to this. When I opened the fridge, it had terrible growth. There was no inventory whatsoever on board, no life raft, no dingy, or outboard. *What a disgrace to have me fly over from the other side of Australia to be presented with this vessel, in such a disgraceful state and defiantly unseaworthy?*

Still, the design was great and as long as I could get it to a seaworthy state, I would go ahead minus the costs but after the surveyor report, the insurance company would not insure it until all items were fixed. The *Penta* mechanics explained that they had placed a 55-HP-*Penta* on *Yanmar* mounting brackets, hence, the vibration, and many other problems such as the windows that had been glued in would need to be replaced. I was looking at $90,000 at least! So much for the beautifully presented, well-equipped, and ready to cross an ocean vessel!

So, after a considerable cost in accommodation, flights, etc. I was back on my vessel In Weipa. I was hoping to get a buyer for my vessel who would fly into Weipa, but I was not prepared to wait and decided to sail back to Cairns to sell the vessel as it was an easy destination to get to. I was keen to get the wind back in my sails.

I sailed one day south of Weipa. The crew from *Rehn's* boatyard came out fishing to the Red Cliffs that dominates the landscape with their red striking colour. At the anchorage area, there where spinning dolphins that would rise out of the water in a spinning fashion, it was incredible to watch them.

Paradise of the West Cape

Alona who I had met while in Melbourne, flew into Weipa to spend time sailing with me. She had also come along with me camping up to the Snowy River in the mountains of NSW, and on the River Red Gum country of the Murray River. Although she had never sailed before, I

CHAPTER TEN

planned to just explore some of the Gulf of Carpentaria around Weipa with her. To my shock, Alona had a tattoo on her forearm that read *Never Die Wondering*. She said that reading my first book had inspired her. We headed out into Albatross Bay and then, up the Pine River, a very wide stretch of river that needed to be navigated cautiously due to the many sand bars, so picking the tides were crucial.

We anchored in a superb location with easy dingy trip to shore where we were able to collect coconuts from a low hanging tree, spear mud crabs in the shallows of a creek, and cook up great meals over the coals on a fire on the beach. They were a great few days of having this magical spot to ourselves, getting around with only our birthday suits. While sitting on the beach one evening, an enormous shark launched itself out of the water. I had never seen a shark of that size and dive clear out of the water as he did. The waters were teeming with many sea creatures. Alona, an avid fishing person, caught several fish and witnessed the incredible birdlife with the likes of the jabiru, Australian, black-necked stork, that wade the rivers and creeks of this region.

We explored the many waterways, I would get as close to the crocodiles as possible while Alona would lay in the bow taking photos. I introduced her to Snarly the crocodile that had been hanging around the vessel. He did not disappoint, he opened his mouth as wide as he could, made his aggressive sound, turned and went straight under the vessel while we stood on the steps of the sugar scoop. Exploring uncharted creeks and rivers is always a risky proposition. Once we were about to drop the pick [anchor] when the sounder showed it was a little too shallow for comfort, so I went out to what seemed like deeper water. When the water level fell, a massive rocky area was exposed, one that would have really done some damage if the vessel was caught on it in an ebbing tide.

After two weeks of experiencing the sailing life, Alona flew out on 15 July. My old mate from Tumbaraumba, Phil Daly, arrived on the same plane as Alona was flying out on. We had planned that Phil was going to cruise with me back to the Torres Straits after showing Phil around the Weipa area along with the teaming reptiles that are plentiful.

Log: Saturday, 20 July 2019; 1645 hours; arrived north of Penny father dropped anchor 12.12′726/ 141,44′105

Shortly after dropping anchor, a call came on the VHF from another yachtie wanting to know about the anchorage. He dropped anchor nearby and we asked him over for a beer. Don was his name, and came with a freshly caught Spanish mackerel, he was on his way to Groote Eylandt southwest of where we were anchored. During the night. we could hear the sounds of the brolga birds that had nested at the back of the nearby sand dunes.

The next morning, we went ashore to hopefully find the brolgas, but they had all disappeared, on their morning flight. We did find many places where the turtles had nested though. There distinctive tracks that return to the beach lead you to the nests, so it is an easy collection of eggs for the Aboriginal people, and if you were starving. I would not hesitate to take some as well but knowing that it is a challenge for the young turtles to hatch and try to make the long distance to the water, being picked off by the massive numbers of birds, not to mention reptiles like crocs and goannas, I leave the nests alone.

We cooked breakfast on the beach and watched as fourteen Jet Skis went past on their way to Papua New Guinea. You would be lucky to maybe pass the odd seafarer in these waters but never fourteen Jet Skis along with back up vessels. Apparently, it was a fund raiser for awareness of the horrendous London terrorist attack where two of the eight victims were Australian women.

We continued sailing north, making our way into Port Musgrave. Although I was making tracks over ground I had travelled to before, there is always somewhere new to explore, especially, in this vast region.

We dropped anchor at Cullen Point, after sailing with a pod of dolphins guiding us into the bay. Phil hooked a large fish on the way into Port Musgrave that took him a long time reeling in, only to have the wire trace breaking. His face showed a shocked look especially when the second steel trace snaped. He had never hooked monsters before.

Log: Monday, 22 July 2019.

Motored up the Wenlock River dropped anchor up in the mangroves. It was an enormous body of water with crocs on banks at low tide.

Log: Tuesday, 23 July 2019.

We departed Wenlock at the ebbing tide, made our way past the Mapoon settlement, leaving Port Musgrave at 1030 hours. I was able to goose wing which is having the head sail and main sail out in opposite

CHAPTER TEN

directions. Phil was catching fish after fish stating how he had never caught this many in his life and all were good-size, mackerel. The day ended with misty rain, and we anchored along the coast.

The next day, I had to complete the repair of the macerator pump, a terrible job. I had problems with the autopilot although I had just replaced in Weipa my entire multi-function device, chart plotter, my ITC 5, and cables in Weipa but still, now and then, the autopilot played up.

We sailed past the Scarborough River where ships were waiting to get into the river on the rising tide. as there was a bauxite mine up-stream.

Log: Wednesday, 24 July 2019; Anchored 1715 hours 11,34'302/ 142,02'636 misty rain.

We woke to continued light rain, and prediction was for fresh winds all day. We watched a large tiger shark hanging around the vessel. It must have been attracted to the guts and heads of the many fish we had filleted. We sailed off from anchor without motoring and quickly picked up some incredible speed. Some dolphins gave us a great jumping display. Then, the wind went from twenty knots to thirty-four in no time at all.

The next day, we had some terrific wind which soon blew up to thirty-four knots and we needed to reef quickly. All this was going on while poor Phil had become sea sick and was vomiting over the stern, at the same time, he was reeling in whatever number of fish he could. He said, "Do you think a little sea sickness is going to stop me from catching more fish than I have in my life?" He then went on to hook a monster fish while we sailed at 7.5 knots SOG. He skull-dragged it for a couple of miles, as there were strong winds. I was not going into the wind to stop the boat, and the wind reached up to thirty-five knots and by virtue of the speed, Phil lost the monster. We headed for the shore as we had enough excitement for one day, and anchored near the same place where Jeff and I had anchored on our way south

Log: Thursday, 25 July 2019; depart 0730 hours; 11'28,983/142'04,646

There were dolphins galore, and the swell was a south westerly. We sailed past Vrilya Point, an area with a distinctive rocky escarpment and small low-lying hills which are predominantly sand hills.

We anchored near an old shipwreck that lay on the beach. In January 1979, the lightship *Carpentaria* that was used as a beacon warning seafarers of a notorious reef, was dragged off its station by tropical Greta, beaching itself near the point. It is believed the lighthouse vessel mooring chain broke during the storm.

When we explored the wreck, the large chimney stack was lying on the beach. We also explored a large unnamed river and found middens in the sand dunes which were Aboriginal feeding spots where thousands of shells collected and eaten are heaped in piles, the shells discarded over many years are still evident as a mound. We returned to the vessel, weighed anchor, and decided to continue with the great winds at twenty knots plus. Along the way, Phil was pulling in more fish like spotty mackerel, but it was time for catch and release since the small freezer was full.

Phil was moving the rod around with the lure, and it hooked my hand. The hook went right through the piece of skin between my thumb and the index finger. I was yelling at Phil to stop moving the rod but he was unaware that he had hooked me. It was horrible, because Phil kept pulling on the rod and the hook was being pulled through the skin of my hand. Finally, he released it and I asked him to go downstairs and get the bolt cutters. After a bit of surgical work, out the hook came followed by a soak in a bucket of *Dettol*, and all was good.

Another action filled day ended as we anchored between Crab Island and the mainland south of Slade Point, an incredible anchorage safe from the winds with many she-oak, type of Casuarina trees on the high tide mark. Crab Island is where the biggest migration of crocodiles in Australia occurs. They come from hundreds of miles away when the turtle eggs are hatching and wait along the water's edge for their feed.

Log: Friday, 26 July 2019; 0800 hours; Departed from anchorage 10'59,833/142'07,648 for destination Seisia.

We went around Crab Island via the south side, carefully navigating the waters amongst the reef while watching the sounder continuously. We beam reach at 6.2 SOG and had many turtle sightings. Just north of Crab Island, the wind picked up to thirty knots and we made great time, arriving in Seisia at 1530 hours. Another catamaran was frantically signalling to us, as we came straight onto the way point. Now,

CHAPTER TEN

I knew how shallow the waters were and what my boat's draft was, so the fellow in the catamaran, later told us, "As soon as I frantically waved, I thought, you must know the depth as I only draw .600 and knew the spot with confidence." Nonetheless, it is a great comfort to have seafarers looking out for each other.

Horn Island

We spent a couple of days in Seisia. We filled the water tanks with twenty-litre containers from a water tap on the shore, the water was piped from the Jardine River. We bought supplies, refuelled, climbed up the mast for repairs, and enjoyed a meal at the fisherman club. Then, we sailed off to Thursday Island but caught the cross tide against me. Even with a full sail, I had both motors going at high revs, and still, managed to get off course by 0.8 of a nautical mile. The speed was as low as 1.0 SOG. Arriving at Horn Island, in the same anchorage, at 1530 hours, and had the traditional beers at the Horn Island pub. Over the next few days, Phil and I visited Thursday Islands *top pub* enjoying the meals there. It was Phil's first time on the island and my third.

We also went to the cemetery where many pearl divers were buried who died of the bends (decompression sickness where nitrogen gas is released from the blood stream rapidly, when divers ascend too quickly or a low-pressure system occurs resulting in severe pain, even resulting in death). So many fatalities occurred, with over 700 graves of Japanese divers, along with Muslims buried with their right side perpendicular towards Mecca, Buddhists, Pacific and Torres Strait Islanders as well. During the second world war, the Japanese had several air raids on the adjacent Horn Island but never bombed Thursday Island as it was rumoured that a Japanese princess was buried on the island.

The museum holds a lot of information of the many pearl boats that operated in the Torres Strait waters. The pearl luggers were gaff-rigged ketches constructed of wood. They measured up to twenty meters in length, and it is believed there were literally hundreds of luggers working across Australia in any given time. Legend has it that you could cross the water between Thursday Island to Horn Island by stepping from one vessel to another on anchor as there were that many operating in the area. A lot of these luggers were built by Japanese shipwrights. The diving for pearls commenced in the 1860s and continued into the mid-1900s, the golden era of pearl diving for the mother of the pearl shell. One large shell could produce a lot of buttons along with the chance of finding a pearl, the advent of plastics was the cause of the end of that era. Now, pearl farms are established, and they assist in cultivating the pearl.

Phil flew back to Melbourne, and I decided to sail to Saibai Island which lies on Australia's border with Papua New Guinea. I had at least three months until the southeasterly trade winds changed to the transit period when the northwest monsoonal starts. The winds then would be favourable to sail back to Cairns to sell the vessel, unless someone could fly into the Islands to purchase the vessel. There were plenty of inquiries, but I could not get any one to fly into the straits. I was told that permission was needed from the tribal council committees to allow me onto the islands. Even being in Australian waters, it was becoming a nation within a nation.

Winds were sometimes near gale force every day, and it really started to blow in the afternoon, so I really needed to island hop for safety across the shallow reef waters of the Torres Straits. In early August, a small boat with Torres Strait Islanders disappeared heading towards Badu, children included and was never seen again. It was getting essential that I obtain permission from the tribal councils to safely sail to the Papua New Guinea international border, only seventy-eight nautical miles from where I was. Hence, I applied to Saibai Island which is just within the Australian waters, they quickly approved my visit within the same day.

I also applied to the Badu tribal council but met with no response. I called them and was told that they would get back to me. They never did. I continued my requests by telephone and email and was finally told that they had two individual authorities. I needed to have permission, even to just anchor off their island. After six weeks of waiting on Horn Island, still no permission came through. By then, I had had enough and decided to spend time around the tip of Cape York and Seisia instead.

Log: Monday, 9 September 2019; 0620 hours; Departed Horn Island.

I sailed with the tide in my favour, between Horn Island and Wednesday Island. All the islands were named by James Cook, incredibly, based on the days he was there. Not sure about Horn Island though! Along the way, I caught a nice-size tuna. How good was this, slicing the raw fish, soaking it in soya sauce, and eating it raw? Delicious!

I dropped anchor at Punsand Bay, and the next day headed back around the east side of the cape towards Seisia. I anchored just off a secluded beach between the mainland and Roko Island. On the way, through the narrow passage, the wind blew up to twenty-six knots. My hands were on the wheel since the autopilot was not working, as I discovered later, due to a broken drive belt. On the ST 4000-wheel drive. I was able to get telephone reception and ordered parts for the autopilot to Bamaga post office.

The area was smoky due to the enormous fires as far away as Lockhart River. Apparently, the storm damage from the cyclone Trevor had left a lot of litter and large areas went up including a rainforest area that would otherwise not burn. This gave a terrific display of sunsets, with the presence of smoke in the air showing a tremendous reddish colour. During this time, another fire started close by on the northwest tip of the cape, giving an incredible glow at night from the burning timber.

I spent the days on a hammock on the high tide mark of the beach, tied up to a couple of casuarinas, cooking by a beach fire, and exploring this wonderful natural environment. Although secluded, the high-water mark unfortunately is littered by plastic rubbish, labels of which showed the origin of most as Indonesian, along with FADS or fish aggregating devices made of plastic or polyurethane tied with ropes that float on the surface for attracting fish to catch. Unfortunately, they find their way to Australian shores during the northwest monsoons, littering the beaches. The other side of the cape Australian plastic rubbish from the east coast, but the west along the entire length of west Cape York has trash that is predominantly Indonesian.

In any case, it was a pleasant anchorage at this location. In the evening, imperial pigeons would fly onto the land in large numbers, a crocodile, and a large shark would hang around the yacht. I returned to the yacht every night, for I was not keen to spend the night in the hammock on the beach in fear of large reptiles.

Stranded in Cape York Paradise

Log: Saturday, 14 September 2019; 0705 hours; Depart anchorage for Seisia.

Within an hour, the wind had blown up to twenty-seven knots making it challenging sailing into Seisia. Along the way, I noticed Possession

Island was also up in smoke with several helicopters in the air. I dropped the anchor back outside the Seisia fishermen's club in the calm safe anchorage.

Peter and Ilona of the *SV Blue Lagoon* fellow yachties I met here. They owned a lagoon catamaran. Previously from Hungary, they had lived most of their life in Australia. Peter had migrated to Australia and took up pearl diving in the 70s around the islands of the Torres Strait so he was a wealth of knowledge, later in life, they had bought a yacht to explore the world. Since returning to the Torres Straits region, I was to spend over three months here, waiting to gain permission to anchor at Badu Island. Meanwhile, I worked on my vessel on the beach as well as waited for the strong southeasterly trade winds to change to a favourable northerly.

The first time I came to Seisia, Brandon and I drove our 4x4 vehicle camping out in our swags, exploring this region just as the monsoonal started. We were sitting on the beach eating turtle given to us by the locals when I received a disturbing telephone call. My beloved horse, Redgum, who had taken me 5,000 kilometres throughout the mountains had been shot along with several Brumbies just a few meters from the boundary to my property. There are some sick and depraved people, extremists that condemn hard-footed animals, having an ideology that Australia should only have soft-footed native species. Poor old Redgum, a palomino mare, had got through the fence and was shot many times, not far from the gate which she was most likely waiting for someone to open to let her home. Many wild horses are in the mountains, and she would have been just grazing peacefully with them and would not have flinched when shooters approached. When I received the call, the first rains had started so Brandon and I had to head south through the muddy conditions, and we were just able to get out. I always wanted to stay longer in this unique region, for this is what I would refer to as a paradise. Now, I was to spend three months here.

Work was needed on the vessel. I had to check the rudders, so I had my vessel on the beach where I also installed another autopilot unit. When the tide lifted the vessel, I would get under and move rudders, there was a large crocodile who was iconic to Seisia for many years. Kids often kept croc-watch while they dived off the pier, but he was coming around every morning and was watching me sometimes from very close. The local town dogs were coming to the beach early in the morning and I was convinced these were what he was eyeing

CHAPTER TEN

off. However, the local women who fished on the beach daily, were convinced that he was after me in fact, and they were telling others at the club that they were concerned about my safety. I even had the odd person stand on my sugar scope croc-watching just in case he came too close, but I was convinced his eyes were on dogs and not me.

I needed brackets to install a new liner drive as I decided to replace the ST 4000. I had brackets made, for a cost of two cartons of beer from a local who had every type of material one needed. It's amazing the assistance you get in the bush! During this time, I met many yachties exploring northern Australia, the likes of Hugh and Maggie McBride sailing a catamaran, *Paws Awhile*. Hugh had sold his plane to take up cruising full-time. So many others I met were also living the dream full-time like Tess and Ziggy, former Polish people, who bought a catamaran on retirement to live the cruising life venturing as far as the Solomon Islands. Over the years I met many people, some I still stay in contact with, who share the same dreams of freedom.

On one occasion, a solo young yachtie on a twenty-eight-foot mono anchored nearby. We were having a beer on my vessel that had become the 'Do Drop Inn'. He had sailed solo from southern western Australia. The only charts he had was a *Navionics* on his mobile phone. He told me of the remora fish also known as a sucker fish that connect themselves to larger sea creatures to obtain a free feed from the spills. He told me that there was this remora which had travelled with him since Broome, far north of western Australia to Seisia, and incredible distance over many months. I was sceptical of this story, so he took me to his vessel. No windlass, just mostly Rhode where he needed to physically pull in his anchor by hand. He threw breadcrumbs out at the side of his craft, and lo and behold, his pet remora came out, grabbed a feed, and returned. Absolutely incredible!

Finally, I received a call one day from the Badu tribal council. *Fantastic*, I thought to myself, but the caller asked in a demanding tone, "Are you on our island?"

I said, "No, I'm waiting for permission from you."

He stated, "We have not given you permission."

I explained where I was anchored and asked why I had not been given permission and he went on saying that it needed to go through to another council. It turned out there was a yacht anchored near Badu Island, and they called since they thought it was mine. *What a disgraceful call*, I thought. No permission was ever given to me nor any type of explanation was offered given to me. A Saibai Islander who I had met at Seisia was arranging for me to meet his grandfather to show me a tree where in the days of head hunting, they placed their head trophies in the tree trunk until the islanders converted to Christianity and the church condemned the trophy collection of heads. I was going to miss out on visiting Saibai along with the Papua New Guinea border as that was the goal. It was going to be a long time before I got to New Guinea, and it would be the long way round.

Let time be your ally and patience be your friend.

After installing the new autopilot, I sailed again, exploring and anchoring at places like Mutee Head and the mighty Jardine River, where I saw a huge, bronze whaler shark in the shallows of the entrance. The bush area is inundated with tall ant hills that are sometimes seven feet or more in height facing a northerly and southerly direction, therefore, they were compasses of the bush. I would do many walks throughout this savannah timber country and the flood plains that where now dried out, with large paper bark trees. Along the secluded beaches, there were many freshwater soaks.

I met a local feller who spent his time on the high tide mark where he had built himself a hut and planted coconut trees. He showed me, a crocodile's nest close to his hut where a large female crocodile came to lay her eggs. I would not sleep in a hammock at night in that hut, but the local seemed not to be worried.

Back in Seisia, I watched the local Aboriginal lads ride and prepare their brumby mounts for the upcoming Punsand Bay races held on Melbourne Cup Day. The local store was where I would have a meal on most days. One day, I was walking along the beach to the store, when I heard a large commotion taking place with people screaming. A young lad had been partly swallowed by the local, giant grouper that lived under the jetty. He was swimming and this creature swallowed his leg taking him to the bottom of the water, he managed to free himself but was severely cut from the grouper's teeth and rushed to hospital.

I learned from the indigenous people that of the five communities of the region, Seisia and Bamaga were developed predominantly by the Saibai Islanders in the late 40s and 60s. New Mapoon which lay between Bamaga and Seisia had a very sad story. It was formed when *Alco*, the large Aluminium company, forced the original families of Mapoon in Port Musgrave near Weipa to move from their tribal area, in some cases they were removed violently with their homes destroyed.

CHAPTER TEN

New Mapoon was developed to relocate the people, and in recent years, there has been a hand back of sorts with some of the people returning to their traditional lands. One of the other two aboriginal communities was Umagico, that mainly had people from the Lockhart River, who have made this area their home several decades ago. Further along the coast, was Injinoo on the Cowel Creek where most of the people were descendants of the original inhabitants. Seisia also had a large white church hall where weddings or religious events would take place along with islander songs and music that could be heard echoing over the water. Jeff Mullenger arrived at Bamaga airport eager to sail with me back to Cairns. It was November, and the trade winds were dying off being replaced by the odd northerly. It was time to move on.

VOYAGE

Departure: Victoria, Bass Strait, Australia, April 2018, *SV Never Die Wondering*
Arrival: Palawan, South China Sea, Philippines, June 2024, *SV Never Die Wondering II*

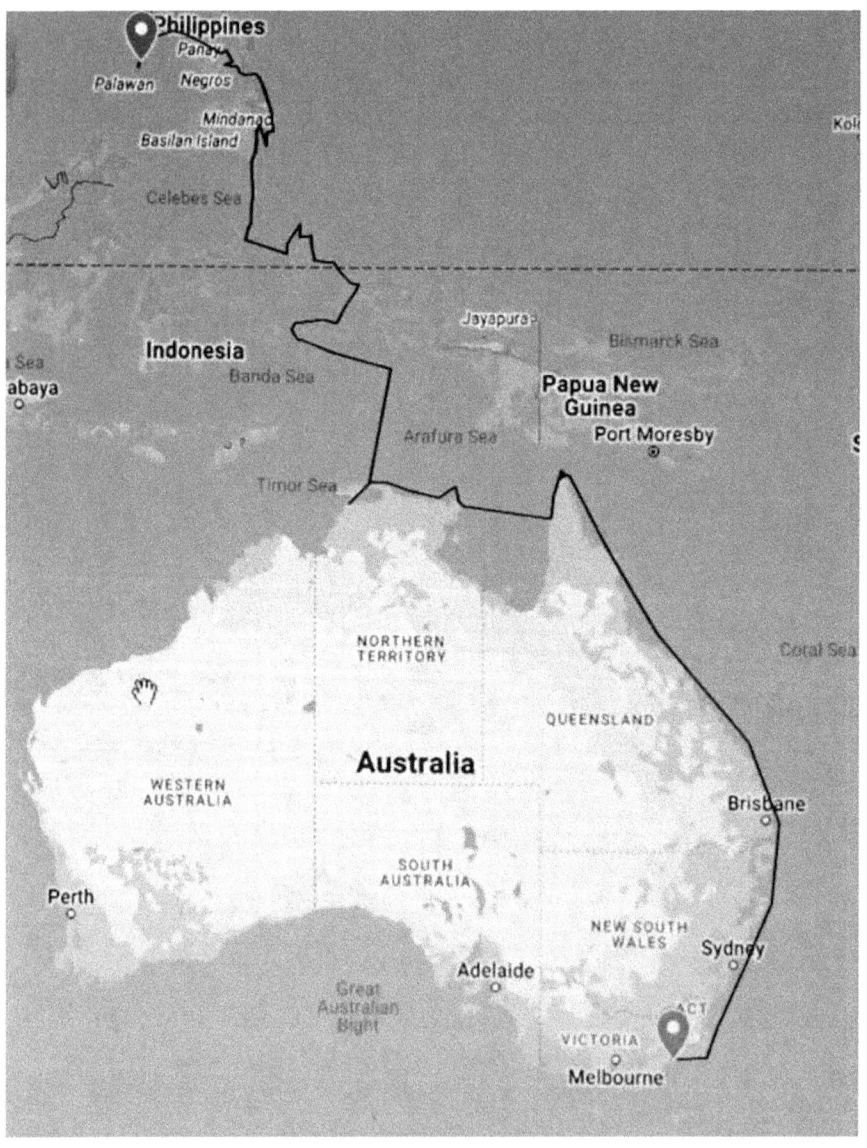

SV Never Die Wondering II

CHAPTER TEN

Police in the Highlands, Papua New Guinea, 2009

With the Asaro Mudmen, Highlands, Papua New Guinea, 2009

Sepik River Region, smoke inside canoe to keep mozzies away, Papua New Guinea, 2009

Sailing the Tasman Sea, geared up for the freezing cold.

CHAPTER TEN

Spinner run with Brandon on the bow, Cape York East, 2018

"Snarly" at Roberts Creek, Weipa, 2019

Brandon with a barracuda, Cooktown, 2021

A magical place, Zoe Bay, Hinchinbrook Island, 2021

CHAPTER TEN

Surfing the south-east trade winds along the Great Barrier Reef, Queensland, 2021

Fresh oysters, Cape York, 2021

Cooking a meal in northwest Northern Territory while crossing the top of Australia, 2021

Purchasing supplies at Tual Market, Indonesia, 2022

CHAPTER TEN

Supplies do not get fresher, Indonesian Islands, 2022

Fish Galore, Islands of Indonesia, Banda Sea, 2022

The traditional Cakalele dance, Banda Islands, Indonesia, 2022

Banda Islands, (Spice Islands), 2022

CHAPTER TEN

Moored to a Dutch cannon below volcano Api, Banda Neira, 2022

Anchored in paradise, Indonesian Archipelago, 2022

Alexa (crew) meditating in view of limestone cliffs, Ceram Island, Indonesia, 2022

The friendly people of the Indonesian Archipelago, 2022

CHAPTER TEN

Happy children on out-rigger, West Papua, 2023

Moored to abandoned huts, morning after the near disaster, Raja Ampat, 2023

The Jewel of Raja Ampat, Wayag, 2023

Cock-fighting, Mindanao, Philippines, 2023

CHAPTER ELEVEN

I had inheritance from my father, it was the moon and the sun and although I roam all over the world the spending of it is never done.

Ernest Hemingway

Torres Straits to Cairns

Log: Saturday, 23 November 2019; Depart 1030 hours; Destination Albany Passage.

We sailed on the west side of Possession Island. It was fairly rough going with wind over tide, first fresh then strong winds, and again, the wind was stronger than predicted so we had to beat. When the tide was in our favour, we flew along at 7.0 knots SOG with the new autopilot not missing a beat. Passing turtles and sea snakes along the way, we sailed to a protected anchorage in Shallow Bay at the start of Albany Passage. We planned to spend the night in this bay and leave early in the morning as the tide turned allowing us to run with the tide ebbing out of the passage.

Log: Sunday, 24 November 2019; 0400 hours; Departed Shallow Bay for either Escape River or Hannibal Islands.

I had decided that if the south easterlies get up too much, we could just get into Escape River. Alternatively, if they are not too fresh, we would continue as far as we could sail, hopefully, Hannibal Island. As the vessel started to turn around with the ebbing tide, in the dark we weighed the anchor and worked our way through the channel.

We were totally relying on the radar showing us Albany Island on our Port side and the mainland Somerset on our starboard side as big red blobs on the radar screen. We slowly moved out of the Passage with motor only.

We could hear the waves from the trade winds smashing against the rocky coastline, and before we knew it, we were safely into the sea, a bit rough but not too bad. As we raised the sails and sailed windward, we were able to sail on rather comfortably with the tide now in our favour. We started to pick up speed and had a terrific sail all day, admiring the views of the mainland, its bright white sand dunes partially tree covered.

We arrived at Hannibal Island at 1700 hours where we anchored for the night protected from the south easterlies. Hannibal is a low-lying island that is covered with a large reef on the southern side of the islet, and anchorage on the northwest side but only if light winds prevail at night, as was the case with us. It has a beautiful beach surrounding the islet. We anchored at 11.35′464/142′55′758 and watched the now common sight of large flocks of imperial pigeons coming into the island to nest.

Log: Monday, 25 November 2019; 0415 hrs; Departed for Cape Grenville.

This was supposed to be a straight southeasterly bearing along the main shipping route of only forty nautical miles but due to being windward we had to beat changing tack on for occasions. We anchored on the northern side of this scenic Cape that is a favourite anchorage to many yachties. I have known many people who have spent months in this spot in Margaret Bay well-protected from the trade winds. When the northerlies occur, you move to the south of the cape at Indian Bay, and you are protected from the northerlies. What a magnificent spot!

As we anchored on the sand in very shallow water, we had a swim with dolphins and many fish close by. The water being crystal clear, you could see safely if any crocs were about. Although I had been anchored there previously, I did not know of the blue trail which is a walking track from Margaret Bay to Indian Bay. People who collect rubbish (most yachties) place the blue pieces of rubbish like water bottles, clothing, buoys, rope, or anything blue as a guide to the trail. We walked along this trail to the other side and returned.

CHAPTER ELEVEN

Log: Tuesday, 26 November 2019; 0616 hours; Departed for Portland Roads.

The sunrise coming up over the Coral Sea was terrific. I learned that you could never get tired of sunsets or sunrises and they all could be different to some degree.

Head Hunters of the North

The sea was nearly flat, so it was a day of motoring. The dolphins joined in swimming alongside for a while. Due east of us was the wreck of the *Charles Eaton*, this region had claimed many ships, but it was the story of the *Charles Eaton* that stood out. Not so much as the shipwreck itself but the events that took place afterwards. The *Charles Eaton* left Sydney in 1834, its destination was Singapore, and it was believed to have twenty-seven passengers on board, including the family of Captain Thomas D'Oyly, his wife, Charlotte, and their two sons, George and William. It became shipwrecked near the Sir Charles Hardy Islands.

Five of the crew members took the quarter boat and sailed it north through the Torres Straits and across the Arafura Sea, arriving on the island of Yamdena, what is now Indonesia. The other survivors made two large rafts and rowed on the trade winds, arriving on Boydang, a small sandy cay that is located between Sir Charles Hardy Islands and Albany Passage on the Great Barrier Reef. At that time, there was a group of visiting Torres Strait Islanders inhabiting the small island cay, who beheaded all the adults and kept their heads as trophies. as that apparently is what head-hunters do?

The young sons of Captain D'Oyly, William aged three and George aged seven were spared. Also, another two boys, John Ireland and John Sexton, were not beheaded and instead captured by the murderous islanders and taken to the Torres Straits. Two of the four boys, Sexton and William, died while the other two boys lived with their captors for many months until eventually being traded for a bunch of bananas. They then lived on the Murray Islands, luckily with a couple who treated them as their family renaming them Wak and Uass.

The boys lived with the Murray Island family until 1836. Following reports of the survivors of the *Charles Eaton* being on Murray Islands, the schooner *Isabella* commanded by Captain Charles Morgan Lewis sailed to rescue them. The only two remaining survivors, the two boys, were handed over to them. They were also told by islanders from nearby islands about heads having been taken back by the murderers to the island of Aureed. It was situated further west towards Badu Island.

Captain Lewis then sailed to Aureed, and he and his heavily armed men explored the entire island but found it deserted, the village on the island had been abandoned. They discovered a dilapidated hut inside which they found a large turtle shell surrounded by human skulls of Europeans. One of the skulls still had red hair and was thought to be the head of the captain's red-haired wife. The island was then referred to as Skull Island. No wonder the Torres Straits were called the "straits of terror"!

At 1245 hours, the border force called on VHF requesting information on our departure port and where we were going. Soon, we had a nice easterly wind and sailed into Portland Roads anchoring just outside the settlement near where I had anchored before.

Log: Wednesday, 27 November 2019; 0700 hours.

We departed for Lloyd Island which is in Lloyd Bay where the mighty Lockhart River flows. The weather prediction was going to be strong winds, so I thought Lloyd Island seemed like a perfect anchorage, as opposed to the small coral islands that become rough. We sailed past Restoration Island, the spot where Captain Bligh made his heroic venture, after the mutiny of the *Bounty* on a small craft. We sailed straight to Lloyd Island which was a picturesque island well-protected from the south easterlies.

I contacted the Aboriginal settlement regarding fuel. They said they would assist in bringing the fuel back out and I was asked to come in. So, we weighed anchor again and motored over close to the town's ramp where I went ashore with the tender carrying fuel cans. Jeff stayed back minding the yacht. I was told someone would pick me up, but no one arrived. Therefore, I grabbed a lift with an Aboriginal family into town bringing my fuel cans along in the back of their Ute.

On the way, they explained to me about the many clans living at the settlement from around the Cape York region. They dropped me off at the store where the store people explained that they did drive to the ramp area but could not see me. I was assisted by a local girl who drove me back out to the ramp and helped load the fuel into the

CHAPTER ELEVEN

tender. Jeff was in a bit of a stressed state as the wind was up and it had dragged the anchor into the shallows. With the tide dropping, it was getting too close for comfort, looking at the shallow rocky ground. We loaded up quickly and went back to the great anchorage at Lloyd Island.

Log: Thursday, 28 November 2019.

As predicted, the wind picked up, with the south easterlies being too strong to go anywhere. Through the mini-iridium I was in touch with several other yachties hiding in safe anchorages along the coast, waiting for the northerlies that were due on Sunday. That was the plan, to hide on the island, then jump on the northerlies on Sunday, and head south. Lloyd island is a very tall hill island with another small island, also a tall hill, on the northern side. We explored the island that had great views from the hill at the top, we smoked fish on the beach and found tracks of a wallaby. It was evidence that there must be water source somewhere just like Restoration Island which had assisted in the survival of Captain Bligh.

We boiled the billy and swam in the waters only when we could see the shallow was safe enough, devoid of reptiles. Over the next couple of days, turtle hunters came to Lloyd Island along with their catch. On Saturday night, before returning, they set fire to the small adjacent island. It was safe enough for us as we were on the windward side, but what a spectacular sight. They set fire at the base of the hill and the fire slowly made its way to the top of the hill overnight, creating a spectacular volcano like scene.

Log: Sunday, 1 December 2019; 0500 hours.

We departed sailing straight across the massive Lloyd Bay passing Cape Direction, another large protruding point along the east coast of Cape York. Jeff pulled in a nice Spanish mackerel and at 1500 hours, those northerlies we were waiting for, finally arrived. How refreshing the sailing was when running with the wind! We pushed as far south in daylight hours as we could then anchoring on the southern side of Wilkie Island in the dark, with the radar for some reason playing up now and then. We slowly made our way closer to the island at night for better protection, our eyes peeled on the sounder.

Log: Monday, 2 December 2019; 0600 hours; Departed Wilkie Island for the Flinders Group.

We set sail as the sun was coming up and the north easterlies were blowing at twelve knots. We got the kite out, and have a magnificent spinnaker run doing 7.0 knots SOG. Log read 300 nautical miles since Seisia and then, unfortunately, the northerlies changed to easterlies. We had to head east across the northern section of Princess Charlote Bay towards the Flinders group of islands experiencing the dreaded windward again. Yet you did not have any options due to the many reefs and had limited beating due to the reef hazards. We arrived at the Flinders group of islands and anchored at a new spot south of Blackwood Island.

The Flinders are an incredible, unique, rocky outcrop of many islands and magnificent bays. I was always out of the cabin before the sun and could hear Jeff on the bow as the morning light saying, "Wow, what a place! Wow, magnificent!" It reminded me of the saying by Ernest Hemmingway in the book, Old Man and the Sea.

Why do old men wake so early? Is it to have a longer day?

This great quote from Hemingway was similar to the saying I was told when I was twenty years old, working on a cattle station in the far Kimberleys. There was this elderly ex-stockman who was then the repair saddler, and he advised me,

Never let the sun beat you in the morning.

It does not matter whether it's a bushman or a seafarer's life, or any an old man, it is all the same. The key is don't waste the day missing out on a morning as one day it will be the last morning you experience.

We noticed a large coral bommie getting too close for comfort since the tide was becoming low. The current had drifted us over a coral fringe reef, that was not on the charts, so we quickly weighed anchor and had breakfast under way. With the north easterlies we had a beam reach run crossing Bathurst Bay, and then around Cape Melville passing Barrow Island and Ninian Bay, where I had anchored before and arrived at a group of small coral islands named the Turtle group.

We anchored in fifteen metres of water between the two most southerly islands of the group, and again, the huge numbers of imperial pigeons with their distinctive white markings dominated the

CHAPTER ELEVEN

evening sunset as they came into nest. The noise of their pigeon hooting sound could be heard all through the night.

Log: Wednesday, 4 December 2019; 0600 hours; Depart Turtle Islands, destination Cooktown.

A fifty-nautical-mile passage passing Cape Flattery, and the iconic rocky escarpment of Cape Bedford was passed sailing through. Many dolphins rode the bow waves, several turtles were seen coming into the entrance of the Endeavour River, and incredibly, I received a phone call from David Williams. The former post office master of Metung and his wife, Judith, were holidaying here in the north. So, he thought he would call to find my whereabouts, and incredibly here we were coming into Cooktown. After dropping anchor and securing the vessel, we all had several ales and a great feed at the township establishments.

After a couple of nights in Cooktown, we were away again. We departed early in the morning and had a terrific run sailing along close to the shore where we could enjoy the smell-scent of the rainforest, passing the entrance of the Bloomfield River, and continued sailing. Arriving at Snapper Island at 1500 hours, just under fifty-seven nautical miles averaging 6.3 knots an hour. Not bad when you have wind in your favour. Now, we had completed 959 nautical miles since leaving the top of Australia. It had been great sailing, and everything had all gone to plan. That was, until early hours of the morning.

Log: Saturday, 7 December 2019; 200 hours.

It was a terrible night. We had anchored in fifteen metres for safety, otherwise we would have been too close to a fringe reef. We were anchored on the southern side, halfway along the island, and protected from the north easterly winds. Then we were awake at 0200 hours with winds well over thirty knots from the west in the opposite direction due to the depth. I had only had minimum scope out. The stern was close to the fringe reef and we needed to get more chain out without hitting that, impossible so we had the motors going which gave us a little comfort of not dragging, but then, the wind got up to gale conditions blowing from the direction of Daintree River, therefore, it created large swells over the bow and the wind did not die down until 0400 hours. It was a sleepless night.

Another boat anchored in our vicinity dragged anchor as you could tell by the lights but then was stable. All its lights were lit up like a Christmas tree and we were the same, waiting out these terrible conditions. Once the wind died off, we were able to get a couple of hours' sleep before weighing anchor and headed the short passage to Bluewater Marina where I had booked a berth. As we sailed off from Snapper Island, there was a gentle south westerly, and then, a calm opposite to the north easterlies of yesterday.

Bluewater is a marina that is about two nautical miles up the winding Moon River passing *Yorkeys Knob Boating Club* marina. As we motored winding our way up this mangrove-lined river, we could see the mountains above the mangrove forest. At that point, Jeff said, "Are you having me on? How could there be a marina up here?"

When you come into the muddy river, it gives the impression of heading into nowhere but then, a large marina appears surrounded my modern new homes, another suburb of Cairns.

Jeff asked, "Do you think you would know anyone in here?"

"I don't think so," I said, thinking I wouldn't.

Interestingly, Macca came to assist us with mooring lines from the catamaran, *Intoxicate*, that I had met in Mackay. Within the hour, I found at least a dozen people I had got to know over the years in and around Cape York were also moored in Bluewater. There really is only a small yachties cruising community.

Lagoon 410 SV Never Die Wondering II

My plan was to quickly sell my vessel and go wherever in the world to purchase the vessel I needed. Unbeknownst to me, this was going to be wishful thinking because Australia fell into a type of tyrannical dystopia due to the extreme Covid-19 restrictions. Like many other yachties, I found myself caught in a marina. During my time at Bluewater, which was going to be over a year, I socialised with many yachties, both new and old acquaintances. Especially, Macca who named his catamaran *Intoxicate*, and Geoff whose yacht's name was *Fortified Port*. We spent many months having sundowners (beers in the afternoon) guaranteed with salties who name their craft after the drop. We spent every afternoon together solving the world's problems.

In June, a forty-one feet *Lagoon* catamaran came on the market. There were no photos available, but it was in a berth at the Marlin

CHAPTER ELEVEN

Marina, Cairns. As the ludicrous restrictions stopped anyone from inspecting the craft from interstate, therefore, the restrictions turned out be in my favour. I quickly became the proud owner of a 410 French design *Lagoon* launched in the USA in 2000. It had three queen-size bed cabins, two x bathrooms, 1.2 draft, two 40 HP *Yanmar* engines, a fantastic layout with galley up, and a large saloon 7.1-metre beam. It was an owner's version that meant having the starboard side captain's area with a large library-office, perfect for me.

It was named *Tropical Soul*, and the records kept were fabulous. Originally, it was named *Bebes L'amour*, French for baby love. Launched in the USA in 2000, she had sailed the South Pacific, Indonesia, Malayasia, and the likes of the Solomon Island and many other places, a proven craft. Geoff and Macca both came with me as we sailed her back to Bluewater Marina. The only problem was, I then had two yachts side by side. It took me another six months until I sold the *Crowther* to an experienced sailor 84 eighty-four-years-old, who ironically had sailed from Europe to Australia, many years ago. Both his adult children had passed. He also had lost his wife recently whose last words to him were, "Get back out there sailing!" She knew he missed the sailing life.

The number of improvements I needed to upgrade the new vessel seemed to be endless. Although the vessel was perfect for me, it had been idle for a long period of time, therefore, many things needed replacing. I up graded all the electronics and navigation gear to *Raymarine*, new anchor chain, and also was in waiting for months in some cases for parts like the radar. In all honesty, I really needed at least six months getting the vessel to how I wanted. Once while diving under the vessel, I felt a sting on my foot and noticed a sting ray. When I climbed back onboard, my foot was gashed with blood everywhere that needed medical treatment. The hazards of working on vessels!

Once I was happy with the vessel, Geoff Hunn and I sailed her from Bluewater to Fitzroy Island, then from there to the Reef and back to Bluewater over a few days. It was a reasonable shake down, having great winds, being light and moderate, and was able to sail all wind angles. While we were on Fitzroy Island, we witnessed a hammer head shark chasing and attacking eagle rays right up to the water line of the beach with a sting ray diving onto the beach itself. I registered the vessel under Australian flag, with home port as Cairns, and renamed her *Never Die Wondering II*.

My son, Brandon, came with me for Christmas of 2020, and we spent a week sailing her up to Cooktown, anchoring at many places along the way. On Snapper Island, just off Port Douglass, I got the whisky bottle out and we christened her *Never Die Wondering II* in true salty style, asking Neptune and Poseidon for fair winds and protection. We had a brilliant sail to Cooktown, trying to anchor at different anchorages, and returning to Cairns with another list of jobs for the vessel. As is always the way with yachts.

CHAPTER TWELVE

I sail not to escape life, but for life not to escape me.

Log: Tuesday, 16 March 2021; 1000 hours; Destination Townsville.

After more than fourteen months, I was under way motoring out of Bluewater Marina, out of Moon River, and into the sea. The weather wasn't the best with stormy conditions and south easterly winds. I had to motor sail, but I didn't care because I was so glad to be under way. Fellow boaties who were sailing two nautical miles away, some of whom I knew from the marina radioed me to ask me to meet at Fitzroy Island. I declined them, as I planned to anchor at Turtle Bay opposite Fitzroy Island on the mainland. I wanted to see a small waterfall that came down onto the beach area from an exposed boulder type of rock formation. I anchored there for lunch, but the weather blew up to more than twenty knots, so I decided to sail over to Fitzroy Island. I moored on the public swing moorings on the western side of the island that is more protected. A few beers at *Foxy's* bar, and I returned to the vessel as light showers came in. The next day I sailed sixty-one nautical miles to Dunk Island.

Legal Pirates of the Sea

Log: Thursday, 18 March 2021, 0630 hours; Departed Dunk Island for destination Hinchinbrook Island

The day brought very calm conditions, even with full sail I needed one engine going for momentum with a south westerly wind of nine knots. There were a couple of fishing vessels working in the area and

I decided to sail along the west side of a group of islands known as Brook Islands due to the fishing trawlers. I noted on the log, *very interesting place, long fringe reef stretching from the northern island to the southern island that had pyramid buoys in one section, I dare say marking the coral reef.*

There was a fishing vessel anchored just south of the northern island that I passed. Seeing the fishing trawlers, and being calm conditions, I decided to throw a fishing line out the stern. As I was doing this, I noticed a large rubber dingy with a shade roof coming towards me, it had an official type of appearance. I threw the line out and went back to the helm. Within a short period of time, I had this official dingy come beside me, written on the side was *Girringun Rangers: Strong Aboriginal People, Strong Culture, Strong Country*. They were all filming me with mobile phones and an *iPad*, as they came up close to my vessel. I had only the wind slowly pushing me along, I asked, "What are you doing?" I felt intimidated with three fellers filming.

The leader of the group replied, "We will tell you in a minute." They continued filming and after a while, he then asked, "Can I have permission to come aboard?"

I said, "Only one of you!" Then, I assisted him to step on board. He then explained that he was filming me with another camera, a body cam, and that they were doing routine checks.

Then a person in the dingy asked, "What is that line out the back?"

"It's a fishing line." I said.

The leader then looked and said, "You are in a green zone, fishing is not allowed."

"I have a new chart on my plotter, along with a *Navionics* chart on my *iPad* on the saloon table, including a paper chart. There is no green zone on any of them," I stated.

The leader said "Yes, there is. I will show you." He then looked at the chart plotter and zoomed all over it and said that for some reason it was not showing it. We then went to the saloon, and he tried to find it on the new *Navionics* tablet but it was not there, and neither was there any indication on the paper charts.

He then said, "You will only get a warning as long as you have not been fishing in green zones before."

I suggested that he did not go any further due to the circumstances regarding the matter, but it was wishful thinking on my behalf. Several weeks later, I would receive a notice via email with a fine of $2,700. I had the right to write to the authorities stating why I should not be

CHAPTER TWELVE

fined which I did, but then received a notice stating I was not successful. Moreover, if I did not pay the fine, I would have to appear in the Townsville court and if I was unsuccessful there, I could be then faced with an $11,000 fine.

At the time of this potential court proceedings, I would be in isolated parts of Northern Australia, and it would have cost me more to fly back to Townsville than the $2,700 fine along with not being able to leave my vessel and face additional $11,000 fine. So, I bit my tongue, and was robbed of the money by legal pirates of the sea, or should I refer them as privateers, fully funded by the Australian taxpayer.

Log: 1145 hours; passing Hinchinbrook Island to the east.

What a spectacular sight! The island had the most dramatic peaks with what is known as the Thump, a sharp rocky peak that was just protruding through a shroud of cloud after a shower of misty rain. I wrote in my log that it reminded me of the old man store on the Isle of Skye in Scotland.

The easterly winds came in hard, so Zoe Bay on the east side of Hinchinbrook was not going to be a good anchorage as the easterlies were up to twenty knots. Hence, I continued to Pioneer Bay on Orpheus Island, catching a large spotty mackerel along the way, and then was greeted by a pod of spinning dolphins at the anchorage.

The next morning, I was away at first light to Magnetic Island. The day was spent in poor visibility with light showers and a South easterly all day with winds reaching eleven to eighteen knots going windward at thirty degrees. It was not the best day for sailing but much more comfortable than the little *Crowther*. Along the way, I received a call on the VHF from Ziggy and Tess who I had met in the Torres Straits. We could not see each other due to the rain but he picked me up on the AIS. After that, I received a call from Brian Dorling who was coming into Townsville from the south. It is incredible the communication you can have at sea along with identification system on your charts.

I arrived at in Horseshoe Bay on the northern side of Magnetic Island a safe cove with rocky boulder hills surrounding it, and turtles greeting me as they swam around at the anchorage. That night I watched a documentary on Yamada, the Japanese pirate, of whom the Australian treasure hunter, Ben Croft, believed it was possible that Yamada had found his way to Australia and buried his loot somewhere on Magnetic Island. I researched this theory and found that the loot was rumoured to be worth 100 million dollars I had read about Yamada when I was in the Torres Strait and it was a fascinating story.

Yamada Nagamasa was a Japanese pirate who operated mostly around the Indonesian waters in the 1620s attacking and plundering Dutch ships. He is regarded today as a national hero in Japan. This was many years after Torres discovered the trade route of which the Torres Strait bears his name in 1606 and 150 years prior to Captain Cook sailing the east coast. Yamada retired to Siam (Thailand) and died in 1630. The story describing what some believe could be Magnetic Island, apparently came from documents in a temple in Japan from Yamada along with a painting of one of his vessels. In the 1930s, a newspaper wrote an article describing the potential island of Yamada's 100-million-dollar loot had similarities with Magnetic Island. Due to the thousands of islands between Indonesia and Townsville, one wonders why any pirate would hide his loot so far away. Personally, I believe it is only a myth.

For the next four days, I stayed in Horseshoe Bay waiting for the availability of my vessel to be hauled out at Ross haven slipway for anti-fouling the hull, and lots of small jobs to be attended to. Then, Geoff Hunn sailed in with a Russian girlfriend and with Geoff it was mandatory to have beers at the closest bar.

Log: Tuesday, 23 March 2021;

I sailed to Rosshaven slip via the east side of Magnetic Island. Geoff had also booked having his vessel lifted out, so we both sailed our vessels over to Rosshaven. As soon as *Never Die Wondering II* was lifted out and pressure washed, Brian Dorling came to meet me, he had sailed up from southern NSW with his wife, Sandra. He was also heading to Darwin and over the next few months Brian and I would catch up at many locations from Townsville to Darwin.

It became a week of solid work getting the vessel prepared, sanding back the old anti-fouling paint, applying a couple of undercoats and anti-foul paint, covering the wash areas several times. In addition, it needed replacing seals on the sail drive and anodes, prop speed paint, changing oils, and I had ordered a new life raft which arrived too. Meanwhile, I socialised with the yachtie community around Townsville marina and then the vessel was back into the water. I returned to Horseshoe Bay and stayed anchored there for another week. Again, many other jobs

CHAPTER TWELVE

continued, servicing the pump for the water maker, and making sure everything imaginable was satisfactory for the voyage to Darwin.

Log: Tuesday, 6 April 2021; Depart 0620 hours; Destination Zoe Bay, Hinchinbrook.

The wind was in my favour, a light southerly and I was able to hoist the asymmetrical spinnaker and peacefully sail along even when I had wind over tide. It created a bit of chop but I could comfortably move along the east side of Palm Island, and then the western side of Hinchinbrook, sailing into the spectacular Zoe Bay. The shroud of clouds trying to cover the majestic peaks, the fresh smell of the rainforest as I sailed into this magnificent, sheltered anchorage where you could see the distinctive large waterfall in the distance.

There was only another vessel in the bay, a fishing boat, some distance from myself. As the sun went down, it cast an incredible light towards the peaks enhancing the remaining clouds that seemed to just sink into the crevices of the rocky peaks. At dawn, it was a totally different sight as the sun rose from the east and cast a bright light onto this magnificent escarpment. The sun, now fully shinning on the peaks, moved any cloud away from the tops of this mountain terrain.

I made my way to the waterfall, Zoe Falls, and walked up a track to find many bushwalkers who were tramping for days from one side of the island to the other, all looked exhausted. The waterfall is spectacular, and this bay is one of my favourites. On my return to the dingy, again it was high and dry. I strained my back dragging it to the water. As soon as I was back on board, I quickly raised the anchor to take advantage of the southeasterlies. I hoist the asymmetrical and sail comfortably passing Brook Islands on the west. This time, I did not place a line out until I was well past Brook Island and caught a good size shark which I released. I was able to beam reach with the asymmetrical arriving at Dunk Island just before dark. Two fishing trawlers were working the area. I stayed here for a couple of nights resting up and downloading the *PredictWind* on the *Iridium*.

Log: Friday, 9 April 2024; Depart Dunk 0620 hours; Destination Mourilyan Harbour

With light winds all day, it was not a huge distance in the morning sail while coming into Mourilyan Harbour from Dunk Island. Still, in the morning hours, the first thing you notice is the large wharf that loads the sugar. It is actually the entrance to Moresby River where the river cuts its way to the sea through these two high hills. Inside the harbour, is a large body of water, a great bolt hole for tropical storms, great anchorages, and many mangrove creeks where one can hide from a storm. I spent three nights in this harbour exploring the many mangrove creeks, catching snook which I discovered is a very tasty fish.

Log: Monday, 12 April 2021;

I sailed out of Mourilyan to nearby Frankland Islands. I wanted to explore these picturesque group of islands as this was going to be my third time passing them. Another great asymmetrical spinnaker run, also caught a large mackerel which I quickly cleaned, and then using my recent vacuum sealed contraption had many feeds sealed into small bags for the freezer. There were a couple of public moorings on the southwestern side of the islands, so I dropped the spinnaker into the sock, and started the motors to manoeuvre onto the moorings.

    Foolishly, I had forgotten to bring my fishing line in and as a result, the line quickly wrapped around the port side propeller. Fishing was costing me a lot of grief! I secured the mooring, started the diving compressor, and went under the boat to remove the line by knife. It was great clear water so I could see if a large reptile was around from the Johnston and Russel rivers that are not too far away.

    I dinged over to Russell Island that has a lighthouse on the southern point. It was low tide, and I was able to walk along the low tide mark between Russell and a smaller island to its north that was a high rocky hill type. Russell Island itself has a high hill that is covered in lush rainforest. The shallow water was littered with sea cucumbers or beche-de-mer which was a highly sourced commodity a century ago. It was a cloudy day and in the near distance a large water sprout formed that seemed to slowly head towards my direction. I watched this event for some considerable time taking photos, and then, it slowly dispersed. I returned to *Never Die Wondering II* which had a couple of turtles swimming nearby. That night, there was a large amount of lightning around the vessel along with strong winds.

CHAPTER TWELVE

Log: Tuesday, 13 April 2021; 0640 hours.

I departed early as the south westerly was making mooring there uncomfortable. It was head sail only for most of the morning, then again asymmetrical up with the south easterly winds which at some stages took me to 7.4 knots SOG. I decided to head back into Bluewater Marina since it was easy to resupply there, and I needed a few small electrical jobs. However, the main reason was the weather predictions of this low-pressure system that was coming in, along with expectations for torrential rainfall. So, by late afternoon, I found myself back into the crab pot.

Marinas are like crab pots easy to get in but hard to get out.

I was trapped in the crab pot for another three weeks, and the torrential rains was exactly that—torrential! Within a week, over 700 mm of rain fell. I was able to get all the jobs done, like mast work refigured, supplies, fuel, and more maps and books on anchorages purchased.

Voyage Back to the Torres Straits

Log: Monday, 3 April 2021; Destination Darwin.

Leanne, whom I had met in Cairns previously, came out sailing for the day along with her daughter as a bon voyage. They both only sailed the short distance to Double Island and I took them back to the shore by tender where they would get a taxi. Even that was challenging, as the strong winds were up and we waited until nearly night before it was safe enough to take them onto the jetty, as the waves were smashing against it. Again, trying to get them safely onto the jetty was extremely challenging, because along the way, I had to collect a fishing line around the dingy. You would think the person fishing off the jetty would have the common sense to reel in his line, when someone amongst waves is trying to land on the jetty. Common sense is not common!

Log: Tuesday, 4 May 2021; 0745 hours; Depart, Destination Cape Kimberley

Southerlies were enough for just the head sail, running with the wind. Brian Dorling from *Sea Leaf* contacted me on the VHF and said, "Where are you? I have just negotiated with fishermen, have a box of prawns and mackerel!"

Just like that dinner was arranged off the northwest point of Snapper Island, just short of Cape Kimberley. It was not an ideal anchorage with the wind southerly, and when I dropped anchor, it jammed then I dragged some distance. Brian came aboard from his dingy and we both worked on getting this chain sorted. Once we were done, it was straight to his vessel for prawns, mackerel, and beer with which we yarned away for many hours. There were discussions on the passages further north, as Brian and Sandra were also heading to Darwin.

Log: Wednesday, 5 May 2021; 1000 hours; Departed Snapper Island after a late breakfast.

I had Brian and Sandra over for fruit breaky and cupper. It was so exciting to sail with the trade winds. Just as I had weighed anchor up, with asymmetrical away I went in light south easterlies. This was a wonderful coastline as the closer you came to the shore, the more the beautiful the rainforest looked. Added to it was the smell of the bush and the unique soaring mountains with their distinctive peaks.

I passed Cape Tribulation, and arrived at Cedar Bay, where Brandon and I had explored at Christmas. I was in a great calm anchorage and a superb large sea eagle would soar around the vessel for ages as if confirming his territory. I awoke the next morning to the fresh rainforest smell with a light south westerly blowing, and experiencing this incredible aroma smell that scented the cabin at Rattlesnake Point. This was now my fifth time sailing these waters and there was no need to visit Cooktown. I was eager so I continued sailing north, I still had the feeling of spending all that time in the marina, on the yacht working along with the covid restrictions I just wanted to sail a big distance.

Your yacht is similar to an island, it can be your refuge or quickly become your prison.

I dropped spinnaker about 1130 hours and just had the head sail out as the wind had picked up. I was a little worried about blowing the kite when Geoff Hunn from *Fortified* contacted me via VHF. He also was sailing to Darwin solo and was a few miles north. Incredibly, Geoff would continue sailing to the Kimberley's and Broome and back to Townsville and complete the trip solo. The border force radioed as I passed Cape Bedford requesting departure and asked where I was

CHAPTER TWELVE

going. I arrived at Cape Flattery at 1700 hours and dropped anchor overlooking another majestic rock formation impression of a wall that runs north to south. In the vicinity, opposite to rocky formations, were white silicon sand hills that stretched for miles.

Log: Friday, 7 May 2021; 0800 hours; Departed Cape Flattery, destination Lizard Island

The trade winds had now set in, consistent all day and slowing down only at night. This is what sailors dream of and with head sail only, I sailed over to Lizard Island. I had not ventured on the island before. Anchoring in Watsons Bay on the northern protected side, I found there were three other yachties there. Nigel who I had met in Townsville came over on his dingy to inform me of drinks on the beach that night. Brian and Sandra had arrived as well, and I met other yachties who were, all on their way to Darwin as well.

The next morning, Brian and I climbed up Mount Cook, 358 meters high. We stood on the hill admiring the view and imagining how James Cook must have stood there looking frantically for a pass through the coral reef and back into the safety of the Coral Sea after the repairs to the *Endeavour* at Cooktown. It was surreal looking down into Watsons Bay at the four sailing vessels that looked so small, and you could clearly see the airstrip, we watched far below us as a small plane landed at the resort. Many goannas were seen throughout the island and on our return, I snorkelled amongst the fringe coral reefs.

Log: Sunday, 9 May 2021; Depart 0630 hours.

The prediction was for moderate then to strong winds. I wanted to sail the strong winds to check the vessel, but they increased up to near gale in the morning. I had the third reef in the main, and was still flying along, at one stage it was 9.0 knots SOG. The swells were up and not comfortable smashing the starboard quarter, the drain in the cockpit became a water shoot. If the angle of the wave was right, it would manage to smash under the cockpit and come up through the drain. soaking the entire cockpit with the swells breaking at the stern. Besides the noise of the smashing swells, the vessel handled it fantastically.

Prior to lunch I found it no point to continue in the near gale conditions, so I anchored on the leeside of an islet called Coquet Island.

Although it blew all afternoon and continued throughout the night, the large reef around Coquet stopped the large swells.

Log: Monday, 10 May 2021; 0800 hours; Depart Coquet Island.

The wind had not eased off and as of 0800 hours it was 14-19 knots. *PredictWind* forecasted moderate to fresh, but then yesterday was near gale force winds when it was only supposed to be moderate to strong, so who really knows! It is recommended to add 40% just in case to the predicted wind as a wise move. At 1000 hours, I was able to goose wing the sails and had a terrific sail running with the wind a far cry from the previous day. I was comfortably making 7.0 knots SOG arriving at Cape Melville at 1600 hours in 3.5 meters of water. I planned to visit the memorial to all those who lost their lives in the 1899 cyclone, Mahina, the biggest cyclone recorded ever hitting Australia. However, the strong winds coming off Cape Melville made it impossible.

SV Cool Change was anchored next to me, Matt and Lisa who I had met at Lizard Island. We discussed the wind on the VHF. Cape Melville has high boulders of granite hills above the Cape itself that seemed to create bullets of the wind runs along the tops in the south easterly trade winds and gathers wind that further speeds that come down into the bay. What is referred to as bullets. There were stories of yachties caught for days with their vessels, stretched on the anchor chain, not being able to move forward to lift the anchor struck into ground.

Although it was only thirty-three knots of true wind and no worry for my vessel, the problem was getting to the shore in the tender amongst the swells. With the stirred-up water you couldn't see the bottom which was threatened by the possibility of hitting a prop once in the shallow water. As the morning brought no reprieve, I decided to sail on, and so did Matt and Lisa on *SV Cool Change*. They would eventually sail their mono to Darwin and then circumnavigate Australia.

After only a short distance sail away from the Cape, the wind reduced considerably. I was sailing due west across Bathurst Bay to the Flinders group of islands on a broad reach. I was sailing through fly Channel on the southern side of Flinders Island and then into Owen Channel southwest of where I had anchored previously.

I was told recently by a fellow yachtie of how he had stumbled onto an Aboriginal burial cave with skeletal remains wrapped in bark in a large, sheltered cave. He had given me a rough sketch of where he

CHAPTER TWELVE

thought it was, and I spent hours climbing and exploring to no avail. Although in recent years, the site was rediscovered, and the shelter was steel fabricated gated to protect the skeletal remains. All the years I had spent in the bush, I would search rock shelters in the hope of finding paintings, and only once stumbled onto a burial site that had a skull on a ledge.

Log: Wednesday, 12 May 2021; 0710 hours; Departed Flinders Island.

Within the hour, I had the asymmetrical up again and was getting along with eight knots of wind, doing 5.1 SOG. I passed a large sand cay on the west side that had literally hundreds of booby birds on it. The wind dropped and became a southerly, and then south westerly. I arrived at Burkitt Island and dropped anchor on the east side of the island in eleven meters of water.

Burkitt is a mangrove island with a beach on the northern side. All these islands have fringe reefs, and I find it safer to drop anchor once I hit the near ten-metre mark rather than trying to get further into shallow water, and risk hitting coral. Due to the light winds, it was a pleasant anchorage, and many dolphins were swimming around. The evening was alive with a variety of birds coming onto the island.

The next morning, I was underway by 0615 hours. Unfortunately, there with no wind so I was forced to motor only, for an hour and a half, there was enough wind then to fly the kite on a southerly. I hoisted the conventional downwind spinnaker that is larger than the asymmetrical and passed Wilkie Island, another small mangrove islet. I watched several sharks that were following the yacht at one stage, wondering if they were following the scent of my recent fish kill. I passed a fishing trawler at Hay Island that was on anchor, and most likely, the reason for the many sharks.

A very comfortable sail in light winds and I was able to have a much-needed shave, cooked tacos for lunch, and on several occasions, had dolphins come along for a ride. I decided to anchor at Night Island and when sailing near the island I hooked a large shark. I needed to drop the kite to slow the vessel down to be able to bring the shark in and release. I was sailing at 6.2 knots. After another catch and release, I anchored at the northwest anchorage. *SV Seins de le via* with Terry and Leonne who I had met at, Lizard Island were also on their way to Darwin. They radioed me and also dropped anchor nearby.

Marooned Cabin Boy

I had recently read a book titled, *Castaway* by Robert Macklin, based on the memoirs of Narcisse Pelletier who was a French cabin boy who was shipwrecked off the eastern tip of Papua New Guinea. He sailed across the Coral Sea with several survivors in a small craft only to be abandoned by the rest of the crew, here at Night Island in 1858. He was taken in with the local Aboriginal tribe of Night Island the Uutaalnganu people who occupied the island, reefs, and most of the shoreline of the mainland within the vicinity I was anchored in. Narcisse's account of his seventeen years living with the Night Island people is one of the best accounts of Aboriginal tribal life and culture, and sometimes a brutal existence. He became a husband and father here but was eventually captured by pearl lugger people and taken to Sydney. He was then taken back to France where he died a depressed man, after being taken away from those he had declared his people and family.

Log: Friday, 14 May 2021; 0630 hours; Departed Night Island.

It started off as a cloudy day. I had full head sail and reefed in the main as I was expecting an increase in wind. I was able to make 6.0 knots SOG and the dolphins joined me. The morning had plenty of chat on the VHF with the several other yachties I had met on Lizard Island. I passed Cape Direction at 1020 hours and now was heading northwest towards Restoration Island, where Captain Bligh ate booby birds that saved him and his crew. With the wind now at 180 degrees on my stern, I was able to goose wing and what a great sail it was. Along the way, I brought in another mackerel and quickly the cockpit became the butchering and packing factory where all the pieces were vacuumed sealed. I took a photo of the pieces on the table displaying the zebra skin appearance.

Brian Dorling called to anchor at Portland Roads, but I declined as I wanted to get most of the good sailing and decided to make it to Beesley Island and arranged to meet him in the next couple of days at Margaret Bay. I had explained to him in the past, the Bay was one of the best places on Cape York. Passing Fair Cape at 1515 hours and arriving at this small coral cay at 1710 hours. I wrote in the log, BARREN PLACE. The island was part of the Piper islets that are two coral reefs with two small, vegetated areas. Beesley is the better of the two, and I anchored on the lee side. I regretted it later and should have gone

CHAPTER TWELVE

further into the cay for better protection. I rolled all night, not a comfortable anchorage, in fact, I had written in the log, terrible anchorage.

The next morning, I quickly departed Beesley at first light and with the south and south easterlies I beam reached to Cape Grenville. The wind was up, and good swells were coming over the deck. I was moving at 8.0 knots SOG, sailing in the shipping route. Two large ships passed me heading south that created a large wake. The great thing about sailing the inner reef is that the Barrier Reef itself reduces the big swells from the Coral Sea making sailing more pleasant.

The seaweed catching in my line was too much, so I brought the line in, and then peacefully sailed through Paluma Passage rounding Cape Grenville and into the quaint, picture-perfect Margaret Bay. By late afternoon, there were five vessels in the bay. Brian and Sandra came over to *Never Die Wondering II*, as it was my turn to cook the fresh mackerel caught on the way. The next morning, Brian and I were roaming the rocks at low tide with hammer and chisel eating many large oysters, *it does not get fresher than that.*

The winds were predicted to be strong to near gale force. The other few vessels decided to keep going while I decided to wait for better, favourable winds. I enjoyed several days having the bay to myself. Besides, there was the bucket loads of oysters, that I had to consume washing down with cold *Great Northern* beer. I explored the west side of the beach and discovered an old plane that had crashed in the 40s. In the low tide, it is completely exposed, the wings all still attached and covered with oyster shells, nearly eighty years of sea creature growth. I cooked back at the camp, smoking fish in my metho-smoker, and in the evening, watched a dingo come around the fire looking for what he could scavenge.

Places like Margaret Bay deserve the respect of spending time, while exploring this wonderful part of the earth. There is a lagoon where I would take my dingy up to. where whistler ducks roam in their hundreds. The water has many sharks that can be easily observed in the shallows along with the sting rays that are prolific.

Log: Friday, 21 May 2021; Depart 1430 hours.

Although Margaret Bay is well-protected, a mile out from the bay you could see the white caps of the strong winds. The afternoon brought a reduction in the wind, so I decided to sail the short passage to Rodney Point. I anchored in the lee of the point as the next day would be a sixty nautical mile voyage to Escape River and I was just trying to shorten the next day's passage. I sailed out of the bay and into the blowing thirty knots of wind. All the anchorages are only recommended in calm conditions to Escape River that would be the only comfortable anchorage. I dropped the pick at Rodney Point and not far from me was the ship *HMAS Benalla* on anchor.

Log: Saturday, 22 May 2021; 0605 hours; Departed Rodney Point, destination Escape River.

As I was away from the protected lee of the headland, the wind was blowing strong. I only had my head sail and making great speed up to 7.0 knots SOG. I passed Macarthur Island on the east side and a few miles on, passed Hannibal Island on the west side, a place I had anchored before. I was broad reaching and having those dreaded swells slapping the quarter. Still, passing the many reefs on high tide in strong winds is incredible, watching them becoming awash with waves breaking from the south easterly winds.

At 1250 hours, I passed Bushy Island on the western side, a coral cay with only a patch of vegetation. If needed, you can anchor on the northwest side, but it is guaranteed to be an uncomfortable anchorage in these strong winds. It was an entire cloudy day, and the afternoon brought light rains as I passed Gilmore reef. With large waves smashing in the strong winds, I enjoyed another feed of mackerel and veggies and continued the fast sailing. I arrived at the mouth of the Escape River at 1615 hours. It was a very challenging entrance as the winds were at twenty-five knots and the bar depth was only three meters at this time. It was a little hairy going!

I dropped anchor close to the low tide mark that is exposed just within the inside of the entrance. Then, at 1900 hours, I found myself having the anchor drag a long distance of 300 meters, I quickly raised the anchor and motored back to the way point placing out more chain this time. When it was set, I fell asleep exhausted, waking up at 0730 hours, still fully clothed.

Log: Sunday, 23 May 2021; 0645 hours; Departed Escape River.

The wind was up to twenty-eight knots, another guarantee of an exciting sail. I motored out of the entrance into large swells breaking, but once I was past the shallow bar and headed northwest with the wind

CHAPTER TWELVE

behind, it was a pleasant sail. With head sail only and with the tide in my favour, I could get up to 10 knots SOG. I entered the Albany Passage passing the waves smashing the rocks on the rocky mainland. Once inside the passage, all became calm with the protection of Albany Island to my starboard side. The tide was taking me through at 8.5 knots, it was a great feeling.

It was then that I noticed a plane coming from the north. It seemed to be flying downward towards me in the passage. I could distinctively see the bombs underneath the army plane, and for a brief moment thought, *is that one of ours?* Now, I had not heard of any news in a couple of weeks. It did turn out to be one of ours, just doing routine patrol.

I continued sailing through the passage then continued northwest around the top of Australia to the north of York Island. I now had sailed mostly solo nearly the entire east coast with the exception of Mackay to Townsville. It was a feeling of a great accomplishment and now this was my third time passing the top of Australia in my sailing vessel. The tide was in my favour and the wind was still up at twenty knots that had reduced since being on mainland protected lee. Before I knew it, I had passed the memorial for Cook on Possession Island and anchored back at Seisia out the front of the fisherman's club.

My old mate, Geoff Hunn, was anchored there as well and a few mandatory beers were enjoyed. My log read a total of 1,278 nautical miles since I placed the new plotter so *Never Die Wondering II* had gone through a lot of different conditions over 1200 miles with hardly any motoring. That was the sea trial, and I was more than happy with her.

CHAPTER THIRTEEN

The greatest risk in the world is to take no risk at all.

Crossing the Gulf of Carpentaria

Over the next four days, I prepared for the next leg of sailing across the Gulf of Carpentaria and decided to head south of Weipa. There, I would be able to have the trade winds in my favour and be able to run with the wind and possibly get a spinnaker run across the Gulf of Carpentaria to Arnhem Land.

Jeff Mullenger was flying in to crew with me and I contacted the authorities to submit a border pass into the Northern Territory for the both of us, required due to the ridiculous Covid-19 restrictions. Meanwhile, I bought supplies and fuel from the local stores and sealed the emergency hatches which seemed to leak a little in rough conditions. Jeff arrived by plane, landing in Bamaga and hitching a ride out to Seisia. He was questioned by the police and had just made it into Queensland when another ludicrous Covid lockdown happened. We needed to repair a roller system on the water-maker belt, and fashioned a rough repair to make water, then at 2300 hours we were underway.

Log: Friday, 28 May 2021; 0155 hours.

It was a great night for sailing. It was calm leaving Seisia and now only eight knots of wind, the passage plan was to sail across Inskip Banks from northeast to southwest during the high tide. It is extremely shallow in some parts as low as two metres, but safe enough as long as the weather was in our favour, and I keep to the route I had in the past.

CHAPTER THIRTEEN

Jeff was exhausted after his flight and he was sound asleep in his cabin, the night was incredible peaceful as I motor sailed to the start of Inskip Banks that was approximately fourteen nautical miles long, only a three-hour trip across the banks. I went to the front of the vessel, the safety harness on, and sat just above the trampoline admiring the moonlit night, passing Woody Wallis Island about two nautical miles to my starboard side. You could clearly see the shape of the island even at night. Everything was in my favour, fair winds, high tide, and the wind prediction was all favourable. That was until 0220 hours, and then all quickly changed for the worst. thirty-one knots of wind from a light eight knots and the wind direction was now against me. Although luckily, I could get sixty degrees to the wind as opposed to right on the nose. The bow was now smashing through the waves, I was not able to bear a way as I would be sailing into dangerous shallow water and just had to keep to the safest route of deeper water.

Jeff was now in the cockpit and we placed the dodger with the clears on. The waves were now coming over the deck, smashing onto the saloon windows and up over the cockpit roof. Our speed over ground reduced considerably, Jeff continued saying we were on a "roller coaster" as we tried in vain to continue sailing forward. I contemplated about turning around, but being halfway through Inskip Banks, we continued and found ourselves slowly moving at 2.0 and 3.0 SOG that would make the passage twice as long in time. Once we were finally out of the Banks, I decided to beat towards the land as the wind did not reduce at all, and after the many hours crossing Inskip Banks, I needed rest and rest on anchor was preferred.

When dawn broke, we could see the land and headed south, beam reaching from the now easterlies with the winds at twenty-six knots. The sailing from terrible was now fantastic and we flew at 7.0 and 8.0 knots SOG. Admiring the morning sunrise and the incredible colours that the day brought across the western cape, we continued sailing south and by 1430 hours, we were both exhausted. I had no sleep whatsoever and we dropped anchor between Jackson and Skardon rivers not far from the shoreline with large sand hill dunes. Incredibly, I fell asleep for twelve and half hours, totally exhausted. So much for a peaceful nighttime sail with calm conditions to light winds predicted!

The next morning, we needed to repair the navigation light at the bow of the vessel as the constant wave smashing had really knocked it around, so after a bit of rewiring and straightening, it was as good as new.

After a big feed, we departed at 1040 hours and had a great beam sail. The wind was a comfortable twenty-two knots as we sailed along the west coast, the entire length of the coastline of sandy beaches all isolated. The view would not have changed since William Janszoon sailed along the coast on the *Duyfken* in 1606. We passed Cullen Point, and the entrance into Port Musgrave, and dropped anchor on the north side of Janie Creek.

Log: Sunday, 30 May 2021; Depart 0800 hours.

The wind was fourteen to seventeen knots south easterly. A large turtle nearly hit the bow as we sailed off from the anchorage to Duyfken Point on a falling tide and the current against to cross Albatross Bay. We decided to anchor a little north of Duyfken Point so to get the tide in our favour for the next morning. The morning brought strong winds from the east, thirty knots, we beamed reached across Albatross Bay hooking a large mackerel along the way. We reefed in the main as winds increased with large swells and we arrived at our departure anchorage just south of Norman Creek.

We cooked a huge feed of mackerel and then lowered the tender. Jeff trawled while I steered the tender. He hooked a monster near a large reef, but it freed itself after a long fight. It was fantastic exploring these isolated creeks all to ourselves, being low tide, we were able to explore Norman Creek and came back near the vessel where we had a fire on the beach. Returning to the vessel at dusk, we watched a spectacular sight of flying fish around the vessel with colourful patterns. We photographed these incredible colours, a fluorescent blue from their head to tail, displaying wings that had a distinct glowing yellow rim.

Log: Tuesday, 1 June 2021; Depart 0730 hours; Destination Cape Arnhem.

It was 276 nautical miles away, the forecast was ideal for the next few days with the wind directly from behind. We just hoped for fair winds. As soon as we were sailing, Jeff hooked a nice spotty mackerel and at 1130 hours, we raised the asymmetrical spinnaker and were making 6.0 knots SOG as we started crossing the Gulf and the sight of the mainland disappeared. Then at 1430 hours, the wind died off and we were lucky to make ground at 3.0 knots SOG. With only a gentle light wind, we left the kite up into the night prior to dark Jeff while on watch called out, "Orcas!" He spotted them distinctly due to their large fins.

Once the wind increased nine to ten knots, we lowered the asymmetrical and had the sails full and made good speed over the night with the great swells assisting us. During the night, it got up to sixteen knots of wind, all from behind as predicted then we had a fantastic twenty knots at one time. We would do three-hour shifts on the helm, and when it was my rest time I slept comfortably because Jeff had got the hang of the vessel over the last few days. I was comfortable fine with him on the watch.

Dawn is never to be missed while sailing across any body of water because it is incredible to see the sun showing its head way out east coming up from the water horizon, and the similar experience in the evening as it disappears in the west. As the conditions were extremely mild, we were able to have a couple of beers on the deck chairs at dusk heading into the direction of the disappearing sun. My vessel is usually a dry one when underway with the exception of a couple of beers if the conditions are fair.

Log: Thursday, 3 June 2021; 0400 hours.

I swapped shift with Jeff and when dawn came, we raised the asymmetrical spinnaker and noticed small holes appearing. As the wind increased a little, we swapped over to the conventional spinnaker down wind and repaired the asymmetrical with patches to try to get a little more out of the old kite. We were now fifty-four hours at sea and at 1325 hours we could see land, Arnhem Land for we were just fifteen nautical miles out. Jeff had his line out with a new, large and expensive lure, and he hooked what we would refer to as a monster as he tried for ages to reel in this enormous weight. I remember saying, "Are you sure you have not hooked a 44-gallon drum?" When it took the lure, it nearly ran the whole line out and we spent an hour taking turns slowly trying to reel this beast in. As it happened, it broke free in the end.

When we came towards Cape Arnhem, a booby bird circled the vessel. We came closer to shore admiring the cliffs and terrain of the Northern Territory. We sailed into Dalywoi Bay, a secluded bay, and dropped anchor at 1645 hours in this protected inlet southwest of the Cape. We were both extremely pleased with our crossing, it could not have been better. I never imagined I would be visiting Arnhem Land by sailing vessel.

In 1986, I did visit the western side of Kakadu and always wanted to see this region. I remember as a kid, reading a book where the author had lived with the Yirrikala people and documented about their culture. The great documentary film of Malcolm Douglass across the top where he himself documented some of the cultural practices of the tribes, still practicing their traditional ways.

Log: Friday, 4 June 2021; 0930 hours; Departed Cape Arnhem for Gove.

We sailed past the Aboriginal community of Yirrikala and then onwards between the town of Nhulunbuy and Bremer Island. The wind was twenty-two knots, and we were flying at 6.0 knots SOG then rounding Gove itself sailing southerly first, then easterly into the Port of Gove with its large industrial treatment plant for bauxite. We anchored just off the jetty to the yacht club where you sign up for a temporary membership for $10. The people were so helpful offering a car to go to Nhulunbuy to buy supplies and fuel.

We spent three days in the area visiting Nhulunbuy, the township built for the mining in the region, an incredible modern town. We visited Yirrikala Aboriginal settlement and the art display centre where they have many traditional paintings along with didgeridoos and other artifacts. Back on the vessel, we carted the fuel and supplies, cleaned out the forward lockers and bilges, and had everything back for our passage to Darwin. It would take a couple of weeks to complete exploring the outer islands along the top of Australia.

Sailing Through the Hole in the Wall

Log: Monday, 7 June 2021.

As we started departing from Gove and raising the anchor, Jeff was at the bow asking me to go forward. So, I placed the gear lever forward then into neutral as he winched up the anchor chain. "Go forward a bit more," he would say. Then I would go forward then back into neutral. This happened a few times and I was sure the anchor was lifted but Jeff repeated, "Go forward a bit more."

CHAPTER THIRTEEN

"Are you sure?" I said and went into gear again. Suddenly, I realised an old mooring line had wrapped around the portside prop. I quickly placed the gear into neutral, but it was too late. We did have the anchor lifted but unfortunately, we had drifted back onto a rotten old line. The water was almost chocolate in colour, impossible to see even two meters in front. The cove had many local reptiles living about, and one of us needed to swim under the boat and remove the line.

I quickly put on goggles and dived to see that the line was tightly wrapped around the propeller. So, out came the hooker gear (breathing apparatus) and with a weight belt on, I went back under. I instructed Jeff that if he saw any movement in the water coming towards me, he had to quickly tug on the line so that I might have a chance to get out of the water before I was eaten. Thereafter, back under the boat I went, and spent a while cutting off this old line away from the propeller. I was as quick as I could be and was relieved to be back onto the vessel and soon, we were away.

Dolphins escorted us out of the port. We sailed northwest past Cape Wilberforce on our portside and Southwest Bromby Islet on our starboard side. These magnificent rocky escarpments with gentle rising land that had a green tinge gave more of an appearance of Scotland than Australia, with the only exception of the tropical humid weather. We continued sailing through a gap with Cotton Island on our portside and Wigram Island on our starboard side. It was a cloudy day and we beam reached around Wigram where we planned to anchor at first, but it was a settlement, so, we continued further and found another good anchorage northeast of Wigram. I had bought a book in Cairns in which the author detailed many anchorages from Cairns to Darwin showing satellite imagery. It proved to be a great reference for anchorages. Jeff who seemed to always have a fishing rod in his hand, reeled in this monster catfish but, it was a catch and release.

Log: Tuesday, 8 June 2021; 0835 hours; Departed for "Hole in the Wall".

The Wessel Islands are a group of islands formed like a narrow chain, and renowned to be the most isolated in the territory. There is an incredible natural cutting between the rocky islands of Raragala Island on the west side and Guluwuru Island on the east side. This is what is known as the "hole in the wall". Sailing through this passage can be disastrous if picking the wrong tide as you need to pass preferably on the slack tide, we only had the head sail out and entered this unique passage thirty minutes after the high tide, as the tide was ebbing to the north. Incredibly, we made it through in great timing at 8.0 knots SOG.

The walls of this unique cutting are like flat stones piled layer upon layer. It being very narrow across, you can imagine picking the wrong tide and coming to grief trying to turn around. It is only two miles long, but only 200 yards wide that can make life difficult if you pick the wrong tide. Once through the "hole in the wall" we anchored at the next suitable anchorage on the west side of the cutting, in a well-sheltered cove. A lot of the water here is unsurveyed, so Jeff had to keep a close eye as we found suitable anchorage.

A heron bird dropped in to visit the vessel to say hello and walked around the deck for quite some time. We could see large fires in the distance as the islands were, what we believed, having their annual traditional burn. We explored above the dunes and found a freshwater pool with numerous paper bark trees and pandanus palms. The pool went for some distance of 100 meters or so. There were many aboriginal paintings under rocky ledges of what seemed to be arrow heads and creatures showing hands with six fingers, along with the traditional human hands. We cooked our meals on a rocky platform overlooking *Never Die Wondering II* as Jeff had caught a flat head in the shallows in the low tide.

Sailing Across the Top

Log: Thursday, 10 June 2021; 0810 hours; Depart for Refuge Bay.

We sailed across Brown Strait to another group of islands still in the Wessel group but separate by the strait. Stewart Island with its lighthouse is a distinctive marker along the northern coast heading the south-westerly and passing several islands. At Drysdale Island, the landscape changed dramatically and was similar to south of Weipa in the Gulf with red cliffs dominating the landscape. We sailed forty-five nautical miles that day with the wind up by a nice twenty knots. We were able to reach all the way south-westerly, admiring these unique islands at 6.0 and 7.0 knots SOG. We then anchored in Refuge Bay at a terrific cove on Elcho Island.

CHAPTER THIRTEEN

Log: Friday, 11 June 2021; 0730 hours; Depart for Howard Island.

The wind was a south-easterly and we were heading south-westerly, so we beam reached along the northern side of Elcho Island and made speed of 7.0 SOG. With Elcho Island well-positioned and protecting us from the swells, we sailed to Howard Island, another large island in the Wessel group and anchored in a protected cove where you could see the airstrip and several buildings.

The next day, we departed at 0640 hours and headed northwest while trying to keep to the safest route on the chart for they were marked "INADEQUATLY SURVEYED" on that part. The south-easterly continued and we hoisted the asymmetrical spinnaker and had speed up to 6.4 knots SOG. It was a sunny day that was appreciated after several days of cloudy conditions. At 0900 hours we passed Castlereagh Bay to the south and slowed down considerably as we were against the tide, and in shallow waters only eight meters deep.

At 1000 hours, we blew the asymmetrical spinnaker, ripping it in half. Well, the old spinnaker was well over its "use by" date. We then unfurled the head sail and were able to have the tide in our favour with its ebbing. After that, we raised the main, passing Mirungga Island to our starboard side and again, making great time. We passed Crocodile Island next and then went onto the mainland side at Cape Stewart where we dropped anchor in an unsurveyed area. I would have liked to move in closer to the shore for better protection as it was a rolling anchorage, but the water was not clear, and I would not take any risk in these "INADEQUATLY SURVEYED" parts. We enjoyed a barbeque on the back of the stern, and yarned about the day sailing we had, and planned the route ahead.

Log: Sunday, 13 June 2021; 0700 hours; Depart Cape Stewart.

We were glad to get away as the south-easterlies hit the Cape creating swells to roll around the cape and into the cove, rolling the vessel all night. It hits the beam while the vessel is kept facing the southeast. There was hardly any wind, so we motor-sailed with one motor and the head sail. At 0845 hours, we had the wind at 180 degrees on the stern, so we hoisted the conventional spinnaker, and another great day of sailing ensued. A hammer head shark passed by the vessel; it was a great sight to see. Suddenly, we lost all wind at 1230 hours, so we dropped the spinnaker and were forced to motor.

The top end of Australia is renowned for periods of no wind. I was extremely grateful for the great trade winds that I had jumped on at Townsville until then. We arrived at a very small island rock and reef cay named Haul Round Island, it had a light house and was surrounded by beach. We anchored on the southwestern side. Since the wind and swells had died down, it was ideal to anchor there for the night otherwise the protection would not be the best. From the vessel, you could see literally thousands of birds nesting on the island amongst the small vegetation of grass and small shrubs. We ventured ashore and walked amongst the several different varieties of birds from frigates to sea gulls. A large sign stood there, and it read,

YOU NEED TRADITIONAL OWNER PERMISSION TO TAKE SEAGULL EGGS. IF YOU TAKE TOO MANY, ONE DAY THERE WILL BE NONE LEFT. DON'T BE GREEDY.

We decided to walk around the island on the beach because the grassland was littered with eggs and we did not want to stand on any. It was surreal, all these birds flying around us. We returned to *Never Die Wondering II* to watch the spectacular sight of thousands of birds from the vessel, so we would not disturb them.

Log: Monday, 14 June 2021; 0530 hours Depart, Destination Goulburn Island.

This passage would be sixty-three nautical miles. We motor-sailed in the morning and could see stormy conditions coming from the east. However, that never eventuated and at 0950 hours, there was enough wind to hoist the spinnaker, and we sailed all day with the kite. We came into the entrance of South and North Goulburn Island late afternoon, the view was spectacular looking to the south mountains of Arnhem Land. This was the first time since the Coral Coast near Cooktown that I had seen mountainous country. There were large cliffs on southern Goulburn. The passage between both islands did not disappoint either, with dolphins, sharks, and turtles. The old saying "you don't see sharks if dolphins are around" is BS!

We anchored on the southwest side of North Goulburn Island known as Mullet Bay that had grevilia trees and sand dunes on the beach. The sunset was spectacular as the countryside burning off that was happening on the mainland. The smoke gave the sun a reddish colour making the sunset another type of beauty. At night, we could here magpies and geese that were nesting in the swamp on the island.

CHAPTER THIRTEEN

In the morning, we departed at 0745 hours for our destination Valencia Island. We passed close to the mainland by Gningarg Point and Cape Cockburn. Large sandy type cliffs and stunted shrub vegetation dotted the landscape. We could see the water bubbling (fish rising) to our starboard side. The charts clearly showed the soundings, so we motored out circling the fish movements, hoping to catch a feed. All of a sudden, we were alerted of shallow water on the depth sounder. I quickly placed the vessel into reverse and we could see the reef just in front. Never trust a chart!

We anchored on the southwest corner of Valencia Island, one of the most scenic islands in the top end. The island is well-timbered on a ridge that overlooks the anchorage with a cliffy type of terrain running straight to the water's edge. The sun shone on the island in the evening giving it a picture-perfect sight.

The next morning, we were underway, and had dolphins travel with us riding the bow wave, including small calves. The distinctive bottle nose could be seen eliminating any doubt of what type of dolphin they were. We decided to sail through a passage between Croker Island and the mainland of Cobourg Peninsula as opposed to sailing around the northern section of Croker.

The passage was roughly about five nautical miles long and one nautical mile at its narrowest. It was an unsurveyed stretch, but we observed a large ship coming from that direction at night, so we knew cargo ships were using that passage. Therefore, we decided that it must be alright, at least on a near high tide. The AIS also showed a cargo ship coming through the passage so we placed way points on the chart plotter as it passed and that clearly showed they motored through at a distinctive route nearly touching Croker Island at the middle section. Once we arrived at the entrance, we simply just went from way point to way point that we marked just to make sure.

We were then at Cobourg Peninsula where the first establishment in Northern Australia happened. We anchored in a bay named High Point where a fort was built in the early 1800s. It had white sandy beaches, and rocky cliff with pandanus palms. It was low tide, and we dinged to shore exploring the area. One part of the bay seemed surreal as it had a circle beach with large trees on the high tide side, and above the small rocky cliffs, the bush was savannah type, such as sappy gum and bloodwoods. After much exploring, we discovered the foundations of the old fort site that were pegged alongside the stone foundations. Apparently, although this was the first fort established by the British, it was a short-lived settlement and the British at a later date, moved to Port Essington only two bays further west. So, the next morning we were underway and sailed a quick five nautical mile trip to Port Essington, anchoring near the jetty at Black Point.

Terry from *SV Sens-de-la-vie* whom I had met at Flinders Island was anchored there as well and came over for a few beers. We hadn't seen anyone since Gove, so we exchanged stories of our passages. He explained how they had a terrible crossing from Seisia to Arnhem Land. I had already received a call from Brian Dorling of *MV Sealeaf* who had told me the same thing describing the crossing as "like a washing machine", adding that he regretted not heading on the route I had taken. Jeff replied that our crossing was fantastic if not perfect while going the extra distance south to get the tail wind. However, when you placed the nightmare of Inskip Bank into the equation it was hard to know what the worst scenario was.

The next day, we visited the culture centre at Black Point and met a couple of Aboriginal rangers who wanted to know of any sea creatures we had seen while sailing across the top. They explained to us that in recent years, more dolphins and whales had been seen and the orca that Jeff had spotted was a pygmy type seen in tropical waters. As we walked back to the tender, Jeff said, "Can't you see that?"

"What?" I asked, as I was about to move the tender.

"Look at the back!" Jeff retorted.

Just below the surface was a crocodile, watching all our moves. Thereafter, getting into the tender took a lot more caution than usual.

We motored down the large cove of Port Essington to Victoria Settlement, which was seven nautical miles south, on the southwestern side of the port. Anchoring a little south of Minto Head, we went ashore to explore the incredible ruins and absorb the unique history. The Victoria Settlement was established in 1838 by the British which proved to be a futile attempt. Previous establishments had been at Fort Wellington that we had just visited, but this one was a large concern where rocks from the waterfront were cut, and made into incredible buildings that still remain standing today. There was a Government House, many quarters for married couples, and a stone jetty. The settlement only lasted for eleven years and was completely abandoned by the British. The traditional inhabitants, the Madjunbalmi Clan, made genuine friendships with the British and assisted in building the settlement. When the British abandoned the place, the Aboriginal people were presented with all the livestock horses, cattle, dogs, as well as the buildings.

Prior to the failed attempt of a settlement, a local twelve-year-old Aboriginal boy named Mildun with two other local boys travelled to Hong Kong in 1847. When one of the British ships departed, the master of the ship died, and the three boys were left stranded for a year but were later brought back to Victoria Settlement. Mildun, later as a teenager, joined a merchant ship and sailed for many years visiting many distant lands. He even spent five years in England where he attended school and was given a medal by the queen for being the chief of his tribe. One can only imagine the stories he brought home to his people, he was obviously one of Australia's first true adventurer.

When visiting the cemetery, we looked at the plaques standing in memory to those who lost their lives at the settlement or while coming or going in ships. There were sixty-one who had died in that eleven-year span.

Log: Saturday, 19 June 2021; 0800 hours; Departed Victoria Settlement, destination Alcaro Bay.

The south-easterlies were up to twenty knots, allowing us to have another perfect sail heading out of Port Essington. Out at sea, the winds increased to twenty-four knots and we had the tide in our favour and was up to 8.2 knots SOG. It was all short lived though. Before midday, the swells were rough but we were making good ground rounding the north-west of Cobourg Peninsula and heading south west into Alcaro Bay, and into a nice anchorage well-protected and surrounded by beaches.

The next morning, we departed at 0630 hours with the south-easterly on the beam and the tide extremely choppy. We sailed onwards and picked up the tide in our favour, making 7.0 to 8.0 knots SOG. The top speed for the day was 10.4 knots while passing Bernard Shoal on our starboard side about a mile off. At 1200 hours, we sailed between Abbott Shoal to the east and Craven Patches to the west. By the afternoon, we could see the lighthouse on Cape Hotham passing many turtles in this section. We dropped the anchor once we were in the protective side of the mainland about three nautical miles south of Cape Hawthorn. That night, we heard the distinctive crocodile barking I had become accustomed to. The mouth of the mighty Alligator River was not too far away renown for the large reptile.

Log: Monday, 21 June 2021; 0745 hours; Depart for Darwin.

For the first time since Cooktown, we passed a couple of small pleasure fishing boats out for the day. At 0850 hours, while passing Howard Island, the wind became light. We sailed past the large Australian warship on anchor and the view of the skyscrapers greeted us in the skyline of Darwin city. I cooked a pizza as we sailed into Fannie Bay, Darwin. A total of 1,539 nautical miles sailed since leaving Cairns seven weeks ago. To have the trade winds in our favour most of the time, I would have to describe the sailing as close to perfect.

Wet Season in Top End

The plan was to sail to the island of New Guinea. This time, the destination was West Papua (also known as Western New Guinea and Indonesian Papua). Unfortunately, due to Covid-19 restrictions, I was unable to sail to Indonesia at this particular time. Surely, I thought, it could not be that long until restrictions lifted. How over optimistic was I! It was going to be over a year before I could commence my international sailing adventure.

In the meantime, I enjoyed Darwin and it was a great place to socialise with many yachties and many people who had come from southern Australia. Darwin seemed to be the place to escape the Covid-19 restrictions. During the dry season, I anchored in Fannie Bay. This region had ten-meter tides, so if you stayed longer than planned in the yacht club you would find yourself high and dry, either waiting for the tide to come back in or dragging the tender for some considerable distance. The opposite was also true. If the tide was coming in, you would find a stretch of water from where you left the tender to the shore. Not an ideal situation at night where you would have to swim the short distance back to the tender, with the constant worry of crocs.

During the monsoonal season, I secured a swing mooring in Sadgroves Creek that was on the southern side of Darwin, in a mangrove creek, protected from storms and also had Darwin's second yacht club, *Dinah Beach Cruising Yacht Club*. I became a member of both these establishments.

CHAPTER THIRTEEN

An Old Salty Legend

There was much talk regarding the many deaths of yachties over the years who spent their final days in the creek on either a swing mooring, or the fore and aft moorings, lining the creek on two sides. I have seen several of these places where many old salties either run out of money or become too old to sail, and find themselves in these places at the end of their life. An exception to the latter would be Old Salty Harold. I had met briefly in Gove, Arnhem Land, and later, in Sadgroves Creek for he frequented the Dinah Beach club. He was in his late 80s and still solo sailing. He would sail solo from Arnhem Land to Dinah Beach club to do his annual maintenance, dry dock his mono, a steel Bermuda rig vessel that he built in 1978.

I enjoyed listening to Harold's adventures. Born in Norway, he came to Australia working as a stockman and then he was drawn to the sea, building and welding his vessel. He named it *FRAM* after the great Norwegian wooden vessel that still holds the record of sailing furthest south into the Antarctic, and furthest north into the Arctic Circle. A non-drinker who reasoned that since his wife left him, he didn't have an excuse to drink anymore, and thus, became a teetotaller. He had sailed as far north as the Arctic Circle, above 70°N, and then later, sailed south around the Cape of Good Hope of Africa. At one stage, having come down with an affected leg, which he referred to as black leg, he heated a poker on his stove bursting the boil on it, only to become very delusional with the affection becoming worse.

Harold then told me how he had nightmare following that while sailing. He dreamt of being involved in a shoot-out with pirates. In his dream, he and the pirates were firing guns at each other in the middle of the night while he thought they were trying to board his vessel. He said there were loud screams as they exchanged fire. He woke in the morning and could see the coast of Mozambique. He was extremely ill by then, so he notified the authorities on his radio, and they came to his rescue. For two months he was hospitalised, the doctors were surprised how he had survived let alone come close to having his leg amputated. On his return to his vessel that was kept on a public mooring by the relevant authorities, he rolled out his head sail to discover it was riddled with bullets. Most likely it was not a dream at all.

I flew to Melbourne for Christmas, spending time with my son and drove back across the length of Australia in my 4x4 visiting many places that I had been to in 1986, when I travelled and worked across the country. I had many trips around the coast of Darwin after that. Gareth Benson, my lawyer mate from Melbourne, had moved to Darwin for work and lifestyle. He and I once sailed to the Tiwi Islands of Melville and Bathurst for a few days. These were incredible islands that bordered the Timor Sea.

Soon, I started preparing the vessel for Indonesia. I removed all unnecessary gear a heater system that was throughout the hull, upgraded the solar panels, placed new house batteries, serviced the motors, bought new spinnakers both asymmetrical and conventional, and then, I was ready to sail. The trade winds were blowing, Indonesia was finally allowing people to enter, and most importantly, Australia was allowing people to leave.

I had to make a flight to Melbourne first, as a close friend, Lyn Borg, died. The Borg family asked me to do the eulogy at her funeral, and I was privileged to do it. Lyn was like a daughter to my late mother, and she had been extremely supportive of me over many years. I still have a great friendship with her entire family, even dated one of Lyn's daughters many years ago for a few years.

Once I returned to Darwin, I started with all the formalities. I completed visas and documentation requiring exporting of the vessel overseas (crazy bureaucracy) and finally, I was ready to explore and discover other countries adventure bound.

CHAPTER FOURTEEN

There are only two times in life, either right now, or too late.

Crossing the Arafura Sea

Log: Thursday, 25 August 2022; 1120 hours; Depart Cullen Bay pontoon, Darwin; Destination Tual, Indonesia.

After waiting for what seemed an eternity for Covid-19 restrictions to lift, and then several weeks of waiting for the Indonesian visas to come through, *SV Never Die Wondering II* was away, sailing for destination Tual in Indonesia. This was the port we needed to clear into Indonesia, though I would have preferred to clear into the Saumlakki situated on the island of Yamdena. It was only 250 nautical miles from Darwin which was much closer then Tual. However, I was advised by my agent that was not possible and that I needed to sail to Tual instead, which was a voyage of somewhat 450 nautical miles crossing the Arafura Sea. A four-day passage.

My crew was an Italian feller, Simon. He had advertised on the notice board at the Dinah Beach sailing club saying, "Wanting to crew on a yacht sailing to Indonesia". He was travelling the world and had no prior experience in sailing nonetheless, he had canoed down the entire length of the Murray River to the sea solo, a distance of some 2,000 km over many months. I showed him the ropes one morning, in moderate winds while sailing around Darwin, and he seemed quick to learn knots and the operation of navigation equipment, etc. He was a very polite young feller, thirty-one years old, and by virtue of his trial run for a few hours combined with his marathon canoe trip down the mighty Murray River, I decided to allow him to crew. On one condition though, it would be based on only one passage at a time. After all, he might not be suited for sailing after his first passage, only time would tell.

Simon had plans of kayaking from Singapore to Bangkok in Thailand after sailing with me. Therefore, the arrangement with me was that he needed to board another vessel to that destination of Singapore, as my plans were to explore the many exotic Spice Islands (present day Moluccas) then sail to West Papua New Guinea. My ultimate goal was sailing from Victoria Bass Strait to New Guinea.

My old sailing mate, Geoff Hunn, came down to the pontoon to bid me goodbye. Once the border force departure formalities were signed, away we went with wind in the sails, next anchorage Indonesia. I received a text straightaway, from Geoff saying, *Crew green in gills?* Although his opinion on my choice of crew was not very positive to say the least, it was not going to be long before Old Geoff's wisdom was about to be correct.

It was ninety miles across Van Diemen Gulf until we reached the start of the Arafura Sea. There was hardly any wind so we were forced to run one motor at a time. In this gulf, picking right tide could get you across to Cobourg Peninsula, which is the last point of Australia, with good speeds, but with the tide against you, it could be a very rough and slow trip indeed. Luckily, this time, we had the tide in our favour and made incredible progress. We passed the Vernon Islands by late afternoon, and Cape Hotham at night. I was able to have one-hour naps as Simon was on watch.

During the early morning, there was a light south-westerly allowing us to run with the wind, goose wing (i.e. with main and head sail out in opposite direction with wind at 180°).

Log: Friday, 26 August 2022; 0550 hours.

The border force called on VHF by fly over stating that the navigation lights on the mast were not, correct. I had placed new LED bulb at the top of the mast, and when securing the NAV lights, I screwed them back 30% too much! A job at anchor not at sea, so I turned off the top NAV lights for I had the deck navigation lights along with the steaming lights and that would suffice.

We now had some great wind, from the east that enabled us to sail with the wind to Tual, and it was not far into the Arafura Sea that

CHAPTER FOURTEEN

old mate Geoff's prediction came true: CREW SIMON GREEN IN THE GILLS?

I was excited to be in the Arafura Sea heading into international waters, the winds were up in the twenties, and consistent. The swells were forward of the beam, which was not ideal, but our speed was fantastic, consistently up to 6.0 knots SOG.

Poor Simon did not share my enthusiasm at all, since he was vomiting over the stern. "Is it always this rough?" He managed to utter.

My reply was, "This is easy sailing mate," and then excitedly yelled out, "It does not getter better than this!" I kept that encouragement up the whole way with Simon, and also calling out at times,

> "The best place to be is here, and the best time to be here is now!"

The Arafura Sea is part of the western Pacific Ocean, overlaying the continental shelf between Australia and Western New Guinea. The Moluccas people of Indonesia named the sea Arafura meaning "The people of mountains". I was to spend several months exploring the exotic Molucca islands and getting to know this wonderful place and its people.

Due to the forward swells, flying fish would often appear on the deck of the vessel and trampoline. I had trimmed the sails to the desired position and had full sail both main and head, and that was how it stayed the entire passage. I have always had a wind shift to some degree; therefore, it usually was a consistent job of trimming or if wind got up then reefing in, especially at night, just in case the winds came up. However, I was so comfortable with the consistency of the weather I was able to trim and leave it for the entire passage.

Poor Simon was still vomiting, and after two days out at sea, I told him to drink water, but he refused saying, "I cannot. I bring everything up?"

Then, I told him, "I am not asking you, Simon. I am telling you to drink some water." The last thing I needed was him to die on me during the crossing as he had not eaten or drank anything for two whole days. He eventually started drinking a little.

I was in my element and cooked up a huge meal of big hamburgers with double patties, eggs, beetroot, and cheese on buns Poor Simon took one look trying in vain to get some food into him and rushed back to the stern to feed the fish.

Now, I had explained to him before hand to never put the toilet paper down the toilet as it would jam the head. "Always place it in paper bags provided, because it is a 12-volt system and if the power is down a little, the toilet paper will jam in the pipes," I had said.

Still, he told me in his Italian accent, "Toilet block with toilet paper."

I shouted, "What part of DO NOT PUT TOILET PAPER DOWN IN IT, did you not understand?"

"The paper should dissolve," he told me.

"For God's sake, Simon! Now, you must unblock it and that is a messy job. Don't worry about it now. Do it when the swells reduce a bit later on, a reduction in the swells will make sailing more comfortable," I told him with my patience back a bit.

Simon went below to fix his mistake when sailing became a little more comfortable. He was there for quite a long time, so I went to check on him. Oh my God, the sight was horrendous! He had removed the hoses, and the floor was covered with everything. I had explained to him how the pumps worked and how he needed to undo the pipes before cleaning etc. but he chose to pump the horrors through the shower drainage on the floor. Blocking another system! He was wearing surgical gloves but more or less kneeling in the horror. I could not believe what I was seeing. Over the course of four weeks, he was able to block the toilet on three separate occasions.

With the forward beam swell and a slight increase in wind, waves would come over the starboard bow, and I noticed the forward locker hatch was open slightly. When I checked, water had been coming over the bow and straight into the starboard side sail locker, I estimated it had taken 1,000 plus litres of sea water, waterlogging everything in the starboard locker. We quickly emptied the water out by pump as carrying that extra water was not ideal.

I could easily notice Simon's weight loss, his face had become gaunt, and he still looked seasick. I discussed his illness with Doug Mathias via satellite *Iridium* and his belief was that Simon would make good in three days. Doug had spent a lot of his life at sea as a professional fisherman. And yes, after the third day, Simon stopped throwing up and started to eat and drink in small amounts. A relief to me.

Indonesia is renowned for fishing vessels everywhere. However, whether large or smaller ones, these vessels had limited lighting or none at all, and most did not have AIS. This created a dangerous situation of possible collisions or picking up a large fishing net along the

CHAPTER FOURTEEN

way. On the third day across the Arafura Sea, the dodging of the fishing vessels began with several large vessels coming into our direction of path, where we would change course and pass wide aware of catching a fishing net.

Log: Sunday; 28 August 2022; 1200 hours.

We sighted land, the two main islands that surround Tual. With the swells now coming to stern of the beam, created from the protection of the Eastern Island of Tual, we were able to fly the kite. The asymmetrical, spinnaker. What a great sail into Tual we had, passing moored fishing platforms made from timber that had several A-frames latched together at the apex with small huts on the platforms.

Our timing was great, as I planned to reduce the risk of anchoring at night, making a priority to anchor with plenty of light. These fishing platforms were unlit and unmanned, and to crash into one would be so easy at nighttime.

Islands of Tual, Indonesia

The water between the two major islands was incredibly deep with 600-metre depths close to the shore. The island *pulau* in Bahasa Indonesian on the eastern side is named NaHuroa, and the large island on the western side is Pulau NaHuyat. Tual is situated on the western side of the two main islands, and a third island named Kaidulah.

As night was approaching, we decided to sail up the narrow channel heading northeast to Tual itself. We knew there was a bridge that would restrict us getting to the northwest part of Tual but anchoring here was the best option in terms of safety for the night.

At 1850 hours, we anchored at Tual, south of the bridge, amongst the little fish platforms with homes very close. It was really the only suitable anchorage on sand as coming into the inlet was deep water.

What an exciting place! The people were friendly and waved at us close by. I made a gesture to a local asking if it was alright to anchor at that place and got the thumbs up. I promptly anchored with the sound of the call to prayer echoing across the inlet.

The homes close by stood on stilts on the water, most had old rusted corrugated walls and roof. Some homes had new iron roofs painted a white and blue stripe, along with long timber boats with outboard motors parked up against their homes. Nearby was a partly sunken ship that seemed to look like an old ferry. Homes on the opposite side of the inlet were of bricks and new iron, with better looking boats. It seemed, one side of Tual was wealthier than the other side of the waterway. There were many plastic bottles used as buoys with fishing lines, the fisherman inspected the lines a few times a day to retrieve their catch.

Up went the yellow quarantine flag with the Indonesian flag below it, and the Australian ensign flag below that on the starboard side of the vessel. My main Australian flag same size of all, was permanently at the stern. The passage had been 448 nautical miles, a total of 79.5 hours at an average speed of 5.6 knots SOG. I was very happy with that.

The next morning, I was able to contact my agents, Kim and Fatima, who advised us to anchor on the other side of the bridge. We had to lift anchor and sail around Tual Island some twenty-six nautical miles, to get to one nautical mile past the bridge. It was great view nonetheless of the beaches and hills of the islands with the many mosques scattered throughout the villages. On the way, an Australian radioed us to say giddy, he had cleared in and was heading to Bear Island.

We anchored half a mile off the port of Tual in the designated anchorage and had Kim and Fatma come out to the vessel to greet us and start the long quarantine custom process to obtain clearance before we are able to go ashore. I had to return Kim and Fatima to the Port on my tender, and naturally, was not allowed ashore.

The next morning the quarantine officials arrived, and the lengthy paperwork began. I was asked if I had whisky and I denied as the official hinted that he drank whisky. I was not going be caught with this old style of "pay your way". I had already paid enough for visas and vessel declaration fees, which all worked out to be much more than just visa.

Once quarantine was over it was photo time. Not of the scenery, of me! This became a custom throughout Indonesia, everybody wanting their photo with you. When I was taking back the quarantine official to the Port by the dingy, a ship was coming in. He asked me not to worry and indicated to more or less keep in the front of him, on my little 3.1 metre rubber tender. I had to increase maximum speed to avoid being swamped by this ship coming into the Port and decided that in the future, I would ignore any official telling me to go onwards

CHAPTER FOURTEEN

placing us all in dangerous situation. I dropped off the immigration officer onto the coast guard vessel moored to the wharf. While there, I noticed many rats running along the timber frames of the shops that protrude out over the waterfront, and the owners of the eating houses throwing buckets of trash into the waterway from the windows of their establishments.

After I returned the quarantine official, we were greeted by two young gentlemen from Immigration, immaculately dressed in their uniforms, having arrived paddling an old wooden boat. The motor had stopped working so they had to paddle to the vessel. I took them back on my tender as well. Then, it was the turn of three Customs officials to board, and go through the Customs signing procedure, new documentation, crew list, checking passports and visa, and stamping along with my *SV Never Die Wondering II* stamp to finalise this lengthy procedure.

All was not over yet, as I was told that I needed a sailing certificate signed and stamped by the Harbour Master. This would enable me to sail Indonesian waters but only in the direction which the certificate stated. I was personally told by the Harbour Master that a vessel previously had not obtained the said certificate and sailed off thinking he had crossed the t's and dotted the i's. However, when he arrived in Bitung in Sulawesi, he was arrested and had to spend five months behind bars in a Sulawesi prison only to be released with a US$99,000 fine.

Nothing in my documentation provided by my agent stated this fact, how easily such a slip could happen to anyone. You can't take anything for granted clearing in and out of any country. The Harbour Master wrote my exit at Bitung, Sulawesi, with other documents showing that I planned to extend visa at Ambon, and Sorong in West Papua, and then exit Bitung. From there, I had decided to head out to the Philippines, seeing it was close at Sulawesi.

Tual is a bustling town, predominately Muslim, and the traditional call to prayer can be heard loudly five times a day wherever in Tual you may be. In Tual's main mosque, a drummer started the prayer with the striking sound of a padded mallet against the skin of a huge double-headed drum three feet in diameter and at least four feet long. The drum hung on steel fashioned hooks that slightly swung with every hit of the drum with a timber cradle and these incredible carvings in traditional Arabic writings.

Kim and Fatma joined us for dinner on the vessel one night with Simon insisting on cooking up an Italian meal. All well and good until I walked into the galley, to see the frying of bacon! Not a good start for potential friendships with Muslims. That idea was quickly dropped, and a non-pig dinner was prepared.

Tual is like most of the Indonesian islands where you can just get lost in the atmosphere of the people and culture. Although the amount of plastic that seems to be dumped by the populace into the water is nothing to be desired. I took a photo of an abandoned ship at low tide exposing the hull of the vessel, two feet deep in plastic trash. Unfortunately, this was going to be a common theme throughout Indonesia. We disposed our rubbish into the port's bins but noticed a large floating black bag amongst all other floating trash, the next day. We wondered if that was our trash, *do they just empty the bins into the water, surely not?* Sadly, so many people really did not care.

I learned to burn my rubbish on beaches when I could, not perfect but better than the obvious alternative. I tried to reduce all plastic purchase, refused plastic bags, and when on beaches, as I did in Australia, collected others' trash and disposed them by burning.

Kim and his cousin drove us to a freshwater cave that had crystal clear spring water seeping through the overhead limestone ceiling. It had hanging stalactites with stalagmites even below the water. There was a colony of small bats hanging on the ceiling throughout the roof of the cave as we swam through this ancient rock shelter, cooling from the stifling heat outside.

We arranged fuel by carting jerry cans by a hired vehicle then tendered back to the vessel. The market, like most markets in the world, was a hive of activity with fresh fish brought in along with all the islands' produce of vegetables and fruit. While in a section of the market, we were approached by many of the women who wanted to have selfies (photos) with us. Some would hug us, and a few even grabbed our noses! There were no men in this area of the market, Simon and I obviously, were the new fresh meat arriving in town.

Back on the vessel, we took a photo of the freshly purchased produce on the cockpit table prior to storing the supplies. It was a showing of healthy food, several varieties of fish, bananas, cantaloupe, fruits, snake beans, potatoes, oranges, cucumbers, eggs, tomatoes, nuts, chilli, the list goes on. For the next six months, I was going to be able to purchase similar healthy produce throughout the archipelago.

CHAPTER FOURTEEN

Hazards of Coral Reefs

The Immigration fellers were divers and recommend that we visit the islands northwest of Tual. We anchored on an island called Ramadan where the locals quickly visited us by their craft. We were invited to their village, so we went there the following day. Most of the villages we visited, everyone came out to meet us. We were taken to one of the village homes where they were making sago bread. Sago tree is a common food source throughout New Guinea and eastern Indonesia where they pulverise the husk that is gathered from the core of a sago tree. After a lengthy pulverising period, they wash the powder resin out from the husk and once the starch settled in the likes of a canoe, they removed the water and dried out the white flour which was baked like bread or *nan* in India.

I love sago bread, it has a sweet taste and when I started eating a piece, I knew what it was courtesy my time in Papua New Guinea. This village was just like all other villages, they freely feed you with their fish grilled on the coals. And always, there was coconut water to wash the meal down.

On Ramadan Island, I allowed some of the locals to come back to the boat, as a sign of appreciation for their hospitality. When we were heading there in the tender, some of the women just threw their children in, and before we knew it, the dingy was overcrowded. Yet everyone was laughing with excitement to visit the sailing yacht. The girls on board quickly removed their hijabs and allowed their hair to be free. On board, we supplied drinks and played my sailing songs, for instance, the *Wellerman* (Sea Shanty), and the locals were all dancing to this seafarer's tune.

North of Ramadan, the islands are known as Baeer, and I quickly discovered that across the Indonesian archipelago many islands are called by different names. This is due to Indonesia having 300 different ethnic groups conquered by either Portuguese, Spanish, Dutch, or English, and after the entire Indonesia obtained independence, Bahasa became the official language, creating a chronical of different names over 300 years.

We headed to these small islands close to Ramadan and I waited until the sun was high to be able to see the coral bommies. I had previously shown Simon coral reefs whereby the charts showed deep water, thereby explaining that the charts cannot be completely trusted so it was paramount to keep a careful watch at the bow, especially, in that area. This was why I preferred entering into a coral area with the sun above us, gave us a better chance to see any dangers.

"Never trust electronic charts," I explained. "You must keep a good visual. Eye on the water!" Simon was at the bow watching and I was on the helm. We were slowly making our way through the area but I was concerned about his concentration, so I kept saying, "Keep an eye on the water!" Then all of a sudden, the depth showed 1.3 on the depth gauge. I yelled at him, "Are you bloody watching?" I quickly engaged reverse and then the dreaded sound of crunch came. We had hit a coral head!

By virtue of quickly reversing the props, I was not moving very fast. The vessel, then in neutral, drifted backwards with the current. I waited until we were clear of the coral and then dropped anchor on a sand patch. I sent Simon into the bilge area to see if we had damaged the hull and made a leak. I quickly dived under with the snorkel gear to only find that the boat's steel plate on the bottom of the keel on the portside had a small dent in the metal. How lucky were we! I was pretty calm about the whole incident and reminded Simon, "This is why you must focus, and keep a sharp eye on things when you are told to." Since we were anchored safely, we snorkelled amongst the coral and that was absolutely superb.

It was now fourteen days since arriving in Tual, so we were keen to explore more islands and made our way to Banda Neira (The Spice Islands). We headed west through a maze of coral reefs. This time Simon diligently kept his eyes on coral bommies. After clearing the coral area, a light wind enabled us to fly the asymmetrical spinnaker and a peaceful sail was enjoyed with dolphins riding the bow waves.

We arrived at Pulau Tayandu and anchored on the northwest side of the island near a small islet known as Pulau Nutrawet. The village nearby was known as Yembo, and there we anchored for a couple of days. We needed to recorrect the navigation light at the top of the mast and repair the steaming light along with tying down electric wires, etc. Simon climbed the mast in the Bosuns chair, and I maintained the winch. The scare of hitting a coral head must have got Simon's mindset focused as he climbed the mast brilliantly without me heavily crunching on the winch, and quickly was able to do the minor jobs. On the way back, he had a photo session of the top with the incredible views of the islands.

CHAPTER FOURTEEN

Nearby was an abandoned dwelling that seemed to be a former place of worship. It bordered an almond plantation where the trees were of an ancient size. The views from the dwelling were superb, especially, looking back at *Never Die Wondering II* on anchor amongst the islet's white sandy beach with coconut trees lining the foreshore. We visited the village and was accompanied by at least sixty children. The pier was the drying platform for the village's coconut husks.

Our luck having the trade winds were still about, and at dawn we were underway. An asymmetrical kite run to Pulau Kur, an island only a short sail west. Once rounding the southwest point of the island, the asymmetrical spinnaker that was new jammed, and we were unable to drop the sock down over the kite. As it usually happens, the wind picked up strong. Now, that was fun to say the least as we had to drop the kite halyard to retrieve the kite all in a strong wind. We discovered later that a knot had formed in the line within the sock and made the kite impossible to bring down the sock.

We dropped anchor near a village called Tanjung Hawatutu. The village is on the west side of Pulau Kur and is nestled into the steep mountains that tower over the village. The village is shadowed by sheer limestone cliff faces that make it a very picturesque place with the mosque as the standout feature of the buildings.

We met a local young feller who was keen to come aboard the vessel. They had spear guns that looked very well-made with heavy-duty rubber and were razor-sharp. Tattoo was the name of another feller who wanted us to see his island.

A long fishing vessel with one outboard motor arrived with two local fishermen. They opened up the tarp to show their catch. The floor of the craft was long and deep filled with freshly caught fish. I gave the fisherman money for a few fish, but they really were not interested in making a deal. They just tried to give a chaff bag full to us for free. When I said, "No, I only need a few fish." They simply threw heaps of fish on board as a good will gesture and motored off.

Tattoo and his friends paddled back in their timber craft. We caught up with them later in the evening and what seemed like half the village came to greet us. Again, we felt like a celebrity with people asking for photos with them. We were taken to a nut forest where the locals would throw sticks or rocks to knock down the nuts that seemed like almond but very soft. Also, bananas were given to us, and we were shown their coffee harvest. Simon displayed his soccer skills on their grassy field and had dozens of children join in.

On our return to the vessel, we were met by more locals wanting to come aboard which they did for coffee. These were different people we had not met before. They produced their spear guns that were roughly built but had fascinating craftsmanship. Simon became a little alarmed and quietly said. *"Alistair, there are seven of them. They could overpower us."*

He was correct they could easily overpower us, but I was 99% comfortable with all of them otherwise I would not have allowed them on the vessel. They were friendly young fellers who were proud of their weapons and wanted to show us their spear guns. Nonetheless, it was a fair and wise comment from Simon, and I was glad his attitude was on the side of caution.

Late that night, Tattoo and his mates returned and wanted us to go spear fishing in their paddle crafts. The wind was up and I decided it was not for me and Simon thought it was a bit risky for him too. So, we declined the offer. Simon was still alarmed regarding the many visitors we received armed with spear guns. He mentioned how easy it would be for someone to attack him with the hatch open while he slept. I told Simon of my history of shooting a violent criminal in self-defence, and several other altercations I have had while travelling. I said that I was leaving my hatch open, and that I was not alarmed at the slightest. I gave Simon a knife for protection as I thought it would make him feel a little easy, still he retired to his cabin and closed the ceiling hatch. I opened my hatch and enjoyed the peaceful breeze without a care in the world.

In the early hours of the morning, I was woken by a flashlight through the cabin window on the side of the vessel. The voice said, "Mister, Mister, Mister have you coffee?" A couple of fellers were even trying to board but I politely told them, *"Tidak tidak saya…"* then made a sleeping gesture. They said, *"Maaf…Maaf"* (Sorry Sorry) and left. Typical friendly people of Indonesia genuinely wanting to meet travellers. My course on Bahasa in Darwin was starting to pay off.

CHAPTER FIFTEEN

To desire nothing beyond what you have is surely happiness aboard a boat, it is frequently possible to achieve just that, that is why sailing is a way of life, one of the finest lives.

The Spice Islands

The next morning, we were away by the kite taking advantage of the great trade winds. "Spice Islands, here we come!" A passage across the Banda Sea, an over nighter as the distance from Pulau Kur to Banda Neira is 133 nautical miles. In some places, the Banda Sea is seven kilometres deep, it is measured 1,000 km east to west, and 500 km north to south. It is one of the four seas within the Maluku Islands (also the Moluccas).

The other seas in the Maluku archipelago are the Ceram Sea, which is between Ceram Island and south Raja Ampat, the Halmahera Sea which lies west of Raja Ampat and the Island of Halmahera, and the Molucca Sea which lies east of the Island of Halmahera and the Island of Sulawesi. I would eventually cross all the seas in the Maluku Islands group.

It was an incredible feeling to know that under your vessel there was seven kilometres of water. Until then, the deepest water I had experienced was 2,000 metres off the continental shelf in the Tasman Sea, and 2,000 metres recently in the Arafura Sea. It was a big jump to 7,200 meters to be precise. Along the way, a humpback whale breached on my portside, a superb breach giving a clear view of this magnificent creature.

Simon was not vomiting as he had on the Arafura Sea crossing but still seemed a little green in the gills. The sailing was more than terrific with beautiful rolling swells from behind that created great momentum. By late afternoon the wind picked up, so we dropped the kite and just had full head sail right through the night.

During the passages, I sometimes started the 2KVA generator as I had installed a 60-Amp charger. So, it was a simple and cost-effective way to charge the batteries as opposed to starting the motors to have the alternators top up the battery bank.

In the early hours of the morning, there was no wind, so we were forced to run the starboard motor. Full sails and one motor still got us along at 5.0 knots SOG. Then, the sight of the Banda Islands came into view, the exotic Spice Islands, and what a sight to behold! The most distinctive sight was of the large and still active volcano known as Gunung Api or Gunung Banda Api where *api* in Indonesian meaning fire.

The islands are made up of several individual islands, such as Pulau Hatta as you pass sailing in from the east. It was named after one of the fathers of Indonesian independence. Then Pulau Banda Besar, the largest of the Banda islands to the south adjoining Pulau Gunung Api, the volcano island, and Paula Banda Nera that lies in the shade of the volcano and is the main town of the Spice Islands. There is Pulau Pisang which means banana island, and the two other inhabited islands were ten nautical miles from the volcano being Pulau Run and Pulau Ai.

All up there are seven main islands of the Banda group traditionally known as the Spice Islands as it was here that the valuable fruit, the nutmeg, was grown naturally on the islands' rich volcanic soil. At one stage, this small fruit nut was more valuable than gold by weight. Stories of sailors who could smell the aroma of the nutmeg twenty nautical miles out at sea made for legendary stories. Sailing to this exotic place of tiny islands extremely isolated from the rest of the world was a treat.

We sailed into the group of islands passing between Pulau Pisang and Pulau Banda Besar. Then, we sailed into the protective waterway and anchored in shallow waters on sand near the jetty of Banda Besar. Opposite to Besar was the small island and main commercial area of the Banda group of islands, Banda Neira, with the old fort positioned on the hill that had striking views from all around. We were then met by several maritime authorities who requested to come on board. Again, extremely friendly people welcoming and willing to assist, explaining the anchorage area. Although marked as an anchorage on the charts, it had recently become a marine park and was no longer an anchorage. They asked if we could anchor at the front of Banda Neira hotel instead.

The peculiar thing was we could stay for a fee that was particularly high, so I vetoed that option and went to the new anchorage. There were overhead electricity cables between the volcano island and Banda Neira township without any markings on the lines whatsoever, nor any warning signs. One could easily sail through the channel and become fried with the mast striking the powerlines.

The anchorage here was twenty-five metres in depth. I reversed with the anchor in the 25 meters of water and had stern lines thrown to the people at the hotel's wharf and they tied it to an ancient Dutch cannon. This was going to be one of the greatest places, staying, in the shadows of this live volcano known as "the mountain of fire" at 640 metres above sea level.

Mita Alwi, the owner of the *Maulana Hotel* came to greet us, along with Hussain, Fatma's father. They had been told by her that we were arriving, and Hussain was to arrange fuel for us. It was being brought in by cargo ship in large 44-gallon drums within the week. Mita and her husband, Anwar, had only recently reopened the hotel after Covid-19 restrictions of two years. What an interesting place this was! Her grandfather had built the hotel in a Dutch colonial fashion that resembled the Dutch era. The walls of the hotel had many old photos with the likes of the great ocean adventurer Jacques Cousteau who was a personal friend of her grandfather. Lady Diana Spencer (The Princess of Wales) along with many other well-known people had stayed at the hotel in the past. Mita and Anwar had been trying to restore the hotel after years of no operation.

Streets of Banda Neira

We immersed ourselves in the culture and history of this fascinating place. The streets of Banda Neira were a hive of activity, the buildings were from the bygone days of the Dutch that were made of rock and brick walls, high ceilings, and timber shutters scattered about the village. The precious nutmeg of which Banda Islands are renowned for, were drying on the streets with the distinctive aromatic smell, along with chilli, cloves, and cinnamon. Amongst the small alley ways, baskets abounded for sale of a variety of spices. We ate at the local cafes, and the hotel where traditional Indonesian dishes were served. After a period of time, the women of the local cafe would show us their cooking methods and ingredients prepared on their fuel stoves located at the back of their eating venues.

Mita invited us to banana island or Pulau Pisang, in fact, Mita's family once owned the island, and I was to discover her family lineage was truly fascinating. She was a descendant of the Indonesian Pearl King, Said Baadilla, the wealthiest man of the region in his time. Mita also descended from a Sulawesi princess.

The Pearl King's grandson was Mita's grandfather, Des Alwi, and he had created his own wealth and had developed a large part of Banda Neira. The hotel once had an aquarium that housed sharks and many other exotic sea creatures. Mohammad Hatta took Des Alwi under his wing as a child. Hatta is considered one of the fathers of Indonesian independence who was forcibly sent to Banda Neira in exile by the Dutch.

Many Banda Island people have diverse bloodlines either descending from the original Bandanese or from other islands in the archipelago along with Arab, Portuguese, Javanese, Malay, or Chinese roots. They all added to the diversity of the people, and the incredible history of the Spice Islands. All due to the famous small piece of fruit, the nutmeg.

This incredible fruit that sold more than the weight of gold, had the colonial powers of the world fighting over the control of the Spice Islands. The nutmeg that grew in the fertile volcanic soils of Banda had been used as a spice by the local Bandanese originally. Soon, they were sought after by the many traders who passed by these magnificent islands. The Arab traders had traded this unique fruit along with Indian, Chinese, Malaysian, Spanish, and the Portuguese who were also the first colonial powers into the Spice Islands as Banda was originally called, and the Portuguese established the first fort on Banda Neira.

Travelling leaves you speechless then turns you into a storyteller.

Abu Abdella Mahomed (1369)

Then, in the 1609 the Dutch East India Company (*Vereenigde Oost-Indische Compagnie* or VOC) tried to control the islands from the original habitants. This was a failure under Admiral Verhoeven and twenty-seven Dutch were killed. A clerk named Jan Pieterszoon Coen escaped with his life but returned in 1621 as the new appointed so-called Governor of the Spice Islands appointed by the VOC. He was hellbent on taking revenge for what had taken place twelve years ago.

Captain Jan Pieterszoon Coen as Governor of the Spice Islands spent no time in ruthlessly controlling Banda. He took control of Banda Neira Mosque turning the premises into his headquarters. He then took forty-four of the senior leaders (Chieftains) or Orang Kaya (wealthy people) as prisoners. They had Japanese Samurai warriors, who the Dutch had brought with them, execute four leaders whom they accused of orchestrating the attack on the Dutch twelve years ago. The Japanese Samurai killed those four by cutting their bodies into four parts, to the horrors of the crowd.

The remaining forty leaders were also executed in the afternoon by Coen's orders. They were beheaded by the swift action of the Samurai sword, their heads and bodies impaled on bamboo sticks to display as a warning to the Banda people. These atrocities continued with the killing of 2,800 and 1,700 enslaved.

The Bandanese were overpowered by the well-armed Dutch VOC, and families in fear of their lives fled the islands. It is believed that the native population was 15,000 prior to the brutality of the Dutch with only 1,000 remaining after the massacre. This gruesome murderous event is depicted in an oil painting at Banda Neira that shows the Samurai warriors wielding their swords and beheading, with the crowd screaming and young children being manhandled by the Dutch army.

The VOC were then short on labour due to the massacre and fleeing islanders and as a result they brought in slaves from Java to fill the shortfall. During this era, it was not just the Dutch trying to get into the spice trade. The English with their East India Shipping Company had taken control of Rhun Island which lies ten nautical miles west of Banda Neira. They had friendly relations with the islanders and offered them protection from the Dutch, therefore, giving them a foot into the spice trade. Over time many skirmishes happened at sea between the English and Dutch. Finally, the Dutch attacked and killed the English captain and crew and took control of Rhun Island as well.

In retaliation, the English took control of New Amsterdam which is located in Manhattan in present day United Sates of America. Then a truce was reached by both parties and an agreement was made between them that the Dutch keep Rhun Island, and the English keep

New Amsterdam whose name was changed to New York. I think, we all know who got the better deal in the end, but the poor Bandanese would have to wait 300 years before the islands were returned to them. By this stage, the Bandanese had become an incredible mixed race of people, derived from the original 1,000 inhabitants and bloodlines from the middle east, other Indonesian islands, Malay, Chinese, Portuguese, etc. with the majority being Muslim.

On Pisang Island, we were shown the nutmeg and how they picked the fruit when ripe by a basket type of catching device on a large pole. The outer shell of the nutmeg is called the fruit, within that is a seed surrounded by a red lace-like skin called mace. All of these three parts of the nutmeg are used as spices. In fact, the flavour of nutmeg has been used in *Coca Cola* and the similarities are incredible when comparing *Coca Cola* with a nutmeg syrup.

Back on Banda Neira, we met four local female schoolteachers. They had visited us on the yacht, an easy task of being ferried by the tender a short ten metres from the port and we would pull ourselves along by the tether lines of the stern to the anchor. The previous morning, I had become frustrated with Simon due to him still not being able to do the three main knots, clover, hitch, and bowline.

It was part of the agreement on sailing that the three knots are a must to know and for whatever reason he still could not master them. As a result, I would have to do all spinnaker bowlines, double check the tender being tied, etc. On this night, the girls were leaving, when one of them said, "Ali, Ali, the boat is gone!"

Simon being the last person in the tender had not tied it properly or not tied up at all. As a result, my 3.1 dingy along with 9.8 *Tohatsu* outboard motor was somewhere heading out to sea!

I had kept my cool regarding the toilet head being blocked on several occasions due to ignoring my advice. I even kept my cool when we hit a coral bommie ignoring my call to keep watch. However, the loss of the tender along with the outboard motor, due to ignoring my request to properly secure lines with knots that I had shown him, time and time again was all too much for me to take. I exploded verbally at Simon this time, even threatening him to quickly go out on the kayak to look for it. *I ranted and roared like a true British sailor*, "If you cannot come back with the tender, just continue paddling far away from me?"

I was having visions of forcing Simon to walk the plank or better still, if I could keelhaul him. This was a known punishment in the early days of sailing whereby sailors who disobeyed an order were tied to

CHAPTER FIFTEEN

a line and looped beneath the hull, then being dragged underneath the water from one side to the other. For a more humane way, I could drop Simon on a deserted island and leave him there. Just like Alexander Selkirk who was a privateer and must have drove his Captain mad for he was placed on a deserted island and forced to stay there for four years until the ship returned. This story inspired Daniel Defoe to write *Robinson Crusoe*. I am sure the teachers on board at the time thought I was also a mad Captain. Simon was kayaking out in the dark looking for the tender. While all of these murderous thoughts were being played out in my head, thankfully, Simon appeared with the tender along with the outboard motor intact. Fortunately, it had become caught on a fishing boat mooring otherwise it would have been lost to the sea. Lucky for Simon!

What incredible people the teachers were! These four young girls had carved out a school in a gully of the rainforest on the volcano island and held their classes in an open-air classroom. They were also involved in cleaning up beaches and trying to educate people on the harms of plastic in the waterways. We arranged to have the thirty-odd school children visit *SV Never Die Wondering II* for the day. I would show them the journey from Southern Australia to the Spice Islands on paper maps and electronic chart devices along with photos, etc. These were happy, eager to learn children who clapped when different parts of the vessel were shown. The teachers had put a great video clip together of the tour and uploaded it to *Facebook* showing the smiling faces of the appreciating children.

The islands are renowned for their coral gardens, and in some parts, the hot water from the volcano seeps through the lava flow into the sea water. We tied the tender up to a tree that had survived the lava flow and snorkelled amongst the hot water seeping from the rocky lava rocks. You could hear the water gushing through the lava, an incredible experience swimming in the coral gardens and having the feeling of hot water while swimming. I noticed several sea snakes in this area that seemed to like the hot water.

The streets of Banda Neira are exciting, narrow laneways with all the islands' produce being traded and variety of spices drying on the streets in the hot sun on tarps. Also cloves and cinnamon were on the islands that had originally come from as far away as Ternate in Northern Indonesia and from Sri Lanka.

I returned the hospitality of Mita and Anwar by taking them and their family sailing around these incredible islands. On one day trip, we encountered over sixty melon-head whales. It was amazing to watch the dozens of whales as the volcano seeped out clouds of sulphur. It played out in the front of a large cave where Anwar explained the Bandanese hid in 1621 to escape the murderous Dutch. This cave can only be reached by sea and was very long inside, enabling families to enter and hide way up into the dark places escaping from the horrendous genocide.

There was an area which was a small village only a few years previously but was now completely covered with lava. Anwar told me about an old man who had lived there his whole life, and refused to leave even as the red, hot lava slowly flowed down into the village. Everyone evacuated to Banda Neira with the exception of the old man who stayed on to be consumed by the lava flow. Not a trace of the village or the old man remained.

I was starting to believe that the story of early sailors smelling the aroma of nutmeg twenty nautical miles out at sea was just a sailors' myth. Sailing between the volcano and Banda Besar Island, the distinctive aroma of the nutmeg drying, confirmed it was no myth. Besides, in the early days, they would have been drying the spice by the tonnes over fires and it would have spread for many miles out at sea.

The trade winds were coming to an end, and a small window of wind remained for the next couple of days to cross the rest of the Banda Sea. Hence, we prepared to leave as soon as possible with all supplies purchased. While. Making water, the small water pressure motor's frame cracked away from the main motor causing a delay in departure as I had to remove the frame and have it rewelded.

I had also strained my back and Mita arranged for the local healer woman to give me a massage, and what an advent that was. I waited ages for her, she was late because she had to attend the call to pray first, being Muslim. The healer was an elderly woman but worked her fingers through pressure points of my body quite nimbly. At one stage, I was convinced she had pierced my muscles as the pain was overbearing, yet she worked on my body for ages. When I eventually left, I could hardly walk, but the next day, I felt fantastic. Apparently, islanders went to her rather than a medical doctor.

By the time I had repaired the frame and was ready to depart, there were no trade winds anymore. There was the odd north-westerly, opposite to what I needed. I knew the dreaded motor sailing was to begin. Mita and Anwar persuaded me to stick around as the Rhun Island war canoe races called *kora-kora* were starting in a few weeks.

CHAPTER FIFTEEN

There was also an ongoing cultural event with traditional dance and song on the other islands. Moreover, I was enjoying the company of the local people, meeting different travellers at the hotel, and given the nightly local music and get togethers, I decided to stay on.

My visa was due in three weeks, so it was pointless going early to Ambon, in any case. I also decided to stay because I was in a great frame of mind and had terrific inspiration at this special place to write my memories. Simon needed to go to Singapore to prepare to kayak to Bangkok, so it would be easy for him to hop on the ferry at Banda Neira to Ambon, and then onto Singapore. Simon eventually did kayak from Singapore to Thailand, an incredible paddling journey just shy of 2,000 kilometres completed in June 2023, and incredible feat.

On most mornings, you could hear the war cry from the *kora-kora* war canoes as the paddlers, thirty men to a canoe, would race and practise for the upcoming event to be held on Rhun Island. It was a spectacular sight witnessing the paddlers pushing their timber crafts along the front of Banda Neira chanting a war-like cry that echoed across the small bay. The evenings were spent with my newfound friends, eating wonderful local dishes, and washing them down with *Bintang* beer that I had taken a fancy to. I was called "Chilli" by a few of the locals, since I convinced them to have the beer extremely chilled. Again, I thought, *the best place to be is here and the best time to be here is now.*

Another school from Banda Neira asked if their school kids could visit my vessel, and another wonderful experience followed. The children were asked to sing a song for my entertainment in Bahasa, and the next day, in appreciation, the children's mothers had baked me various types of cakes.

Pulau Banda Besar was holding the cultural day traditional music and dance. Several of us from the hotel precinct jumped on the bamboo roof of a transport vessel and attended the event held on the western side of Banda Besar, adjacent to the beach above the sand spit and below the rainforest's steep embankment. It had areas of shade coverage and seats were given to all from our group. What a great event this turned out to be!

The *Cakalele* dance is a traditional war dance where the male dancers wear Portuguese helmets, and clothing representing material from Indian traders. This unique dance is similar throughout the Moluccas islands with the crowd chanting an addictive tune that grew louder as the dance slowly became faster.

Historically, only five warriors remained during the massacre of the Bandanese and although there were many dancers on this cultural day. Traditionally, only five dancers represent the symbol of the remaining resistance fighters of 1621, along with a golden type of fixed flower in their mouth to represent how the Bandanese were made to be quite by the Dutch.

Anwar commented that born and bred as Bandanese, it was the greatest display of music and dance he had seen yet. "I have goose bumps!" He said as the yelling and chanting increased and echoed with the crowd joining in. Other dancing and music continued with traditional drums. A graceful nutmeg dance performed by women who were dressed in Muslim headscarfs and colourful costumes carrying the harvesting baskets.

I sailed to Ai Island which is next to Rhun Island on the west of Banda Neira. Mita, Anwar, their kids, and their entourage of nanny and staff, along with others who I had befriended at Banda Neira were with me. Ai Pulau had a terrible anchorage, and we had to moor along the huge light buoy. To reach the shore, you had to cross the coral garden, a fringe reef covered the entire island. The host was calling us in from his veranda on the second storey of his beach house. I had learnt never to trust anyone saying it was okay to go ahead, and this was no exception. If I had listened to him, I probably would not have had a yacht now as the coral was less than one metre under the waterline. My host was used to the *kora-kora* boats of nearly flat bottoms not a yacht. So, we tied to the island's light buoy.

The locals put on a traditional Ai Island lunch for us, a fantastic traditional meal of fish and rice with spices. We spent the day snorkelling in the magnificent coral garden and exploring the old fort on the island. Cannons were strewn along the fort walls; the Dutch VOC had a large administration building once but all that remained were high stone walls that stretched along a long narrow street. This island was where Banda Neira obtained most of their vegetables. Although both islands were volcanic, for some reason Ai seemed to produce better quality. We returned to Banda Neira at nighttime, under an incredible starry night with everybody enjoying the ride back sitting on the trampoline by the bow.

I had a metal detector for I found it exciting trying to find treasure. Though everything I have found has no real value, but it was exciting to say the least. The locals told me about Samurai swords that fetched a fortune, and I was also asked to detect in the family

CHAPTER FIFTEEN

backyards. We did find coins and old pottery which we thought to be Portuguese.

A couple of the locals wanted to detect a shelter they thought held treasure. They told me how an American archaeological group were once prospecting around the beach area and discovered a skeleton way up on the high tide mark. The skull had two Dutch coins pressed into its eye sockets. An elderly local woman appeared at the site and demanded that no one remove the coins, that anyone who did so would have the fate of blindness placed on them. A woman archaeologist stated that they had to remove the coins to find the date, so in the name of science she removed the coins from the eye sockets of the skull. Legend has it that by the next morning, the American woman started suffering and was totally blind before she left the island. The locals were a bit scared regarding this tale, so we never got to detect the shelter.

My agent based in Bali had mistakenly sent my endorsement letter to Lombok. Therefore, it was not going to get to Ambon with only two days before my visa expired and the fine was a million rupees per day if late. So, it was time to sail to Ambon as soon as possible. While purchasing my supplies in the local market, the sellers who knew I was leaving gave me extra produce as a gift, very generous people. It was an emotional farewell with Mita and Anwar, and their family who gave me great gifts of nutmeg jams, and a memoir of Mita's grandfather, Des Alwi.

Finally, the anchor was raised, the stern lines removed from the ancient Dutch cannon, and away I and *Never Die Wondering II* went, leaving a place that has appropriately been called heaven on earth. I sailed for new places, new adventures, and this time, solo across the Banda Sea.

It is always sad to leave a place but also exciting to think of what lay ahead. Banda Islands to Ambon was only 120 nautical miles, therefore, an estimated 24-hour passage. Solo sailing and overnighters are an exhausting exercise to say the least, and on the route, you had the large ferry that travelled from Ambon to Banda back and forth, and many fishing vessels along the way. At night, I lay at the front of the trampoline, while the vessel sailed on autopilot. This enabled me to have a somewhat better view if I approached a fishing vessel with poor lighting or with no lighting at all. I had a large spotlight that I used as well. I set my alarm for only brief power naps. In fact, I set two alarms on two separate phones just in case, but on this particular night, I had no power nap at all since there was always another vessel in the vicinity or the large ferry coming from my stern.

The first day of light is always a grateful feeling. Watching the sun, rising from the east over the Banda Sea was spectacular sight. It does not matter how many sunrises or sunsets I see; they are all unique and gives you the feeling of gladness to be alive.

CHAPTER SIXTEEN

The world is a huge place. How will you know where you fit in unless you explore beyond your comfort zone?

Ernest Shackleton

Ambon to West Papua

Ambon is an island southwest of the large Ceram Island. The city is located on a large inlet when sailing towards the city on an ebbing tide the vessel was pushing through a sea of plastic rubbish and many other debris, old fishing platforms, etc. It was a terrible sight to see this beautiful waterway polluted with a sea of garbage. This was by far, the worse I had ever seen. You have the feeling that the entire city throws their trash straight to the sea!

The island itself is incredibly scenic with high mountain ranges. The population of the island is 350,000 inhabitants and was the site of civil unrest in 1999, it cascaded into an all-out-warfare where atrocities occurred against the civilian population. Religious militia from both Muslim and Christian faiths fought each other, resulting in many deaths with a displacement of 20,000 residents that fled Ambon to escape the violence, many houses of worship were destroyed both mosques and churches with countless homes torched.

I anchored south of the main part of the city off a beach called Amahusu in twenty-five metres of water. I chose this spot as it was away from the hustle and bustle of the main port. I had also arranged for a local to assist me in renewing my vessel that was due to expire the next day. My anchor chain was sixty-five metres, and a hundred metres of chain was needed, therefore, I used my anchor rode (extra rope connected to the chain) to give me enough scope as the tide ripped through this anchorage. By then, I was exhausted with no sleep and finally, lay down. I did not wake up for many hours. There was only one other yacht anchored nearby, an American. Instead of the call to prayers that I had become acquainted with, it was now the sound of the church bells as this was the Christian part of Ambon. The next day, after I had recovered from the night sail, I made my way to Ambon and arranged to meet an assistant to my agent. He had the sponsor letter for me as a requirement to extend the visa for another two months. The hustle and bustle of this noisy city was a far cry from the peaceful village of Banda Neira.

I spent two weeks at Ambon preparing for the passage to West Papua, carting fuel, and filling up gas bottles which was a challenge in itself. The connection that I had for taping into the Indonesian bottle and an Australian connection to fill up my Aussie gas tanks was faulty, therefore, I had to purchase another. This meant rides on motorbikes, visiting appliance shops, and when I finally found one, I discovered it too was faulty when I was filling gas. I ordered another one to be shipped from Java. After several days, the part arrived and the owner of the store where I purchased the gas from allowed me to fill the bottles in his backyard. The operation consisted of tying up the Indonesian bottle to a tree upside down and connecting the device to my Australian bottle so that when both opened, the gas would slowly seep to the empty bottle. The only concern was that this little backyard was also where the family cooked on an open fire. I had to make sure that the fireplace was watered down as there had been recent cooking. All was going fine until the hose busted due to the hose clamps and gave out an enormous loud bang. The shop quickly was evacuated, and the owners ran from their store thinking the worse had happened. After a quick reconnection, I filled my bottles with no other drama.

During my stay at Ambon, I heard many stories and firsthand accounts of the terrible warfare that took place in this usually peaceful island. The common belief was that it started when a Christian taxi driver chased a young Muslim man after a dispute regarding the fare. This was in January of 1999 and by March, at least 160 people had been killed on both sides. Christians and Muslims fighting each other, burning homes, and places of worship, so much for the *Bible* and the *Quran* that promotes peace. Militia groups were formed, and atrocities happened. I was told by an Ambonese Christian that he was approached

CHAPTER SIXTEEN

by the militia who were adamant in attacking a Muslim family who lived in what the militia believed to be a Christian area. He refused but he admitted that he was involved in the fighting in previous weeks and was sickened by the civil unrest. He explained that the mob then went on and murdered eight people. There was an interview on *YouTube* with a senior Muslim preacher admitting to beheading people. All madness on both sides.

I had been contacted by many people wishing to sail with me, and decided to bring on a crew, as it was much safer and easier for keeping watch with fishing vessels every were along with many other debris. I really loved my solo sailing but preferred crew for a watch around the islands. Alexa from Zurich, Switzerland, contacted me. She had crewed on a couple of vessels in Indonesia and Malaysia and we talked via *FaceTime*. She was very enthusiastic and asked, "Do you think I would be a suitable fit? I can be there in 40 hours."

That meant Alexa was jumping on a plane from Switzerland to Singapore, then from Singapore to Java, from Java to Sulawesi, and finally, Sulawesi to Ambon. She had worked as an airline hostess and was used to travel. She obtained a job as a way to explore the world. This would be the first time that I allowed someone who I did not know on the vessel. Even though she passed every question I required, it could be very daunting to say the least. After all, you become responsible for someone else's safety, and you both have to be able to be comfortable with each other.

Fortunately, what a delight Alexa was to have on board for three weeks sailing to West Papua. She had a natural common-sense attitude and worked extremely well with me. Although from Switzerland, she was German-born of Polish parents. Her love for the islands and the people was infectious, and great company to have on board. This tall, blonde traveller from Switzerland was easy on the eye too, had an elegant style about her that made the passage very pleasant indeed.

We both went to the vibrant Ambon markets and bought fresh fruits and vegetables along with fish. I had found that every time I threw a line over the stern, I picked up plastic trash. Indonesia was not the greatest for luring due to the trash, but the markets were full of fresh fish and very affordable. The night before we departed was a partial eclipse. Living on the water enhances events like an eclipse, as your view is not limited usually.

Log: Wednesday, 9 November 2022; 0625 hours. Depart

Weighed anchor had difficulties with plastic rubbish along with wires wrapped around anchor. Bolt cutters were needed. Later, at 1035 hours, passenger ship passing on the portside radioed for yarn. The captain was friendly and wanted to know of the journey of *Never Die Wondering II*.

I had a terrible cough and sore throat from the plastic smoke that engulfed the boat usually in Ambon. It came from the burning of the house rubbish that seemed to be an endless activity. It wasn't until we were many hours away from Ambon in clean clear air that I felt alright.

We sailed north-west from Ambon passing the Island of Manipa (Pulau Manipa) and motored into a channel with Manipa on our portside and a small islet, Bataboui, on our starboard side. The charts showed an anchorage with depths of ten metres but it was thirty to forty metres deep, so we motored in through this small waterway in the mangroves where we came onto a village, beaming with boats and people. We were able to drop the anchor at a ten-metre spot close to large coral bommies only a few metres from the shore.

As soon as the anchor was set, the locals arrived by their crafts and bordered the vessel. It was friendly but very odd since they did not try to communicate with us just sat either in the cockpit or on the trampoline. They were mostly kids but a few older men too! We did get the information by gestures of crocodiles in the vicinity. Eventually, they left when we explained to them that we wanted to sleep showing sleeping gestures with our hands. That night, I was awakened by someone on the boat. I quickly came to the cockpit to find this feller having invited himself on board. I told him to leave in a friendly gesture, again explaining that we had to sleep.

In the morning, a fisherman hopped on board trying to take my swimming goggles and was quickly told to leave. With both of these incidents happening, there was a bad feel to the place. We promptly weighed the anchor and headed north-east. On the way out of the island, we had a pod of dolphins riding the bow waves, always a great sight. Sailors of the past believed seeing dolphins was a good omen and a symbol of protection.

We were sailing off the island of Boano to the south-east at least a kilometre off the land in twenty meters of water very cautiously when all of a sudden, it was only a few metres deep. I quickly moved to a safer course, but these dangerous situations of uncharted area happened again. We came on to a magnificent island called Pulau Nusatea which according to the charts was only a speck of land but was, in fact, twenty times larger than shown. A large steep hill with coconuts surrounded it, a beautiful scenic setting, the chart showed it was supposed to be ten metres of water. We dropped anchor and went to find a route closer to the island by dingy and found a safe passage as well as superb anchorage within only a few metres of water, close to the beach and sheltered. We spent a few days enjoying this wonderful place.

The local inhabitants from the nearby island came to visit shortly after. First, a canoe with all the young fellers who climbed the coconut trees and got coconuts for us. Then the girls came on a separate canoe wearing their hijabs, all extremely excited as they were welcomed onto *Never Die Wondering II* taking selfies with their camera phones. It was fascinating to see how every island I visited always had someone with a mobile phone.

An older feller who paddled in by himself. He seemed a little sneaky, so I kept my eye on him, after a while, I noticed that he quickly stole a lure and placed it in his pocket thinking I was not looking. I retrieved the lure, and he was removed from the boat and banned from coming back on. The others were all welcome though and used the boat to dive from.

The island had several starving cats that seemed to rely on the locals coming there to feed with their fish cath. The coral was superb on the island's small fringe reef, and we floated down snorkelling, admiring the coral and the fish it attracts. We were anchored on the southern side of this island. The view looking east to the islands of Pua and Boano was spectacular. The towering limestone cliffs vertically fell back into the sea. During full moon, the bright moonlight casting a glow through this rocky gorge created a lighting display that gave the entire event a dazzling show.

The Moluccas Archipelago

The wonderful islands from Banda Neira to the Philippines Sea in the north and west of New Guinea, to the east of Sulawesi are called the Moluccas Islands with an estimated 1,000 islands. After a few days, having successfully repaired the tender that needed to be rolled over, submerged in water to find the leak, burning of rubbish and cleaning the beach of trash, we weighed anchor again. We sailed east to the Paula Ceram.

Log: Sunday, 13 November 2022.

We spotted two humpback whales an hour apart. We tried to find an anchorage but every spot we entered there was no patch of sand just coral fringe reef. At one point, the *Navionics* chart showed us on land, but we were in forty metres of water.

Just before sunset we managed to anchor though on the chart, it showed we were on land. Just as the anchor was set, forty odd people swam to the yacht from the shore as we were only a hundred metres from the beach. Again, the yacht was used as a diving platform for the local kids. As the sun went down, all of our newfound friends made their way back to the village. Many local fishermen in their small crafts were fishing nearby on the fringe reef.

The next day, we made our way into the village of Sukaraga and were treated like rockstars with locals asking to take photos of us with them. Back on the boat in the afternoon, thirty-two people swam to the vessel and *Never Die Wondering II* became a party boat with dancing and singing to sea shanty music with the likes of the *Wellerman* song.

Log: Tuesday, 15 November 2022; 0600 hours; departed Sukaraga

We avoided a large log, the size of the vessel closely on our way out. If hit, damage was guaranteed. We headed east then and into a large cove to the village of Seleman. What a spectacular anchorage! When you think you have seen the best anchorage, it just keeps getting better. We dropped anchor at 2°58′044″ / 129°7′7″ just a few metres off the beach with several huts nearby. The limestone cliffs were a breathtaking vertical drop down into the sea, and the smell of the rainforest was evident in every breath. We dived off the boat and the water to our surprise was cool. We then realised that it was fresh water, beautiful, clean freshwater bubbling from springs beneath the sand without overpowering of any salt water.

We had mobile reception, so I rang the nearby resort that was a hut dwelling and asked about meals. The woman from the resort came out to us via boat and cooked a traditional Indonesian meal for the two of us. The next day, we made a trip to the village of Seleman, a very clean place, in fact, the cleanest I have seen in Indonesia. We ate in town for a huge price of $5 for two meals and got to meet the locals. I arranged for a slab (carton) of beer. The alcohol seller operated next to the mosque, and most Muslims do not drink, so I found this to be funny. They arranged a motorbike to ride to another village to bring the beer. Great fantastic service, and so many people obliging to help throughout the islands.

We returned just as a huge thunderstorm hit, and what a huge downpour of rain it was. We quickly put up the rain catcher (tarp to collect rain) and in no time at all, we had the water tanks full. We took long showers. After the storm, during the night, the rainforest was alive with nighttime birds, the sound of owls along with that of frogs, and the smell of the rainforest, stronger than ever.

The next morning, butterflies were prolific around the vessel. The Ulysses butterfly, the size of one's hand with their distinctive blue colour abounded, and so did the turtles swimming around the vessel. This was truly a paradise, and the high rocky limestone range was covered in clouds. I had recently watched a film about the bamboo people who lived high in the jungle ranges of Ceram Island and nearly everything they possessed was made from bamboo, starting from huts to fish nets! A way of life that was thousands of years old and still continuing today somewhere high in the ranges.

We needed to cross over the east Ceram Sea to Misool (southern Raja Ampat) and if possible, cover the passage in daylight hours. The departure point being the shortest distance from Ceram Island, we sailed towards this point with Alexa on the bow, warning me of the coral bommies. They were around our anchored position, and we only had a narrow entrance out since it was low tide.

The day sail was passed river and creek flood out country after the recent storms. The sea from being clear had turned to a chocolate brown from the massive fresh water entering the sea. Keeping to the safe option, I decided to anchor where a shipping port was within a large inlet that had soundings on the charts that could be reasonably trusted as a large pier and a township of Seliha. This proved to be a great safe anchorage on mud, and we arrived just on sunset.

While anchored, I tried to contact the authorities over *WhatsApp* regarding a permit needed for Raja Ampat Islands when we were invaded by literally millions of insects of all description. The entire saloon was swarmed by large and small critters within seconds. Alexa started screaming in frustration as the attack intensified. She then simply retired to her cabin as the only form of protection. By first light, we were glad to leave this horrendous place.

Log: Saturday, 19 November 2022; 0900 hours.

Whales blow and breached close by on our starboard side. At first, I thought it was a log until a fountain of water from a blow from the whale that was just lying on the surface. The day had stormy conditions with squalls now and then, we had full sails, and the passage was only sixty nautical miles. We were making great speed at 8.0 knots SOG with a fantastic pick up of wind from the west, beam reaching. All of a sudden, I saw the rolling black storm clouds coming in.

I lost no time and shouted to Alexa, "GO, GO, GO! Reef in! Reef in!" Both of us quickly reefed the main and head sail to the third reef, and then watched as we were hit by this squall. I referred to it as a "black monster" in my log. Along with forty-knot winds we were sailing in a cloud of darkness along with torrential rain. When the quick burst of wind died down, Alexa stood up right with her face to the storm taking in a mouth of fresh water. I took a photo of her, along with a large pod of dolphins swimming nearby.

Like most squalls, this one too came in quick and left just as quickly. We made our way to Southern Raja Ampat with the numerous and distinctive rocky islets in view. The region is renowned for extremely deep waters where anchorages are very difficult to find, and again the charts were incorrect. As we approached Pulau Batbitiem, another squall hit, and visibility became very poor. Keeping an eye on the sounder, we carefully and slowly, made our way to the east side of the island where a resort was located. Just then, another storm hit as swing moorings came into view. Alexa went to the bow with the pickup pole braving strong winds and torrential rain to secure to the mooring. Thankfully, a local from the resort came out to assist. Then, again, the squall was over as quick as it had started.

We were approached by the manager who explained that there would be diving boats returning for the mooring. He told us about an anchorage to the north only two nautical miles away that also had a mooring we could use. So, we headed to this spot, but we weren't very surprised when we saw that all were deep water forty to sixty metres. We motored into a protected lagoon with high vertical limestone cliffs where a swing mooring was located but it had a fuel vessel already tied to it. The crew of the fuel vessel called us over and asked us to raft

CHAPTER SIXTEEN

up against them for the night. We did so and had a well-earned meal and sleep after the ordeal of the day of squalls. I was a little weary of the fuel barge as it contained many drums of highly inflammable petrol.

The fuel vessel left the mooring early in the morning to drop off the fuel for the resort. We then secured our mooring and took the tender out to explore and snorkel the coral fringe reefs that circled the entire lagoon with a sheer drop of coral walls. Sea eagles made this lagoon their home along with the prehistoric looking hornbill that gave out a unique honking sound. To look at them in flight was truly a magnificent sight.

On my satellite system, you could see areas of sand that made finding an anchorage so much easier, still, you sometimes have to visit several potential spots until you can find a suitable one. There was a lagoon named the Love Lagoon due to its heart-like shape and I was told by other yachties that I could come in from the northern side. We sailed to the entrance, but it was too shallow for me to attempt along with a loading facility jetty which had been built at the entrance.

Hence, after checking several potential anchorages without any luck, we sailed between Walib and Wayibatan Islands. It is a gorge with steep vertical limestone cliffs, a narrow passage that you sail through to finding the most idyllic anchorage. Nearby natives were camped there, I visited them by kayak with my rough speaking Bahasa and learnt that they lived on an island nearby and were fishermen. The next morning, they brought back, two large snappers caught from the reef early in the morning. I paid them Rp10,000 (Indonesian Rupiyah) or AUD$5 each. They were very happy, and so were we with the fresh fish.

At night, the fireflies glowed and so did the water with a phosphorescent glow which was quite spectacular. We stayed there for a few days exploring the lagoons, snorkelling in the turquoise waters either by kayak or tender. After several days of enjoying this tranquil anchorage, it was time to sail to West Papua.

New Guineas had been my destination when I left Victoria in 2018 but due to unforeseen circumstances. I was shy of the border only by ninety nautical miles when I was in the Torres Strait. With Covid-19 restrictions, the route to New Guinea became the long way, over the top of Australia and then through Indonesia. I was now only a day away from completing my goal.

West Papua

We had the tide on our side as we left the anchorage and made our way through the narrow gorge at first light, passing several fishing vessels. As we went by Pulau Balbulol known as the "Jewel of Southern Raja Ampat", a distinct collection of limestone rocky monoliths protruding from the sea gave us postcard views. The wind was up, and the sky was cloudy, so visibility was not the best to enter into the gorge. Although I had prepared all my long forty-metre lines out to tie to rocks, I decided to veto that idea and continue to West Papua.

Log: Thursday, 24 November 2022; 1205 hours; First sight of West Papua.

The passage had another sixty nautical miles to sail, and we were making great time as we sailed into the channel. The west side of New Guinea once named Irian Jaya Barat (West Irian) now an Indonesian province is more or less half the entire western side of New Guinea. We approached the village of Seget with the friendly faces of West Papuans. After dropping anchor close to the village on the sand in very shallow water, again we had the village children swarm the vessel to greet us. A very distinctive group of people with fuzzy hair, darker skin, but just as the Indonesian Islanders, infectiously friendly people.

The vessel was on the sand at low tide as well as being pushed by a westerly but safe. Until, I was woken at 0300 hours by anchor alarm, we had dragged! I shone my spotlight and could see distinctly the village church's belltower that we were passing by. Just a matter of letting out more chain, and the anchor was set now outside the church! In the morning, I went ashore to be greeted by the locals and was shown around their village and the church.

We departed for Sorong but was slowed down in speed, due to the tide against us and even motoring could barely get 2.0 knots SOG. So, we decided to anchor on the eastern side of the channel in a remote spot in a flooded-out country with mangroves. As I was picking a good anchorage, I forgot to bring my fishing line in which quickly tangled around my starboard prop. It wasn't the first time I had done that and after I cursed myself, I quickly put on the goggles and dived under to check. It was a right mess and would take some time

CHAPTER SIXTEEN

cutting. I came back up, started up the hooker unit, geared up my weight belt, and put on the suit. The water was a muddy chocolate and visibility was terrible. If there ever was a place for a crocodile to lurk in, this was it.

I told Alexa, "If you see one of the reptiles, quickly tug on my air tube so I know to get out. If I don't come back, tell my son I love him, and to others say that I did not die wondering." With that I quickly dived under the vessel took quite some time below. I needed to cut and remove the line from the prop and make it free in turning. Once all was done, I was back on board removing the diving gear when I noticed Alexa was a little emotional. I may have been under water a bit longer than I would have preferred, and she obviously, was getting extremely worried with every minute that passed without me surfacing and thinking the worst.

The next morning, we sailed into Sorong and anchored in the north part, outside of *Tampa Garam Boat Harbor Marina*. After calling and securing a spot we entered the marina. It was really only walls protecting vessels, with old, abandoned huts surrounding the anchorage. You dropped anchor in the middle of the pond and reversed to tie the stern lines to the abandoned huts. Alexa flew back to Switzerland from here and went straight to work on the airline. My visa renewal was due in a month's time, and I really needed two months to sail my next passage from Sorong to Bitung, Sulawesi where I would exit for the Philippines. Of course, plenty of repairs and maintenance needed to be done prior to that. So, I went to work on building a polisher system to clean the diesel purchased prior to getting it into my main tanks, as well as ordered parts from Java like macerator, prop for outboard, etc.

Sorong had a fair bit of tension that could be felt in the air, quite different to Papua New Guinea on the east where the locals had their independence. West Papua occupied by Indonesia was fairly hostile, the nationalist Indonesian government was the successor state to the whole of the Dutch East Indies. Therefore, once the Dutch control ended, Indonesia's began as it took control of the entire Archipelago.

In a nutshell, the Melanesian people occupied the island of New Guinea both west (West Papua under Indonesia) and east (independent country of Papua New Guinea) with literally hundreds of different tribes, languages, and customs with a history of thousands of years. The Dutch colonised and claimed the area of West Papua for themselves in 1898, while the east was colonised by the British in 1884. In 1963, Indonesia gained control of West Papua, then called the West Irian and Irian Jaya respectively.

The Free Papua Movement had been conducting a low-intensity guerrilla war against Indonesia since 1963. This separatist movement has raised their own independent flag and has accused Indonesia of a genocide campaign against their indigenous inhabitants claiming an estimated 100,000 to 300,000 Papuans being killed. Not long before I arrived, eight people, workers for a telecommunication company were ambushed and murdered by a Papuan rebel group. A few months ago, a New Zealand pilot was captured by the rebels and was still in captivity a year later.

Hence, West Papua was a dangerous place indeed, and Sorong township had many incidents of civil unrest. When I was learning Bahasa at the Darwin Yacht Club conducted by the Indonesian embassy, I asked the question regarding the belief that Australians were banned from venturing into the hills of West Papua. I was informed that an Australian posted on his *Facebook* page the pro-independence flag of the West Papua freedom movement and this was the reason why Australians were discouraged to go into the remote regions. There was also a situation where twenty-four construction workers building a road in the remote mountainous country were killed by gunmen. It was understandable why Indonesia recommended not to head into these remote regions.

Despite the gloom warnings of the place, I did hire a motorbike and explored areas of Sorong. There was a great market where fish freshly caught were displayed on tables, and all you had to do was point to the fish you wanted, and they would clean and cook it on the spot. Brilliant! In the bank, I was having problems with drawing funds. The Bank Manager came over to help but we were still unable to take out money. She quickly arranged for her mother to take me to another bank on the back of her motorbike to the other side of town. What a great customer service!

Unfortunately, I caught the dreaded stomach bug. Obviously, it was something I ate, but nowhere as severe as what I had experienced in Varanasi, India. It took a few days to overcome nevertheless. After that, I employed another agent with a sponsor letter (yes,

CHAPTER SIXTEEN

again because my original agent let me down). I extended my visa for another two months.

I was away sailing again, this time back to solo. Many people contacted me wanting to crew but really none never ticked all the boxes of what I needed for a crew member. So, a solo voyage to the Philippines began.

CHAPTER SEVENTEEN

The hardest sailing is the one you make alone. That is the sail that makes you strong, confident, independent, and fearless.

Sorong to the Philippines

Log: Sunday, 1 January 2023; Depart Sorong 1000 hours; after a month at Sorong, I was chomping at the bit to have the wind in my sails again. It was fantastic sailing with the odd squall coming through. I had two months to explore islands from West Papua to the Philippines, a total of 1,100 nautical miles. Only a few miles from Sorong, you find yourself back in paradise.

Raja Ampat is made up of four major islands Misool, Salawati, Batanta, and Waigeo known as the four kings and comprising 1,500 smaller islands among themselves. The group of islands is renowned for the most diverse coral reefs in the world, home to 540 different types of coral, and more than 1,000 types of coral fish with 75% of the world's species living in Raja Ampat. The name comes from local mythology where a woman finds seven eggs. Out of the seven, four of the eggs hatch to become kings that occupy the four main islands. *Raja* means "king" and *Ampat* means "four".

I anchored at Pulau Ayemi within a cove of Batanta Island, it was an island within an island. I was greeted by locals on an outrigger who requested to take a photo with them along with photos of the vessel. Ayemi Island had a peaceful, clean environment, a far cry from the month spent in Sorong. It was great to be back on the hook (on anchor) while admiring this beautiful island. Turtles came around the vessel and white sandy beaches stretched with abandoned huts along

CHAPTER SEVENTEEN

the foreshore. In the evening and at dawn, the sound of songbirds was musical to say the least. I was sure they were the sounds of the Birds of Paradise.

While exploring the island, I met a couple of natives who were out climbing palm trees to obtain the small fruit seed. What an incredible ability they had to climb the trees! They took a dry palm throng and deftly fashioned it as a band that they wrapped around both their ankles. Then, in a flash, they would make their way up the tree to the highest point, to obtain the fruit. The speed and the fitness required was astonishing. Many fishing vessels stood along the high-water mark protected by palm throngs that covered the boats. The unique crafts had protruding bows, considering bush skills, they created such an amazing vessel.

I sailed to Pulau Frewin, another very small island off Pulau Gam which is adjacent to Waisai, the major island. This small island had somewhat of a picnic area that had many people visit from the neighbouring islands. The anchorage was not the best, during a squall, I found myself too close to the coral and had to reset to another spot. I found a lot of soft coral in this area. The huts around this picnic area had their sides made of shells threaded through with fishing lines hung vertically, creating a type of wall.

I was approached by a local named Dave who asked, if I wanted to see the Birds of Paradise early in the morning. I agreed and he said that he would pick me up in his boat one hour before dawn for a small fee. He also asked if I could supply a couple of litres of petrol and I agreed with the deal. Within an hour of Dave leaving, another native arrived asking if I wanted to see the Bird of Paradise. Naturally, I declined saying that Dave was taking me.

I was up 1.5 hours before dawn and along came an older feller, speaking only in Bahasa and wanting me to go with him to see the Bird of Paradise. I declined explaining that Dave was coming, *"Pagi* Dave Morning, Dave coming) After a while, the old feller became frustrated either with my poor Bahasa or refusal to go with him and left. Dave, on the other hand, never turned up.

In the end, Dave arrived in the afternoon, on his boat along with his family and explained that he was ill and had asked his father to pick me up. The penny dropped! I explained that I thought he was someone trying to take Dave's job. Anyhow, everything worked out well as the following morning Dave picked me up. With torches on our heads, we headed to Pulau Gam and motored up the long waterway in the dark with the towering limestone cliffs over us. At first light, we saw spectacular clear water indicating safe passage. We then went up a couple of miles to an old bush made jetty, and then climbed for about thirty minutes up a hill holding onto vine type ropes as a guide until we were on the dome of a small hill. The distinctive sound of the Birds of Paradise came alive. Dave pointed out the male birds and showed how they attracted the female into their domain. A truly incredible experience to sit and watch this mating ritual for an hour. I paid Dave a bit more than the agreed fee and also supplied a bit more fuel. Like most of the generous friendly islanders, he brought back fish for me later in the day from his daily catch.

> **"I try to leave a little extra on the table during a deal, most times it is returned in appreciation."**

I had several way points given to me from other yachties and decided to visit a lagoon on the west side of Pulau Gam with a small island, Pulau Yanggefo, to the west of the lagoon. The satellite imagery showed huts out in the water. I was under way at low tide and again the depths were wrong with coral under the yacht too close for comfort. At one spot, I had to stop and reverse. A month later, I met a yachtie who unfortunately got caught in this very spot and was lucky to get his vessel off the coral on the rising tide.

Yanggefo, another spot, another paradise. The huts on the water were abandoned. In fact, they were only partially built and apparently all fell to disrepair due to Covid-19 restrictions that had destroyed many accommodation places. The huts were situated on the far west side of the lagoon and within the middle was a swing mooring as the depth was forty metres. The fringe coral surrounded the sides of the lagoon and towering hills with lush jungle type of vegetation filled the interior. It was a little different to the limestone cliffs which I had become accustomed to in South Raja Ampat. A native approached me and explained that he had a hut accommodation around the northwest side of the island and along with a swing mooring placed in to protect the coral. It was really too deep to anchor, but riskier to anchor near the coral besides damaging this fragile environment. He asked if I would pay him a fee to use the mooring, I did not hesitate and agreed on a price for two nights.

The mooring looked fairly new with large solid ropes and the wind conditions were extremely calm, with the lush rainforest, steep hills surrounding the lagoon. It was totally protected from the sea, in fact, you could not see the sea at all due to the surrounding hills. That night, after a cooked meal, I lay back in my cabin with the hatch open. The strong smell of the rainforest along with a chorus of night birds filled my cabin and I felt relaxed and at peace with the world. Given the feeling of safety on this mooring in calm conditions, I quickly fell asleep. I could not have been more wrong regarding safety, as what was about to happen was going to be the worst sailing experience of my life.

Near Disaster on a Coral Reef

Roughly at 200 hours, I was awakened to the horrific sound of coral crunching on the keel and severe strong winds along with rain. I ran to the cockpit to find that the vessel had dragged the swing mooring. My vessel was now over the coral fringe reef, and my stern was in the mangroves!

At that stage, I didn't know if it was the keel or the hull rubbing on the coral, the latter would easily crack and I would quickly take in water. The lagoon was awash with waves due to the extremely high winds and the crunching sound of the coral could only be described as creating a sick feeling of concern. I thought, *NO, this can't be happening*, at one point I even thought it must be a nightmare and I would wake up, unfortunately it was not. I was in a desperate situation thinking I was going to lose my home. I quickly worked out the tides and realised it was coming off the low tide, so that was in my favour. A further calculation clarified that it would most likely take four hours before the tide was high enough to get the vessel off the coral reef, that is if it survived the four hours.

The wind would not die down and continued roaring with waves creating the vessel to pitch up and down, stern to bow. My concern was although the wind was on the bow, it was pushing me further back into the mangroves and onto the coral reef, and if the vessel turned sideways with the wind on the beam, I would then have both hulls over the coral. At this stage, only my portside was on the reef, and shining the spotlight I discovered it was only my keels and rudder on the coral not the hull. The keel and rudder have steel boots that protect the fibre glass to some degree but for how long in these conditions.

I knew I had to maintain the position of the vessel pointing into the wind and although I started both engines it would be suicidal to go forward as I would guarantee damage or worst, sink the entire boat. I was glad to be by myself as having an inexperienced person assisting or one who panicked could have been disastrous. As time passed, the vessel was washed slightly to the side and therefore, had the wind forward of the beam 30° to 40° degree, a worrying situation.

With the spotlight I saw an opening in the mangroves, I calculated that if I was able to tie a line from the base of the mangrove trunk to the starboard bow, I might be able to stop disaster from happening. I had forty-metre lines prepared and coiled correctly in case I needed to tie to rocky cliff walls, so everything was in its place. I jumped into the tender and rowed with line into the mangroves. Amongst the rain and waves, the tender nearly capsized, I had to lean over the bow of the dingy into the water and dig my way through the foliage. My concern was heightened thinking about crocodiles as they abound in any mangrove system.

Back on the deck, I secured the line to the starboard cleat but realised that I needed another line midship. So, back in the tender I went with my head lamp on along with handheld spotlight. A second line was secured halfway along the first line, and then to the cleat midship. Standing on deck, I was then able to physically work the two lines by hand to stop me the vessel from going beam to wind. This worked well and what seemed like an eternity trying to save my home from disaster.

I tried to call my son, Brandon, but to no avail. I reached Jeff Mullenger by satellite phone to explain my ordeal in case my vessel found its way to the bottom of the lagoon. I am not afraid to say that besides my swearing and yelling out loud, I also called for assistance to the Lord, Allah, God… "PLEASE, PLEASE, don't let this happen! PLEASE Poseidon! PLEASE Neptune!" I yelled out to the heavens. As the hours went, I really was not sure if I was going to save *Never Die Wondering II*.

Finally, either Neptune or Poseidon assisted. I felt the wind change direction and looked at the flag on the stern to see the wind was now coming from the south. Incredibly, the vessel was lifted by the high tide and the changed wind direction cleared it off the fringe reef. As this was happening, there was the first light of day. I was afraid to engage into gear as lines were everywhere but there was enough light for me to see, so I dived under the boat to clear the lines. Knowing they were clear of the props, I placed the starboard engine into gear and then, literally dragged the mooring. I then engaged the portside engine and

CHAPTER SEVENTEEN

was able to drag the mooring back out to the centre of the lagoon forty metres from the reef. I did not want to unhook the mooring from the vessel in case the rudders had no steering and found myself back on the reef. To my surprise, both rudders seemed fine.

The sun came up bright, and I motored slowly towards the west side of the lagoon. All worked well. I tied a bow line to the frame of an old hut, with the stern line onto another hut. All the huts where on stilts on the water. Finally, I was able to sit down exhausted emotionally, physically, mentally. It was several hours before I had the energy to dive under the vessel for a proper examination. My heart was still racing, but to my disbelief, no damage was done with the exception of superficial marks on the portside rudder and keel just where the steel boots were. Thank God for the steel protectors!

Late afternoon, the native feller along with his daughter brought me fish and explained how all his crafts were blown upside down and washed up onto the beach in front of his huts. He had never seen a blow so severe in the lagoon. Well, that was my luck. At the wrong place, at the wrong time!

The day was spent recovering, and incredibly all my arthritis pain disappeared. It is amazing how the mind acts! I decided to stay for the time being, secure with lines to the huts for a couple of days recovering from the ordeal. The lagoon had enormous manta rays swimming in, and diving out of the air, a truly spectacular sight. The coral was fluorescent green and purple, and the area where the vessel went over, I could not see any damage to the coral. With turtles swimming by, I photographed them along with grey cranes swooping into the schools of small fish, and large flocks of hornbill birds nesting in the canopy of foliage far above in the jungle. When the dark came around again, the hill was covered in a glow from the thousands of fireflies.

This lagoon with the abandoned huts on stilts was the safe refuge of the local natives as they were transiting the islands. One group who took refuge on a trip back to their home island with several children visited *Never Die Wondering II* and enjoyed being shown the vessel as was the case wherever I travelled. Another local boat with tourist divers on board told me of a film clip they made of a fourteen-foot crocodile. Guess where it lived? At the same spot where I tied the line during last night's disaster!

I had recovered from the ordeal and after several dives' underneath, I was certain the vessel was fine to continue. So, I sailed north and crossed the equator.

Log: Tuesday, 10 January 2023; 1420 hours; Crossed Equator – Latitude 00.00.000 Longitude 130'12.059 E

I was no longer in the southern hemisphere. I opened the whisky bottle from the alcohol cabinet that only had been opened twice before over a few years, once when initiating the *Crowther*, and again while christening of the *Lagoon Never Die Wondering II*. First, I appropriately poured a small glass of whisky and gave homage to Poseidon and Neptune, especially for their protection the other night and asking for safe passages hereafter. A sip of scotch whisky, and a sprinkle of the fluid over the stern, over both beams, and the fore deck.

Traditionally, in bygone eras, the equator was the unknown for sailors. The developed world was on the northern side, therefore, travelling from north to the south was the unknown. For hundreds of years, a tradition of crazy shenanigans had taken place aboard ships whereby sailors who had never crossed the equator were known as pollywogs, and after crossing the equator for the first time were known as shellbacks. Sometimes, the captain would take the role of Neptune and forced the initiated sailors through crazy procedures he felt was appropriate. All in good fun. Since I was a solo sailor, and this was my first time crossing the equator at sea, my pollywog to shellback transition being completed with a sip of the Scotch whisky, and a request to Neptune for a safe passage was going to suffice.

I made my way along the northern side of the equator to Pulau Kawe, an isolated larger island. I had been told by other yachties that it was in this spot with a defined anchorage where a Russian was taken by a large crocodile. I worked my way slowly north-west in this inlet, in the near dark, carefully on the watch for coral bommies and dropped anchor in eight metres of water, only twenty metres from the mangroves and rocky ledge. It was a fantastic valley and several hundred metres at the head of the inlet was a narrow patch of land where the sea was close. You could hear the swells smashing loudly at night. The evening had the odd squall come through and I was glad to be in this safe haven.

The next morning, I was having my first coffee when along the front of the vessel a fourteen-metre crocodile slowly swam by. Most likely, doing his morning patrol of his territory. As he was so close and I was safely aboard *Never Die Wondering II*, I was able to take some great photos of this prehistoric reptile. I could not help wondering if it was the same croc that took the Russian feller.

Later in the morning, I took the tender to explore up the head of the inlet and wanted to walk to the sea on the other side. However, I had lost sight of the croc and wasn't too comfortable climbing up into the mangroves to reach the land. So, I vetoed that idea and went to an island to the south of where I was anchored to see a marker for the equator. It was an elaborate structure with the latitude and longitude written on it, made of concrete and a steel rod ball that represented the world with another steel rod representing the equator. It was perched on the partially rocky beach which lapped the water on the high tide.

The Jewel of Raja Ampat

My next destination was Wayag, the Jewel of Raja Ampat. Although I had seen many photos of the region, I thought how the places could get any better than where I have been. But Indonesia does not disappoint, it does get better. I had a great south-westerly that pushed me along comfortably. There were limited south-westerlies this time of year, as it was the monsoonal season, therefore, motor sailing mostly. It is a great feeling when you get a little bit of wind in the direction you need to go, even at 8.0 knots.

Wayag is the last group of islands northwest of the Raja Ampat, it consists of three main islands Pulau Alogo, Pulau Lage Genan, and Pulau Laye Peley, and dozens of smaller rocky islets in between. They created a maze through these tall limestone islets, with its crystal-clear turquoise waters, small little beaches, and safe isolated anchorages with sandy floors easily visible to anchor. I sailed along the southern side from southeast to northwest and made my way through the maze to an entrance on the western side passing several live aboard boats, that are motor sailors with two masts. These large accommodation vessels bring divers in from around the world. I made my way to the far east and anchored off a small beach on Pulau Lage Genan, the middle island. The most protected safe anchorage one could wish for. I could see the anchor and entire chain laid out in this clear crystal waters. The beach had fishing racks where local fisherman dried their fish. I found a smoking system in this seasonal fishing camp, that consisted of a fire and timber racks made from local wood made in layers and covered up with palm throngs.

I spent the day exploring by tender this incredible waterway and climbed a hill that had a track along with a climbing rope to the top to see the most spectacular view. It truly is justified calling Wayab the jewel of Raja Ampat. From the top of the hill, I could clearly see the live aboard vessels coming in cautiously to set a safe anchor, and also to the far distance of the sea that I had travelled and also out west to where I would be travelling next. Another fulfilling moment.

There was a couple of days of repairs too. It seemed that if you are not sailing, then you are doing repair and maintenance. I had blown a water hose for the water maker that needed replacing, the next job was trying to figure out why there was power lost on the outboard motor, finally, discovering I needed a new spark plug. I have most essential spare parts on board, and then my hand turned to pizza bread making. My *Iridium* satellite system was playing up, but I had another back up, an *Iridium Mini Go*, a blessing due to the fault.

I then sailed west to anchor on a small island named Pulau Sais, as I needed to cross the Halmahera Sea, and I calculated I could sail it in a day if I departed from there. Pulau Sais was a beautiful sandy island opposite to the high limestone rocky pinnacle islands that I had become familiar with throughout Raja Ampat. I anchored just off a break on the southwest side, I did not venture to the island and stayed on board so as to leave two hours before light and have enough time to arrive at my destination Pulau Otto (aka Woto) well within the daylight hours. It is easier to leave in the dark as you know the area in the light of day on arrival, but to arrive in the dark is too dangerous with bommies and fishing vessel unlit.

Sunrises and sunsets are always welcome, and this was no exception, I passed an old boat that had the diving flags up, also why reducing nighttime sailing is paramount. The day brought small squalls in fact they were welcome for any wind that came along and pushed me was much appreciated. Passing a lone fisherman and a large humpback whale which had the tail up, quite close to his little craft.

The charts stated volcanic activity, so I sailed to the south of an active underwater volcano that is known to cause some grief now and then. I thought it was wise not to sail too close just in case, besides, it was marked only thirty metres below the surface. I made good timing and anchored on the southeast side of Pulau Otto, just between the two surf breaks of both the east side and west side. It was a southwesterly and the prediction was a northerly which was why I anchored there. Unfortunately, again the weather prediction was wrong, and an uncomfortable anchorage was had. So, as dawn approached, I weighed

CHAPTER SEVENTEEN

anchor and sailed north to a comfortable anchorage in a cove, off the large island of Halmahera.

I used satellite imagery to look for the sand to give me an idea of the anchorage but when you are in volcanic sand country, you cannot see due to the blackness of the sand. This anchorage was near Tanjung village, pleasant enough but when I went ashore by tender, there was a swell that made me surf into the black sandy beach. Although successfully surfed, I broke one of my paddles doing so. I know of many yachties who have flipped their dingy in these situations, so I have been very fortunate but have lost count of the times waves have swamped me making it to shore.

Halmahera is the largest island in the Maluku region. It is nearly 200 miles long north to south, and very narrow in some places, only twelve and fifty miles wide east to west. It consists of sixteen volcanoes, many of which are still active. I had been told of a retreat on Miti Island that lies just off the East Coast of Halmahera. I sailed there by rounding the head northeast of Tanjung along the way passing the notorious FADs.

Fish Aggregating Device are either timber platforms or, in a lot of cases, large steel cylinders some being the length of my yacht. They are anchored to the sea floor and are used to attract and catch fish. They are a real concern if and when they break free, because to hit these monstrous steel cylinders could be fatal. They are even anchored in areas where vessels are on route, hence, reducing nighttime sailing in these waters is a must.

Arriving in Miti Island from the north is the safest route, as two sections to the south has overhead cables across the waterway from island to island. This is a great safe anchorage, and I had several beers in the bar an eco-style place that served meals. The island itself was fascinating and I walked throughout a coconut plantation island in the village named Temat. The entire village was built along the Japanese airstrip that was created during the invasion by Japan in World War II. I bought what supplies I could from the tiny stores but discovered that there was not an abundance of supplies.

After a few days, I headed to Tobelo that was only a couple of hours north, and what a sight to behold. As I sailed into the port anchorage, the volcano behind the township was bellowing huge amounts of smoke. In the evenings, loud call to prayers amplified from the various mosques throughout this reasonably large town of 85,000 people.

These ports with large populations are a crowded place, but exciting with all types of seafarers coming and going with their cargo. I would make my dingy ride to town arrange a Tuk-Tuk and have a fuel run. I visited the local markets and bought my fresh produce as well as dry stores from the grocery stores, and experienced helpful people arranging the supplies to assist me with backpack to bring back to the tender.

I sailed around the top of Halmahera. On the tip of the northern peninsula was the little village of Supu and considering it was a light south-westerly wind, I decided that would be my destination for the next anchorage. On leaving Tobelo, there was no wind whatsoever, but turning around the top of the peninsula towards Supu, the wind was a north-westerly. Again, *Predict Wind* was not good at predicting. The coastline to my portside was awash with large waves crashing onto the rocky coast and as dark was falling my belief that Supu was going to be a great anchorage was diminishing.

The wind was up to fourteen knots making it, a not so good place to anchor, but as it was becoming dark very quickly, I decided to drop the pick just back from a surf break that I thought would be alright. I could see the local natives fishing along the beach and had a view of the tiny village of Supu. I stayed on the yacht and had the alarms very tightly adjusted in case of a drag. It was a very rolling night, and I stayed in the cockpit to sleep just in case. As the nighttime call to prayers finished, I fell asleep in this rolling anchorage.

The morning brought the south-westerly wind and away I sailed rounding the top of Halmahera peninsula and headed south along the western coast. Halmahera (which means "motherland") is the largest island in the Molucca archipelago.

Log: Sunday, 29 January 2023; 0935 hours; The Captain of *MV Bahas* **called and talked on VHF, as he steered his container ship on my starboard side.**

The views of a few volcanoes were spectacular from the sea sailing south, I made anchor late afternoon in an incredibly sheltered bay off the main island opposite Pulau Nusa Kahatola. From here, I took several photos of three different volcanoes and one photo of all three together. Again, I was visited by local boats who told me they could get me crayfish or Udang Karang in Bahasa. Early the next morning, they were back with two crayfish and a string of fish tied by a vein. The crays cost me equivalent of AUD$2.50 each, and the string of

CHAPTER SEVENTEEN

fish AUD$7 and what a grand breakfast they made, the crays freshly cooked along with freshy baked bread while looking at the wonderful sight of three volcanoes in a row.

I made a dingy ride into the village and was greeted by friendly people at the wharf. I was given a ride on the back of a motorbike over the hill to the village itself where I met a girl who could speak English. She came to greet me and proudly showed me around her town. Before I knew it, there were dozens of people walking with us. She invited me to her home and the entire family along with the neighbours came to greet me. Her name was Nadya, and her sister, Kathryn, they escorted me back to the boat and offered to show me a waterfall on another island the next day, I naturally accepted and picked them up the following morning.

The waterfall was across the bay on Pulau Nusa Kahatola. After navigating the tender over the coral, we were at the base of this magnificent waterfall at a height of 100 feet. It had a great amount of water flowing over it. The girls told me they couldn't swim, so I motored the tender straight under the waterfall where it was full of water in no time. What a refreshing feeling of the cool fresh water washing away the sea salt.

CHAPTER EIGHTEEN

When asked, what is the biggest mistake one can make in life, the Buddha replied, the biggest mistake is you think you have time.

Islands of the Volcanoes

Log: Thursday, 2 March 2023; 0710 hours; light rain, winds of south and south-easterlies; Destination Tauroici village.

A couple of hours underway, the skies cleared to a nice sunny day, and the wind turned to a northerly. That was a great relief, and I flew the spinnaker downwind. It was peaceful sailing. Although the wind was only five knots, I was able to get 4.0 knots SOG for nearly the entire passage with a large pod of dolphins riding the bow waves.

Arriving at the village at 1720 hours, I saw it had a large pier stretching out some distance from the land due to the large fringe coral reef prolific around the village. The next day, I visited the village and again, met very friendly, welcoming people. The village had both Muslim and Christian population. Walking along the street, I met many people in the Muslim area where a religious event was taking place on the main street, and they were cooking up meals for the large community. Here, like most places on these islands you get the rock-star feeling, as many requested to take selfies with you.

I continued along the village where I was greeted by a large group, one of the girls could speak good English. Her name was Putry, a delightful person who invited me to visit her community in the Christian area. Putry showed me around the village with a large entourage of people following us throughout along with her family home and

CHAPTER EIGHTEEN

store. Putry along with her mother, aunt, and nephew came back to *Never Die Wondering II* to visit the vessel. Like most of the population, they had never been on a yacht before.

I left Tauroici and sailed the short distance of ten nautical miles to the island of Ternate, the home of the spice clove, along with an impressive volcano. The volcano is live and the large community lived along the base of this impressive volcano pumping out plumes of sulphur. At Ternate, finding an anchorage was very difficult. All of the vessels in the harbour were on swing moorings, and coral bommies were everywhere. After an hour, I was able to drop the pick between the Customs and police boats in six metres of water, close to the police station and the port pilot jetty.

From the bank, I had a feller giving me directions saying it was okay to drop anchor there. When I was comfortable that the anchor was set, I ventured to the jetty. The Port pilots offered their assistance if I needed, and ensured me it was safe where I was anchored. The person who was telling me where to drop anchor offered me his assistance saying that he helped out yachties who visited. I needed to do a fuel run so we agreed he would be back the following day to assist. The rest of the day was spent exploring this large town and meeting its people.

The following morning, the person who offered to assist, texted me saying he had a tray truck, and a price was negotiated. Two people assisted me in the fuel run which consisted of fuelling up 140 litres of diesel and carting back to the tender. During the process, I bought them both lunch. When loading the tender with the fuel, this person insisted on jumping into the tender wanting to see *Never Die Wondering II*. There was no room to do so, so I refused his request. Also, he was a little too pushy, I thought, and that gave off bad vibes.

Later on, after I spent the rest of the day polishing fuel, Stephanie a local girl who I had met the previous day contacted me from the shore. She had come with her brother, a senior Air Force police officer. I picked them up from the shore and brought them to the vessel for coffee. During this time, I started receiving texts from the person who had arranged my fuel run. He obviously had been watching me. "Liar! I see you have people on your boat," he said. This continued late into the night as I ignored all calls and messages from him. He started threatening me, saying, "I swear I kill you; I will blow your boat up!" A complete nutter who had his nose out of joint for not being allowed on my vessel.

While I was sleeping that night, the threatening messages kept coming. In all honesty, I was not worried at all. I truly believed he was just a fruit loop venting is anger at not being allowed on my vessel, but then again, an unhinged person is capable of anything, so I kept my crossbow along with my machete close by.

My history of defending myself in my home with a firearm nearly twenty-eight years ago, was an event that was still very raw in my mind. Even though I had shot a known criminal attacking me in my own home along with another violent criminal, I was charged, and was on bail for a year waiting trial whereafter a judge along with a twelve-person jury decided to set me free or send me away for twenty-five years. The result was "not guilty on all charges as self-defence", and I had my firearms ordered to be returned to me. It was a horrible ordeal and to stand in a prison dock facing twenty-five years behind bars is something I never want to experience again.

If that fruit loop swam out the short distance to the vessel, history may repeat itself, and defending myself in a foreign country might have a different outcome. So, I contacted the authorities, the port pilot fellers, and the police. They were all very helpful and assured me, they would make sure nothing happened since they were all proud of their peaceful island where instances of murder were zero. The pilot fellers even took me out for lunch on the back of their motorbikes the next day.

A couple of days later, I ran into the fruit loop. "It's you!" I yelled pointing at him and he quickly ran away. Derri, one of the pilots, discovered from the police that the nutter had quickly jumped on a ferry and left the island. In all honesty, I do not think he was a real threat just making silly threats. This was the only bad situation with a person I had experienced in six months of travelling and meeting literally hundreds of people throughout dozens of islands in Indonesia.

Ternate is home to over 200,000 people. Their homes lie at the base of the volcano known as Mount Gamalama that towers over the city and surrounding villages at 1,715 meters above sea level. Ternate is the home to the spice, clove, as is Banda Islands the home to nutmeg. The clove is a flower bud from the clove tree which is dried and used whole or grounded to preserve food, create extra flavour, or garnish food. China valued this spice as an aphrodisiac. It is also used as a perfume for either the mouth or into the manufacture of cigarettes in later years. As with the nutmeg spice at Banda on the south of the Molucca Archipelago, Ternate cloves growing in the northern archipelago in the rich volcanic soil, had the Portuguese, Spaniards, and Dutch fight over this flower bud. Just like Banda Neira atrocities were also committed to the local people.

Ternate had been ruled by Sultans since 1200 AD with many of the island people descending from Malay origins. I met a local who was a history buff and showed me around the island riding on the back of his motorbike visiting the four forts that had been occupied by many colonial powers since the arrival of the Portuguese in 1512. Incredibly, it was the king of Portugal, Manuel I, who sent a fleet to intercept the Spanish fleet of Ferdinand Magellan on his way to the Spice Islands after exploring the Americas. The fleet was ordered to construct a fort on the island of Ternate and the construction started in 1522 on the southwest side of the island.

In 1570, after several Portuguese governorships, the stupidity and the brutality of the Portuguese came to a head when they captured and imprisoned the Ternate Sultan, Hairun, and executed him within the walls of Fort Kastela. The local Ternates didn't take kindly to their beloved Sultan being murdered by the invaders. The new appointed Sultan Babullah Datu Shah took military action, knowing they were no match to the Portuguese weapons like war cannons. Cleverly, he had the fort surrounded whereby the Portuguese were besieged in their own fort. Incredibly, they were prisoners within their own fort for an entire five years, eventually surrendering in 1575. They handed the fort to the locals before fleeing to Ambon that was occupied by the Portuguese.

Walking through the rubble and ruins of the fort with some of the walls intact, one wonders how these Portuguese soldiers survived the five years. They had to eat what they produced within the walls and obviously some died of starvation. Oh well, that's what you get for murdering someone in their own home! The true definition of a home invasion.

In 1605, the Dutch VOC arrived and captured Ternate and its neighbouring island, Tidore, also a volcanic island engaged in clove production. Then, in 1606, history repeated itself as the Spanish in a recently created union with Portugal captured the island and Fort Kastella taking the then Sultan, Saidi Berkat, hostage. However, they sent him in exile to Manilla, Philippines. The Dutch came back in 1607 and island was divided between the two powers—Spaniards and Dutch. The former departed the islands in 1663, and the Dutch occupied until the British took control in 1810. After only seven years, control returned to the Dutch again. During World War II, the Japanese took control of Ternate until its independence in 1945. So, the poor islanders had invaders after invaders over four hundred years.

There were a couple of scenic lakes formed by past volcanic eruptions, the motorbike rider told me he had seen crocodiles in the lake which did not have an overflow, a water-locked lake within high volcanic rocky walls. Every time he told people of crocodiles, he was laughed at, until a young boy was killed by the large reptile when swimming with friends. So, now it was common knowledge of the crocodiles living in, what they believed, was a bottomless lake.

The weather had turned terrible with a north-easterly to easterly meaning *Never Die Wondering II* was exposed and winds were well over thirty knots. Three days went by, and I was unable to leave the yacht, in fact, it dragged a couple of times, and I had to reset anchor and get out more chain for scope. Six ships rafted up to each other on the wharf and it was very close to my stern, only sixty metres, but there was no other option to anchor anywhere else so I had to grin and bear it. Terrible rolling nights! In the afternoon, a boat passed by having broken off the mooring and was retrieved by the pilot boat. The stormy conditions continued.

Later in the day, I was looking at the police boat for I was using it to gauge if I dragged when I heard a slight yell. I looked carefully and saw a head, bobbing out of the waves at the bow of the police boat. This old feller was holding onto the mooring rope in desperation. I quickly dropped the tender into the water and attempted to pick him up but the waves were smashing high on the concrete pier walls. I had to come from the leeward side for safety and not to go over the top of him, it was easy to capsize the tender. I dragged the poor feller onto the dingy and then back to my vessel, wrapped him in a blanket, and gave him warm coffee. He told me he had gone in the water to check the police boat when there was a small window of the wind reducing, but up it came again before he could climb aboard. He was holding on to the mooring trying to survive, gulping sea water, and thinking it was time to meet his maker. When he had recovered enough to swim the short distance to the concrete pier, I gave him a life jacket for keeping and away he went with his family now on the pier structure waiting for him, a very close call.

Anchoring close to the port area is not the safest place to anchor but like so many islands in the Indonesian Archipelago, you have limited options. Watching Derri and his team of pilots, piloting monstrous ships into the wharf with only a small timber craft as their tug pilot boat with a small outboard is in itself a spectacularly skilled job nor is it for the faint hearted. They visited my vessel for coffee and were amazed to see the modern technology I had, as the only thing they had on the pilot boats, besides a couple of lights, was a handheld VHF radio.

Crossing the Molucca Sea

The Customs visited me on my last morning at port, when I was about to depart. They requested me to come to their office and have the Harbour Master stamp my documents. This was the first time I had done this, as all the ports I had been anchored in were not manned by port officers. After that, it was photo time again with the Harbour Master, and then, I was away to sail across the Molucca Sea. It was going to be another overnighter, but the weather was in my favour and I needed to take advantage of it. The pilot, Derri, came to the jetty and brought me food for my trip, as well as Stephanie and her mother brought me pizza. The hospitality and generosity of these people are second to none.

At 1020 hours, I departed for Bitung Sulawesi rounding the southern side of Ternate with a bearing of 285° direction and a light southwesterly. It was a pleasant sail watching the volcanoes of Ternate and Tidore slowly disappearing in the background.

Man cannot discover new oceans, unless he has the courage to leave the shore.

Log: Saturday, 18 February 2023; 1500 hours; Sighted large humpback whale blow ahead.

At night, I passed the island of Tifore. I was planning to visit this isolated island in the Molucca Sea, but time was of essence due to the good weather window. Besides, it was too difficult to pull in during the night, as I would have to heave too. Hence, I kept going, passing the odd fishing vessel at night, and only having a very short power nap at a time.

Log: Sunday, 19 February 2023; 400 hours.

I encountered fishing boats galore and a large passenger ferry with no AIS. During the morning, I passed long floating nets. I was so glad it was daylight as I was able to steer out of the way. To reach the Port of Bitung, you must come through the channel where the main island of Sulawesi is on the west, with the Pulau Lembeh on the east. As a marker, the southern cape of Lembeh had a huge, tall statue of Jesus with arms spread out, giving the feeling of a greeting into Bitung.

I anchored for the night on the Pulau Lembeh side, on an anchorage marked on my charts, that is adjacent to a water village. I was exhausted after the night sail of a twenty-seven-hour passage and was glad to have found a great sand spot. When I commenced to drop anchor, a local villager called out, "Tadik, tadik!" His gestures told me, he did not want me to anchor there. So, I went a little bit further away and dropped anchor. I had the impression he didn't want me anchoring anywhere there but by then, I had the local village children paddle out on a large piece of foam to greet me, much friendlier than the feller on the shore. The water village had long lines from the village, strung all the way to the shore. They would stand on a raft of sorts and hand pull themselves across the water to the shore. Incredible transport to get to land!

I spent a couple of nights in the cove arranging the departure for immigration, then the following day motored over to Biting and anchored in the port amongst the fishing boats.

Log: Tuesday, 21 February 2023.

Anchored at fisherman wharf, I arranged a truck to collect containers of diesel, and the supplies I bought. I visited Immigration and after having the documentation approved, I had to appear at the Harbour Master for my departure forms. Once that was completed, it was the turn of customary photo session where the officials would request a photo with me. The supplies bought from the local market, I was back on board for departure at 0630 hours, the following morning. Philippines, here I come!

Once you depart from a country, you are not allowed to visit any of its islands on the way. However, I planned to anchor off the islands in both Indonesia and the Philippines without going ashore, and if all went to plan, I would be able to reach Samal Island in Davao, Philippines by daylight sailing. The predicted weather was for extremely light northerlies. Since, I was sailing windward, I knew this would be motor sailing all the way but with hardly any wind predicted,

CHAPTER EIGHTEEN

I thought it would not be a problem. How wrong those predictions were going to be!

Once I sailed through the channel away from Sulawesi and back into the Molucca Sea, there was a westerly wind at twenty-one knots and the current strongly coming from the east. Hence, the washing machine situation occurred and what a rough passage away from the island of Sulawesi. It seemed the seas of the Molucca were being sucked into the Celebes Sea, passing through many small islands, and creating this rough confusing sea effect. Although my speed was 6.6 knot SOG, at least I could sail.

Late afternoon, I arrived at the channel between Pulau Ruang and Pulau Tagulandang, both volcanic islands with the lava flow from recent years showing as hardened from the top of the volcano to right at the water's edge and into the channel. Nearby was a fishing vessel, so I decided to drop anchor in ten metres depth. A large pod of melon head whales was feeding in the channel and soon made their way back out to sea. There had been light rain on and off all day and the top of the volcano gave an eerie look covered in mist. The remaining vegetation next to the lava track was of coconut palms.

Pirate Waters

Log: Thursday, 23 February 2023; 0550 hours.

Departed but was unwell due to something I ate. I got some medicine in a tablet form as I hardly take any other. I drank only tea and dry biscuits thereafter as I beat towards wind at 30° direction with light winds.

The view of a smoking volcano was magnificent, and I sailed along the east side of Pulau Siau and entered the protected cove of Pulau Kahakitang from the east. The sun was setting creating an incredibly bright light on the palm foliage in several gorges while the surf pounded the coastline. Entering into this little cove from the north of the island was a great feeling of safety. The island had a distinctive claw-like shape. I anchored near a couple of huts and again had the local inhabitants come to meet me. Coffee was put on and biscuits were offered. An old woman paddling a timber craft with two outriggers, went past with a small child in the bow section. She had a large cane basket of vegetable produce. I was anchored near a larger abandoned vessel, that looked like it had been a small ferry.

The next day, I sailed along the eastern side of Pulau Sangihe and made my way to an island named Kawalusu that seemed a reasonable anchorage for the northerlies. On the satellite, it showed a pier so I hoped the sounding would be somewhat more reliable. When I arrived, there were a lot of people fishing off the pier, the village was further along in a northerly direction.

I was on the bow looking for a patch free of coral in the clear water. The people on the pier were indicating at me to keep going. It might be alright for a shallow draft fishing boat but too many close coral bommies for my liking. I found a patch of sand and dropped anchor, and as soon as I was secure, I was greeted by three fellers on a timber craft paddling up to the sugar scoop. The person in the back was paddling and had a light-coloured shirt on, the one in the middle was wearing a camouflage shirt, and the one in the front of the craft had a short-sleeved shirt.

The front one asked, "Can we step aboard?"

I agreed and stepped down the sugar scoop step, and held the bow along with the tether line. While I was tethering the line to the cleat of my vessel, this person stepped onto the vessel and all of a sudden, he leant over back into the bow section and pulled out a semi-automatic rifle. In quick reflex, I placed an open hand up on the firearm against his chest, "What's with the gun?" I yelled and was about to push him overboard.

The middle feller stood up promptly, "It's okay, sir. We are the army." The person with the firearm also repeated, "We are the army, although in plain clothes."

I did not know what to believe or say. They then explained that their superiors asked them to come aboard because it was the pier to their barracks. Everyone on the pier were soldiers out of uniform. I was very relieved to say the least and the two came aboard and I showed them all documentation of my departure.

Over a mobile call, a senior officer asked me if I could come to the fort. I declined stating that since I had departed Indonesia (although still in the waters), I cannot break the law and venture ashore. They accepted my excuse and returned to the fort but gave me their direct contact and explained they were there if I needed assistance. They explained their presence was because of the pirates in the waters I was now venturing across and asked me to be careful. They then returned

CHAPTER EIGHTEEN

to the barracks. Within an hour, two paddling crafts came with soldiers, and they had brought *Pisang Goreng* or fried banana for me. Terrific people! They also gave me an army hat as a gift.

The next morning, I was away. The weather was terrible, blowing strong on the nose and I had to beat several times towards the next island. I had decided to sail straight for Sarangani Islands in the Philippines as it was only seventy nautical miles. However, due to the strong head winds, two small passages would be more suited, I reasoned.

Log: Saturday, 25 February 2023; 1000 hours; storm hit, creating large swells over the bow, 30 knot winds.

I made anchorage at Pulau Kawio, a small island with a great concrete jetty. I dropped the pick in sand in six metres of water. I received the weather report of gust warnings for the next few days. I was glad to have an early day as I had been smashing through gusts of up to thirty knots for the last couple of days, so I decided to wait for a better weather window. In the meantime, I blew another water hose fitting on the water maker and had to replace it. Then, I made pizza and waited out the weather. As usual, seven local boys came onto the yacht for photo session. I think I have become camera shy after Indonesia.

After three nights on anchor, the weather prediction showed another small window of wind reduction, but again this would be totally, incorrect. I was beating towards Sarangani Islands and keeping as close to the wind as possible at 30°.

Log: Tuesday, 28 February 2023; 0940 hours; sighted the Philippines' high ranges; 1045 hours; crossed international border of the Philippines.

A great feeling being in another country, but the sailing conditions were still terrible. I wanted to sail into the Sarangani Islands in the middle of the two main islands, unfortunately, my sailing angle was not going to allow for this. The next option was to head to the west of Balut Island.

At 1445 hours, the Philippines Navy warship called me via VHF and requested all my details, they also offered me assistance if need be. It was very reassuring to have the Indonesian army and now the Philippines navy within the vicinity of *Never Die Wondering II* as the waters were known for pirate activity and there was a warning to avoid the area if possible. On the far southwest side of Balut Island, I dropped anchor but dragged some distance due to the strong current. So, I went forward and had the Navy warship requesting to raft up with me. I had to decline until I reset the anchor and got good holding. Once I did so, the Navy warship approached all armed with some serious weapons along with guard dogs. They carefully placed fenders along their vessel as not to damage mine, then without assistance jumped aboard and searched the vessel very carefully. When they had an all clear and realised, I was not a potential pirate, they presented me with a coffee mug. The men of *BRB RAFAEL PARGAS (PC379)* also explained that I had to be alert for pirates and offered their assistance. If in need, I knew to call them.

It was a great greeting into the Philippines, now I only needed to go another 120 nautical miles to clear in Davao. Maybe three days day sailing!

CHAPTER NINETEEN

A great sailor isn't made from sailing on calm waters.

Smashing Windward

Log: Wednesday, 1 March 2023; 0430 hours, Depart.

Balut Island is one of the two Sarangani islands, I would have liked to visit but for the obvious reasons of not clearing into the Philippines, I needed to keep going to clear in at Davao first. I sailed towards the mainland of Mindanao, the second largest island in the Philippines. The sea was lumpy with wind over tide and then at 0730 hours, I was able to sail at 7.0 knots SOG along the Mindanao coast. One of the first things you notice is the coconut plantations high up on the hills, covering the steep side. Obviously, it took intense physical work climbing up these hills harvesting the coconut, in some places you could see banana trees too.

At 1050 hours, the winds were back to twenty knots on the nose, so I was forced to beat windward. I was covering a lot more miles than what I wanted, and then winds increased further to "strong" and *Never Die Wondering II* was again smashing her way forward, not ideal. I reached Bonos Point, a great anchorage, dropping the pick in fifteen metres of water surrounded by other fishing boats. I was glad to be there, to relax as it was a calm anchorage compared to the northly winds out of the cove.

The next morning, I was away at 0535 hours. Again, the wind was fresh, and another day of beating windward in rough conditions continued, I was becoming exhausted. Since leaving Sulawesi, Indonesia, a lot of times it would get to thirty knots of terrible going, windward smashing through the swells. The great sailing I had following the trade winds was now a distant memory. If I had the predictions showing these strong winds, I don't think I would have sailed to the Philippines. The weather predictions showed ten knots maximum instead. So much for modern-age weather forecasts!

I started to encounter many fishing vessels that make it dangerous sailing without good visibility. Before I knew it, another small one-man *bangka* vessel would appear forcing me to quickly tack, then only a few more miles along and another would appear. Besides, the cloudy conditions made it difficult to see buoys indicating fishing nets. At 1530 hours, I anchored in a beautiful cove about which I wrote in my log, "paradise, very calm, after a difficult sail". The passage to here should only have been a short run but due to the windward beating, I added 30% more in distance. Anyway, being in this tranquil cove made up for the terrible day. There was a beach that lined the cove at Tubalan Head, although some areas were netted off. I quickly came to the decision, after dodging many fishing vessels, only to sail when there is good visibility.

The *PredictWind* finally showed that the next day would be thirty knot winds right on the nose, so I stayed resting up as I really needed to recoup. I removed items from the sail lockers to dry as the sails became soaked by the swells smashing over the bow.

Log: Saturday, 4 March 2023; 0530 hours; departed with seventeen then twenty-one knots wind northerly.

I was heading towards Samal Island but with the wind increasing on my portside, I sailed 60° to the wind in what is the Gulf of Davao then changed tack to beat towards the south-eastern side of the island. Another Navy warship called requesting details, and I passed fishing vessel after fishing vessel, trying to keep my distance as I could tell many were dragging nets. I sailed along the west side of Talikud Island that is on the south-eastern side of Samal and is an extremely large island just off the city of Davao. after passing Talikud, I could clearly see the skyscrapers of Davao.

I anchored in a bay of Samal and had to dive under the yacht to remove a large nylon net that was wrapped around the keel and rudder. So glad that I was sailing without motors or they would have tangled the net on the propeller. I needed to go under with the hooker gear as it took a lot of cutting. I was anchored off Penaplata township and

CHAPTER NINETEEN

raised the yellow quarantine flag with the Philippines flag with the Australian flag below on the starboard side. I called the coast guard, and asked where I should anchor for clearance, they said they would call back but they never did. I tried to call Immigration but to no avail. So, after waiting there two nights, I departed for the marina on Samal Island where I also tried to call in vain.

Samal Island

Log: Monday, 6 March 2023.

I passed Davao City on the portside and sailed into Oceanview Marina on the northern most point of Samal Island. The marina contacted the Immigration department and notified them of my arrival. The following morning, I was to visit the Immigration department for all the formalities. I was to stay on Samal Island for a ten-month period working on the vessel with a refit.

I had to repair the bulkhead that I had managed to open up. There was an old wound, a crack through the bulkhead itself. I only discovered it after pulling out a wall trying to find where the rainwater was coming from. All those miles windward, reopened what was so obviously a previously damaged bulkhead, not repaired properly. It required fibre-glassing along with repairs to the wall in the cabin that required re-bracing. I sanded back, epoxy coated and stained most of the timber work and had the upholstery inside the saloon and cockpit all redone. I serviced the engines, and then it was the start of the monsoonal. The Oceanview Marina was in a safe zone for typhoon season, so I decided to stay for the monsoonal.

I started seeing a local woman, Lovely Jane. She was an exotic looking islander whose first name was Lovely and her middle name Jane. I visited many places in Samal Island and the Davao region with Lovely, along with experiencing the vibrant culture and festivals. Lovely was once a cultural dancer of her tribal area or Barangay. These festivals were fantastic, tribal groups dressed in vibrant colours with incredible costumes, traditional dancing, music from the likes of many drums, and acting out their cultural stories. I socialised with the yachtie community of Samal the likes of Niven Robertson, a Scotsman, and his local wife, Hazel. They had sailed halfway around the world and now were doing a major refit on their catamaran on the hard. There was only a hand full that lived at Oceanview, the likes of old Jim in his mid-eighties who had sailed from southern Australia. Coincidentally, he was a teacher where my son went to school and had built his yacht in the school grounds. It really is a small world. It had taken Jim many years to complete building his vessel, he then only had a year of sailing, when Covid-19 restricted his movements. After that, he unfortunately had a major stroke that ended his sailing ability. He said, "The biggest regret I have in my life is that I should have gone sailing a lot earlier than I did!"

I found Samal was an ideal island to wait out the monsoonal and work on the vessel. There were armed security guards, and the marina had a gate across the entrance. All this security was due to the horrendous kidnapping that took place at Oceanview in 2015 when the terrorist group, Abu Sayyaf, entered the marina armed with assault rifles, taking four yachties hostage. They later let one of the hostages free who was a Filipino woman, the other three, two Canadians and a Swedish feller, were held captive for ransom. Canada refused to pay the terrorists so one of the Canadians was beheaded and the other was threatened with death unless a ransom was paid. When that also was refused, the other Canadian was beheaded too. The Swedish feller was eventually let go after a payment was believed to have been made. A shocking event that resulted in Davao and the region being extremely well-armed due to the continued threat of terrorist groups. To be honest, I found Samal Island and Davao, a large city of nearly two million people, to be the safest city I have spent time at. This is after I have spent time throughout the world. It has very little crime, extremely polite and helpful people. You know a place has minimum crime when most taxi drivers place their change on the dashboard.

While on Samal, I had the interior timber brought back by sanding and stain. I had new seating in the saloon galley area along with the cockpit. Unfortunately, I cooked the batteries due to overcharging by way of surges in the main power. I imported batteries from China for half of the price as in Australia. A new dodger was made, engines serviced, and many other small jobs done. I carted parts and supplies in a tribike which is a motorbike with a cabin by Jeson, a local islander who was my driver for the ten-month period. He picked me up from the marina and drove me to the ferry or the local island town of Babak which was a haze of smoke in the evening due to *lechon* or the spit-roasted method of cooking chicken (*lechon manok*) or pork (*lechon baboy*).

CHAPTER NINETEEN

Not far from the marina was a bat cave, Monfort Bat Sanctuary, that had two million Rousette fruit bats much smaller than the Australian version. The bats would cover the walls of the caves that had two enormous open ceilings. Lace monitor lizards could be seen feeding from the unfortunate bat that was the closest to the reptile. During the war, when the Japanese invaded the Philippines and committed atrocities, a lot of the native population families hid in the cave to avoid capture. When one stands above the enormous cave and smells the terrible stench along with the extreme heat that millions of bats create, you wonder how they lasted hiding in this place which was apparently for a very long time.

Log: Saturday, 20 January 2024; 0950 hours; Depart Oceanview Marina.

After ten months, I now was on my way to explore a lot more islands of the Philippines. As soon as I was out of the marina, up went the head sail in a nice northerly and I sailed around the eastern side of Samal. I had done a few day trips before too. At 1205 hours, I changed tack with a wind shift to north-westerly and I dodged the FADS across the Davao Gulf into Borot Cove. I was looking to drop the anchor amongst the fishing vessels in this little cove, when I heard the horrible noise of the keel on the ground. I revved the motors in reverse as I had grounded on the portside and dropped anchor in another spot in ten metres of water. However, with a wind shift, I found myself touching the ground again. There was no damage, but I was frustrated on grounding.

The next morning, I was away hoisted the spinnaker and was sailing in relatively quiet with the exception of an unfamiliar sound coming from the stern of the vessel. I went below and removed the hatch and looked through the manhole to the stern area that is below the sugar scoop. To my shock, it was full of water. I was in full flight then, so I quickly dropped the spinnaker and went to only drifting along. After that, I removed many buckets full of water. I was concerned that I may have damaged the rudder when I grounded the vessel. *Had I managed to damage it causing it to take in water?*

Once the water was bucketed out and the place vacuumed dry, there was no visible signs of water coming through. I headed back to Borot Cove and anchored in the same spot to assess the situation. I discovered a slit in the exhaust hose that filled up the stern with sea water. To my relief, it was an easy fix by cutting the split out and re-clamping. I had the worst thoughts where I had to go back to Oceanview Marina as several other yachties, I had known, had returned with problems they could not fix at sea.

The next morning while having coffee, I watched a turtle swimming around the vessel. I was back out sailing with the spinnaker up at the same position as the previous day, just so happy it was only a minor repair. My back though was giving me hell as I had pulled a muscle with all the bucketing in a frantic panic. Although I have pumps and a pipe to the stern that I only needed to turn on, I chose to quickly bucket so to see were the leak was. Now, I was paying for it with a strained back.

At 0900 hours, the navy called on the VHF requesting my details, and I decided to anchor in Tagbano Bay. Another problem surfaced with the anchor winch not working, but after minor electrical work, all was fine.

Surf Coast of Mindanao

Log: Tuesday, 23 January 2024.

I was underway as the sun was just coming up dodging the many small fishing vessels, sometimes many would gather at a reef surrounding the area in a considerable distance, so I needed to go wide to avoid another net tangle. I was heading south, out of the Gulf and needed to go around Cape San Agustin then turn 180° and head north towards Mati. They wind was twenty-five knots, and I could see the large swells that I was heading into. So, I decided to go wide around the San Agustin reef to try and keep to deeper waters. As soon as I had rounded the cape and reef, I was in some serious swells with wind over tide and the dreaded smashing of waves underneath started.

The wind was north-easterly, and I needed to bear away more then what I wanted, taking me on a longer route. Still, I needed to obtain somewhat of a comfortable sail, and found myself sailing easterly up and over the large swells that were happening due to the wind over tide. There was also light rain to contend with, and the next thing I knew, I was over a large swell and down into an area with three small fishing vessels, one on my portside, two on my starboard side. I was only metres from them and started yelling to ask if there were nets.

CHAPTER NINETEEN

I was concerned that I might have run over the dreaded nylon, but they were just line fishing thankfully.

I continued out east as opposed to north, trying to get a better and more comfortable angle knowing that I was going to have to beat to Mati, making it a very long day. At one stage, I had 10.0 knots SOG. The constant smashing of the waves under the vessel caused the saloon cabinet and seats to come away from the floor with all its contents, food and gear, all over the place. Then at midday, I was able to head north as the swells had reduced and the sailing was better. By afternoon, I was able to sail closer to the coast. I dodged a dozen FADs during the day, I was exhausted due to the conditions with the constant concern of hitting these hazards and keeping a close watch.

As I was coming into the entrance of Mati Bay, a large whale passed the bow of *Never Die Wondering II* and passed the starboard side of the vessel spraying out its blow hole. I took photos of this magnificent creature which I thought was a mini type of orca, but I could not see any white on his body. Though the large fin with its distinctive slight fall to one side, indicated to me a pygmy orca.

I made my way up past the land mass known as the sleeping dragon as the shape of the hills gives the impression of a dragon lying down, I anchored near the mangroves in an extremely well-protected bay from the northerlies called Balete Bay

The next day, more repairs were due, securing the cabinet back in the saloon, fresh water was dripping into the stern area due to the heavy rain, so that needed waterproofing with silicon on the sugar scoop. I made banana bread and had a couple of local fishermen visit the vessel. I was anchored not far from their large fishing nets. The next day, they took me out fishing Filipino style.

Incredibly, they placed poles into the ground at low tide in a circular fashion, the circle had wings as funnels stretching out 150 metres long. At high tide, they created a commotion scaring the fish along the funnels into the circular trap and closed a netted section trapping everything inside. With goggles they dived, picking up all the catch. There were several types of fishes, crabs, squid, shrimp, and even blow fish renowned to be poisonous. They told me that older members of their family knew how to remove the poison glands and cook it into a delicacy.

While one of the fishermen was in the circular net, he was bitten severely by jelly fish. We got him back to *Never Die Wondering II*, sprayed vinegar on his wounds all over one side of the face and along his neck. The fishermen then took me to their crab logs which were large logs cut in half with individual sections for keeping mud crabs. They sold them in Davao city at a nice price as they were considered a delicacy, often purchased for major events like weddings, etc.

I was shown around their small village and many of the villagers knew my face. It turned out one of the fishermen was filming live via his mobile on *Facebook*. Many were following his live streaming on the vessel anchored at their village.

Log: Friday, 26 January 2024.

After changing a fan belt, I decided to head into clearer water than the mangroves. I needed to get supplies, so I needed to be anchored an easy distance from Mati Township, I sailed over to the southside of the town. The anchorage was recommended by Chris and Samantha who were on a mono, I had known them from Samal Island. For the next week, I experienced the biggest torrential rain I had seen in the Philippines. It rained for eight days straight, probably a good thing as my back really needed a rest. When getting supplies in town, the fuel stations had a metre of water covering the site, so I was not able to top up fuel, but I had enough for the sail to east coast of Mindanao.

Back on the vessel for more repairs, the small pump for the water maker had come loose snapping wires so a little electrical work was needed. The starter motor played up, so I replaced it, also repairs to the bilge pumps were done. It never stops, this maintenance and repairs.

Log: Saturday, 3 February 2024; 0530 hours.

After eight days of rain, finally a little sun, as I sailed out of Mati Bay into the Philippine's Sea. I was having troubles hoisting halyard and knew that bearings in the track was another job to attend to. The wind was blowing at twenty-six knots, and *Never Die Wondering II* handled it reasonably well, riding over the swells fairly comfortably. I had both engines with higher than usual revs as I needed to go against the current and wind.

The Philippine trench is in the floor of the Philippine's Sea that stretches from the northeast Philippine's southerly along the coast of Mindanao and has been measured in places to be more than 10,000 metres. I was warned by many yachties of the strong current against and with the north-easterly trade winds it was challenging to

CHAPTER NINETEEN

say the least. If you hug the coastline, you can sail in depths mostly under 500 metres but thirty-five nautical miles from shore it dropped to 9,000 metres. So, hugging the coastline to try to find the least resistance is favourable.

To my surprise Chris and Smantha passed me many miles off my starboard side returning to Mati. They called to say that they got into turbulent conditions and were not making much ground so decided to head back. All was great at my end, and I was more than happy with my speed. Thank God I had two 40HP motors along with sails.

I reached Mayo Bay and anchored in this sheltered and protected bay. The next morning while checking over the engine, I noticed the fuel in the glass filter separator was a milky colour. Bloody fuel contamination! I then spent the day removing all the fuel from the starboard tank and replacing it with new fuel that I had polished. I had built a separate system of cleaning the fuel that I bring in containers, by having a paper filter and a water separator filtering, so I knew it was clean going in. The portside fuel tank was fine and I thought it must have been fuel from Indonesia that had become varnished on the tank walls in the so called "washing machine" at sea which loosened all, contaminating the fuel. I changed the two micro filters as well before heading off the next morning at first light.

Enchanted River

Log: Monday, 5 February 2024.

It was one of those days where I was wondering what the hell was going to happen next. Ever since leaving Samal Island, I have had so many repairs, along with eight days of consistent rain, and working my way along the coast against the wind and tide. This is not what you would call great sailing. I had not seen a sunrise as every day was cloudy. However, for the first time in weeks a magnificent sunrise brightened up the morning both physically and emotionally. The swells and wind were fair, and I made my way up along the coast walking to the bow while watching a pod of dolphins ride the bow waves. My spirits lifted from "what am I doing here" to *"This is the best place to be and the best time to be here is now"*.

By afternoon, I reached Baganga Bay where the surf was breaking on both sides of the vessel coming into the bay. I kept the safe route in the middle from the point of the surf crashing and a reef with similar surf. I anchored again in a great bay with a village close by called Santo Nino. The next day, I visited the township after I could not land on the beach due to the swells coming into the bay having waves on the beach. Instead, I went to the small port that had a deteriorated concrete wharf. The locals gave me a hand to climb up onto the dilapidated jetty, and there I walked into town. I hired a Tuk-tuk to take me to eat, show me around, as well as buy supplies of fruits and veggies.

I wrote in the log how exhausted I was and badly in need of a rest day. It seemed I was repairing something new every day since leaving Samal Island, or on constant lookout for FADs or fishermen, challenging sails along the coast, or facing torrential rain most of the time. In addition, I was woken up during the night by the alarm on my mobile which read "Earthquake" warning about 130 km away. It was a little concerning to think about tsunami possibilities, but all was fine with reports of no damage.

At 0545 hours, I was away again, in hopes of a pleasant day but within the hour the conditions became wet and miserable. I was still able to get 6.0 knots of SOG, but after midday decided to anchor early and made my way into a small inlet called Barcelona. It was protected by an islet on the east called Maopia Island. After dropping anchor, I was somewhat concerned of being pushed closer to shore so re-anchored closer to the islet and stayed in deeper waters as visibility was not the best to risk anchoring in spots that were marked anchorages. The miserable non-stop rains continued all night.

Log: Thursday, 8 February 2024.

I departed in the wet weather itself because the seas were fine, and I planned to get into Enchanted River at midday. A very scenic bay but I was being extremely careful of the surf breaks and sailing up to where the Enchanted River, comes into the bay. There was a large water village where homes were built on stilts out into the water. I dinged up the river that was reached crossing over coral reefs along with other boats and *bangkas* from the resorts that enter via the river. It was an incredible variety of blueish-coloured fresh stream with an enormous darker blue hole. Apparently, no one had dived to the bottom as legend had it that the river was haunted by supernatural beings that act as protectors to the river. If you swim at night, you will disappear.

CHAPTER NINETEEN

The next morning, I was away in the early hours, as the sun came through the clouds and it was a great day of sailing in pleasant conditions. Although I needed to dodge many solo fishermen in their small *bangkas* paddling out to sea. It was incredible how far out these fishermen went, far from their villages, sometimes experiencing terrible conditions only to paddle the big journey back home and also at night. I anchored in a small, protected cove, an area known as Cagwait. It was extremely calm anchorage that guaranteed a great night's sleep not worrying too much about the anchor dragging. It is always subconsciously on your mind, especially, when the wind picks up at night. It was now only fifty nautical miles to the island of Siargao and I was chomping at the bit to get there knowing that once I did this passage, then there would be no more going against the current, and the wind would be in my favour heading west.

Siargao Island

Log: Saturday, 10 February 2024; 0530 hours.

It looked like a good day with the sun coming through at dawn out east towards the Pacific Ocean. I was to get a nice wind shift in my favour that had me moving along a comfortable 6.0 knots SOG. The wind although up to twenty-four knots but the swells were manageable, and then the portside engine started playing up. *Surely, I could not have run out of fuel*, I thought. Yes, I had for I had been using more than usual and since the rev gauge had stopped working, so I was only guessing the lever was equal to the other engine revs. This was the first time, I had ever continuously run both engines at 2500, and against the wind and strong current, therefore consuming a lot more fuel than calculated.

I anchored in a nice sandy spot between Mamon and La Januza Island in five metres of water with a sand bottom and crystal clear. I was glad to be away from the flooded rivers of Mindanao. I changed the filter and refuelled then bleeded the fuel lines. The next morning, a quick run across to Siargao Island anchoring southwest of the township of Dapa in a well-protected anchorage.

Lacey and Angelina came to meet me, I had known them from Samal Island. They were yachties who had sold their vessel and moved to Siargao. Lacey being Hawaiian had set up a Hawaiian food van, and he showed me around the island. An incredible place, very touristy that had a few miles of surf beaches with surf boards and surfer clothing stores.

There was a variety of eating places and bars mostly western style hamburgers and pizzas. I preferred staying at Dapa as I had become accustomed to Filipino food such as, Adobo dishes, *barboy*, etc. It is incredible how one changes their eating preferences, trying to avoid most processed foods. I also stopped having sugar, conscious about keeping fit mind and body for sailing. I was to spend two weeks on Siargao Island. I hired a motorbike and rode around exploring the island that had large coconut plantations, and incredible estuaries of mangrove lined creeks. The surf coast reminded me of Apollo Bay in Victoria of the 70s but with a tropical feel. Siargao had villages on the actual beach itself with sand or dirt roads. After the two weeks of really resting, I obtained my supplies and fuel and was off sailing with the wind on my side.

Log: Saturday, 24 February 2024; depart 0550 hours.

I headed out of the anchorage following the route between Abanay Island which is marked with the red and green buoys. In the Philippines, they follow the American system were coming into port, the green should be on your portside and the red should be on your starboard side, the opposite to Australia and Indonesia. The ferries that come through this very long narrow channel do not have AIS, therefore, you do not know if another vessel has entered the channel until you are nearly through the channel. Then they speed through causing you to move off the channel slightly, with strong currents and rocks nearby on a low tide it can be very intimidating to say the least.

The day was greeted with appreciation as the desired winds were now in my favour and for the first time in many weeks, the sailing was great. The light winds only made slow speed, but it was terrific with no noisy motors, just the power of the wind taking me to my next destination. I passed several islands and the city of Surigao to the south. I received the call from the Navy on the VHF with the same request for location of destination and port of departure.

I crossed over the Hinatuan passage, the waterway of Mindanao Island and Leyte Island, anchoring at Panaon Island, the southern section of Leyte at a village called Son-Ok. There were white buoys that marked a fish sanctuary, a local on a small *bangka* said anchoring there was alright, but a couple of hours later, another *bangka* came up to me, requesting that I move to another location only half a mile away.

CHAPTER NINETEEN

The next morning, this was what I wrote in the log: *A magical mist covering the mountains as some of the mountains on the island rise to just under 700 metres.*

I hoisted the asymmetrical in the light winds and sailed up along the Leyte coast. I had arranged to have *Never Die Wondering II* hauled out at Port Carmen on the island of Cebu. She needed an anti-foul paint job that was at least a year overdue, and I had noticed while cleaning under the vessel some fibre-glass damage at the bow under the waterline. Besides, there were many other jobs like rigging as it was nearly ten years old, along with survey report for insurance reasons. I anchored at the entrance of the Matalom River as it would be just a comfortable one-day sail to Port Carmen. I went ashore to check out the town and was approached by a group of unofficial ports people who produced their coconut brew for me to drink. Well, a courtesy sip was had, and then, I explored the town after a meal at a local premises.

Log: Monday, 26 February 2024; depart 0540 hours.

Heading west across the Camotes Sea, a booby bird flew along with me for a long time, now and then diving into the water to feed as if he was showing off. The huge island of Cebu appeared soon, and I entered into Port Carmen at 1400 hours. A little concerning entry as it was a bit of a maze trying to get to this shipyard. Many enormous old ships were moored, and a few small reefs had to be carefully dodged. There were no markers, just the charts to guide you through. The owner, Zeke, and the American feller who had lived for many years in the Philippines had established the yard many years ago. They built a bar cum restaurant too. As soon as I arrived, he and his crew were there to tie the mooring lines right in front of the bar. *Very appropriate,* I thought. Anyway, it was back to work on the vessel.

CHAPTER TWENTY

Its normal pace, even with the threat of a gale. How long will it last, this peace I have found at sea? It is all of life that I contemplate—sun, clouds, time that passes and abides. Occasionally it is also that other world, foreign now, that I left centuries ago. The modern, artificial world where man has been turned into a money-making machine to satisfy false needs, false joys.

Bernard Moitessier

Port Carmen

I ended up seven weeks at Port Carmen which I had thought would be two weeks at the most. Well, that's sailing! More waiting for the right weather or repairs to vessels than sailing at sea. The tide was very fickle where the high tide wasn't as high as needed to get *Never Die Wondering II* up onto the dry. We did try during the night but the tide was still not high enough. I had to do the hull and fibre-glass work, and anti-foul paint with just enough time for the keels to be exposed on the low tide with blocks underneath to get the jobs done. I was frantically working during the two low tides. The workers in the yard were fantastic as they hand cleaned by sandpaper, put on primer, then had the anti-foul painted.

Prior to this, we angle-grinded the small damage on the bow under the waterline to discover that it was an old injury and only been bogged for a repair. This time, it was properly fibre glassed. Incredibly, the workers would dive at night under the vessel to wedge in timber pieces so as the vessel would not move on the high tide. I changed the sail-drive oil, put *Propspeed* on the propellers, changed anodes, and back into the berth or rafted up to all the other yachts.

CHAPTER TWENTY

A little too quick than I wanted as there was many smaller jobs remained, but I could not do them due to the rush of the tides. It was time to renew the standard rigging, but the type I required was not available. I had a surveyor fly in from Manila for I needed a report for insurance purposes. Several parts were needed like pumps, starter motors, etc. so the waiting game happened again. There was a great electrician who assisted me for many small jobs. The workers who were employed were super and incredibly cheap. As far as staying in Port Carmen is concerned, it was the dustiest place I had ever encountered. Large ships were being sand-blasted along with cement being delivered that created clouds of dust, and the vessels were covered in a blackish dirt, so not good for one's lungs. I just kept saying, it is a shipyard so what does one expect.

The bar was great, and I met many interesting people. They had meat pies available purchased from an expat Australian. I did a trip south and swam with the whale sharks. Finally, when all the parts arrived, I was away again, destination Palawan on the South China Sea.

Log: Monday, 15 April 2024; Departed for Camotes Islands.

I was glad to be away, motoring out past the many ships being worked on, away from the noise and dust. A quick sail across Camotes Sea and I anchored at a beautiful place named Santiago, a small village on the southwest side of Pacijan Island. Pacijan along with Poro and Ponson islands are referred to as Camotes Islands. I was glad to be making water, as fresh water was a scarcity at the shipyard. I spent a couple of days washing clothes and cleaning the entire vessel with high-pressure spray. Santiago had a great beach with several sheds that prepared meals. I ate the *adobo* squid or grilled, and cheap beers of *San Mig Light*.

After a few days, I moved further around the island anchoring on the west side near Mangodlong Rock, away from the rolling anchorage of Santiago. I was to spend over two weeks at Camotes Islands, so I hired a motorbike for exploring these wonderful islands that had many small villages. They had a large freshwater lake on the northern parts of Pacijan and several caves filled with fresh water to have a dip along with the many bats. I made a ferry trip back to the Immigration at Cebu to extend the visa and collect propellers for the outboard and returned ready to continue exploring more islands heading northwest while the trade winds continued.

Log: Friday, 3 May 2024; Depart 0540 hours; Destination Malapascua Island.

With full sails, I headed northwest. An incredibly large dolphin pod swam by that may have had fifty dolphins or more. The wind was up to fifteen knots, creating comfortable sailing except for the dreaded FADs that were very hard to see. I anchored in front of the lighthouse on Malapascua, near a Japanese wreck. I dived to explore the wreck the next day, it still had the entire layout of the once vessel that came to its end during World War II.

The islands have become a diving spot for sighting thresher sharks. After being out with the whale sharks at Oslob, I didn't like the tourist side of it and was not interested in any touristy venture to see the sharks. The school kids on the island were selling timber carved sharks to raise money for their school, so I bought a small carving. I spent my time meeting the local fishermen and women making nets on the beaches under the shade of a tarp. Incredible little villages with no cars, only walking paths throughout the village with little stores selling goods.

Log: Sunday, 5 May 2024; Depart 0610 hours.

A sunny day with light winds, so up went asymmetrical and I made 5.0 knots SOG all the way past Hagdan Island. Then, onto Bantayan Island dodging one FAD after another, I sailed down the west side of the island anchoring a long way out from the shore in shallow waters as it wasn't clear enough. I contemplated exploring this large island but decided against it because how many islands can you really explore? Hypothetically, if you explored the 7,000 islands and spent a week on every island that would take you 134 years! So many places to see and so little time to see them, I would just anchor for the night and be away at the first light.

The Island of Giants – Islas de Gigantes

At 0555 hours, I raised the main and sailed off after weighing anchor in the light, north-easterly winds. I beam reached as I headed northwest to Gigantes Islands. Just when you think it cannot get better, it does. This was the most picture perfect of islands, several in total, and I anchored at the first small island known as Antonia. It had a rocky knoll, a white sandy beach, a rising tree-covered hill, and coconuts between clear water. Legend has it that human skeletons were found in a cave that were of gigantic humans, hence, the name Gigantes. I stayed for three days exploring by tender an enclosed lagoon on the main island and visiting Bantigui Island where the fishermen families cook you a meal. I ate their local squid catch along with *San Mig* beers. Many large turtles can be seen around the island.

Log: Wednesday, 8 May 2024; depart 0540 hours.

I headed west over the top of Panay Island, a huge triangular island larger than Cebu. The winds became light and the asymmetrical went up. The amount of bamboo poles in the water indicating traps were prolific and I was dodging these obstacles. Clearly, impossible to sail at night. I made my way into Capiz Bay amongst the fishing traps, it was difficult to see through the water as the river systems with the recent rains guaranteed murky waters. So, I anchored in four metres between two large bamboo structures.

The next day, I repeated the routine of dodging timber structures and sailing to the well-known tourist destination of Boracay Island. On a north-westerly sail, I made good speed despite the hazards and did fifty-seven nautical miles. Coming into Boracay from the northern side, large high-rise buildings came into view. Sailing down the west coast of this island, the view was of hundreds of boats and paragliders. I counted twenty-four individual parasails in the air. A very difficult anchorage as the entire west side has large coral gardens. The one on the south-western side seemed to be on swing mooring and that was dominated by passenger vessels and the craft that drag parasails. I found a small patch of sand and dropped anchor, but I also dived making sure it was secure in the sand.

People who know me had said that I would not like the place, and they were right. Boats speeding past while dragging people on inflatable crafts, rolling anchorage where you were only able to take a dingy to the beach on the southern section. It was a party capital full of western tourists, and even had a *KFC*. Although, I met a few expats at their local bar away from the hustle and bustle of the tourist capital. Far away from the main strip, is the real Boracay. A market with great produce of fresh fish, fruit, and veggies, Filipino markets do not disappoint.

Log: Monday, 13 May 2024.

I tried to get an early start but had the chain wrapped around a coral head which took several dives to untangle. You need to dive down to see how and where it is tangled, so as to decide which way to drive out, right, left, forward, or back. So, a simple move in the correct way, and then free to winch up the chain. After that, it was brilliant sailing downwind with the conventional spinnaker. I really pushed it that day, the waves were white tipped, and I reached speeds 10.5 knots SOG. I wrote in the log how it was one of the best days of sailing I have had, comfortable and at high speed.

I passed Semirara Island on the northern side and could clearly see the coal mining effects. Big tipper trucks were dumping the tailings from the extensive mines into the sea. After checking the charts, I quickly realised that the island had become much larger since the charts commenced as the tailings were now being dumped further north into what was once the sea. Another good reason not to sail at night in the Philippines. I decided to anchor in a lagoon on Ambulong, a small island south and close to the island of Mindoro, also the island where General McArthur landed on during World War II.

Coming into the lagoon, I relied on my satellite imagery that clearly showed the passage was coral free but then, I felt a pull to the portside. I had somehow managed to have a mooring line tangle under the rudder. No drama, as I was travelling at a very slow speed, but I needed to put on goggles to jump overboard to remove the line. It didn't need cutting as it had only just caught. I continued into this well-protected lagoon. This was a special moment as I had decided to head south afterwards to explore the island of Palawan. With the onset of the southwest monsoonal, I needed to be south of 10°N. This was the furthest north I was going, Latitude 12'11.826 Longitude 121'1.554.

I was a long way since 38°S in freezing Bass Strait, Southern Australia. I spent a couple of nights in the lagoon, resting up from a chest cold. In the evening, I watched the local fisherman paddle out on a bamboo raft with all his children aboard, and another small vessel coming from

CHAPTER TWENTY

the opposite direction and smashing the water that sounded like the hollow sounds of bamboo hitting water to funnel fish into their traps.

Log: Wednesday, 15 May 2024; depart 0600 hours.

The South China Sea was now to my starboard side. Elon Musk must not have liked me sailing there for he quickly stopped my *Starlink* sending a text saying, I must use it only on land or update to another plan. No wonder he is worth billions!

I was able to goose wing the sails comfortably moving along at 5.1 knots SOG in the following seas. What a marvellous sight coming into Coron! It can only be described as spectacular with their steep greyish limestone rugged terrain. Most areas are a sheer drop into the sea, I sailed on the northern side of Coron Island, and on the southern side of Busuanga Island, only half a mile wide. I tried to find a place to anchor at Coron Island but it was too deep to anchor, so I opted for the safer anchorage at the Coron Port on Busuanga Island anchoring on the north-west side of the port itself.

I spent six days around the Coron Island and township, I would tender over to the island, exploring the lagoons, two of which are freshwater lagoons. You can walk from the sea lagoons up and over the rocks to two of these fascinating freshwater ones. I saw a large, lace monitor very similar to the Australian goanna. Back at Coron township, I carted fuel by Tuk-tuk and tender and stocked up with fresh produce. I also headed to a bay fifteen miles away where I had heard that an American war plane had crashed and was still visible. I searched the satellite imagery and found it clearly lying in the waterway.

I sailed up through these magnificent islands and anchored in a sheltered bay, near two other yachties. Incredibly, one of the yachties' name was Skip and he was an American Horseman. He had moved to Australia in the 80s working on a cattle station near my property at Tumbarumba. Later, he took up sailing and spent many years living between Philippines and Malayasia. I visited the plane that was in the next cove from where I was anchored and what a sight the plane was. It had a long wingspan of thirty metres, being alloy it had not weathered much in forty years. Even in the high tide, most of the plane was above the water line. Apparently, the pilot survived and although the plane was in good order, it landed on the water and rested only on the muddy area near the mangroves where it was abandoned.

There was a resort nearby up a steep hill with many steps. It had spectacular views of the sunset, and several of us anchored in the cove had dinner at this premises. In order to leave, you had to partially slide down a concrete slide, back to the water. A potential typhoon was predicted, building up in the Pacific that could possibly come across the Philippines. So, I decided to stay as there were great bolt holes in the mangrove river and creeks close by. The low-pressure system brought torrential rains and lightning bolts along with many squalls. One night, the wind was of gale force that caused me to drag a little, but the high winds were over as quick as they came. My 2KVA generator came to its end of life, so I needed to start motors to charge batteries as there was no sun due to the clouds. I stayed in the cove for a week writing my memoirs after which the low pressure dispatched, and the rain eased. It was time to explore again.

Log: Thursday, 30 May 2024.

I had dodged fishing vessels nets, bamboo timber structures, FADs, and this time, it was the dodging of pearl farms that were all connected with black buoys nearly impossible to see. While passing the top north side of Culion Island, they seemed to just appear out of nowhere, jump out in front of you. I dropped sails and only motored, in case I needed to quickly stop. At one stage, I found myself surrounded by black buoys. I had managed to drive into the pearl farm incredibly without hitting a single one. I quickly circled back finding a passage through this nightmare of obstacles. At another instance, I noticed what seemed to be the hull of a boat just below the water line, that connected the pearl nets! Imagine sailing over the top of it, guaranteed hitting it with my keels. I sailed between Galoc and Popototan islands and anchored in a cove in the latter protected from the south-westerlies.

The South China Sea

Log: Friday, 31 May 2024; depart 0700 hours.

I sailed out of the passage into the South China Sea. It was an incredible feeling knowing that China was only 600 nautical miles away, and

CHAPTER TWENTY

Vietnam, 500 nautical miles. I headed south as the plan was to explore Palawan and got closer to the 10°N, away from typhoons passing the western side of Culion Island that was twenty km in length. It was called the island of the living dead or the island of no return as the Philippines declared it to house anyone affected by leprosy, back in the last century. Culion quickly became the largest leprosy colony in the world.

I made my way to Linapacan Island and anchored in a cove where the water was so clear, I could clearly see the ripples of the sand several metres deep. Surrounded by hills and scenic rocky type islets, it was a good place. Palawan was not to disappoint, I would make my way to El Nido, a known tourist town on the west coast of Palawan with its high sheer drop limestone cliffs that seem to fall into the sea. I explored another bay, Inlulutoc Bay anchoring in a quite bay with no one living there.

It seems everywhere you go in the Philippines, the islands are occupied with people, and so much terrain is farmed regardless of how steep it is. However, this bay was surrounded by native jungle, sandy beaches, and coral gardens. While I kayaked along a rocky foreshore, I got up close to a large monkey that watched me for a little while then clambered back into the forest. At this point of my sailing journey, I am sitting on my yacht at Port Barton, a quite village that has a striking mountainous forest that stretches down to the village itself. A brilliant wide sheltered bay ideal for anchoring. The monsoonal is here, just as it was when I started writing my memoirs over two years ago during the monsoonal in Darwin, Australia.

The great sailor and adventurer, Bernard Moitessier said that he found the holy grail to be the sea and all it has to offer. Well, I found my holy grail so to speak a very long time ago. It was in the mountains above the worry line which is 1100 metres above sea level where the peppermint gums grow, the air is clear, and the excitement of my horse taking me higher into the alpine ranges.

I have since substituted the High Country and horses with the sea and by sailing. It turns out that my holy grail has always been freedom, living life on my terms. Now, I am heading towards the age of sixty, the hourglass naturally has not as much sand left as it originally had, but as long as there is passion with purpose, and my health allows, I will continue to live an adventurous life.

"An adventurer, a free-spirited person must never conform to other people's expectations. It is essential to live your dreams, to explore and to discover. Anything less would eventually lead to a life of regret, pursue the ultimate goal to never-die- wondering".

Alistair J MacLeod

If by Rudyard Kipling

If you can keep your head when all about you
　　Are losing theirs and blaming it on you,
If you can trust yourself when all men doubt you,
　　But make allowance for their doubting too;
If you can wait and not be tired by waiting,
　　Or being lied about, don't deal in lies,
Or being hated, don't give way to hating,
　　And yet don't look too good, nor talk too wise:

If you can dream—and not make dreams your master;
If you can think—and not make thoughts your aim;
　　If you can meet with Triumph and Disaster
　　And treat those two impostors just the same;
If you can bear to hear the truth you've spoken
　　Twisted by knaves to make a trap for fools,
Or watch the things you gave your life to, broken,
And stoop and build 'em up with worn-out tools:

　　If you can make one heap of all your winnings
　　　　And risk it on one turn of pitch-and-toss,
　　And lose, and start again at your beginnings
　　　　And never breathe a word about your loss;
　　If you can force your heart and nerve and sinew
　　　　To serve your turn long after they are gone,
　　And so hold on when there is nothing in you
　　Except the Will which says to them: 'Hold on!'

If you can talk with crowds and keep your virtue,
Or walk with Kings—nor lose the common touch,
If neither foes nor loving friends can hurt you,
If all men count with you, but none too much;
If you can fill the unforgiving minute
With sixty seconds' worth of distance run,
Yours is the Earth and everything that's in it,
And—which is more—you'll be a Man, my son!

INSPIRING QUOTES FROM MY LIFE AT SEA

1. *Twenty years from now you will be more disappointed by the things that you didn't do than by the ones you did, so throw off the bowlines, sail away from the safe harbor, catch the trade wind in your sails, explore, dream, discover. (Mark Twain)*
   Adventure may hurt you, but monotony will kill you.
2. *Fill your life with adventures, not things, have stories to tell, not stuff to show.*
3. *Life is not measured by the number of breaths we take, but those moments that take our breath away. (Maya Angelou)*
4. *When you follow the crowd, you will lose yourself, but when you follow your soul, you will lose the crowd. Eventually, your soul tribe will appear. But do not fear the process of solitude.*
   Fear kills more dreams than failure ever will.
5. *It's impossible," said doubt. "It's dangerous," said fear. "It's pointless," said reason. "Give it a try," whispered the heart.*
6. *Jobs may fill your pockets, but adventure will fill your soul.*
7. *Who is a happier man, he who has braved the storm of life and lived or he who has stayed ashore securely and merely existed? (Hunter S. Thompson)*
8. *The distance between your dreams and reality is called action.*
9. *At sea I have learned how little a person needs, not how much a person needs.*
   The cost of not following your heart is spending the rest of your life wishing you had.
   Mine was not the sort of life to make one long to coil up one's ropes on land, the customs and ways of which I had almost forgotten...I was born in the breezes, and I had studied the sea. (Joshua Sloccum)

10. *Not all who wander are lost.* (JRR Tolkien)
    Let time be your ally and patience be your friend.
11. *I had inheritance from my father, it was the moon and the sun and although I roam all over the world the spending of it is never done.* (Ernest Hemingway)
    Why do old men wake so early? Is it to have a longer day?
    Never let the sun beat you in the morning.
12. *I sail not to escape life, but for life not to escape me.*
    Marinas are like crab pots easy to get in but hard to get out.
    Your yacht is similar to an island, it can be your refuge or quickly become your prison.
13. *The greatest risk in the world is to take no risk at all.*
14. *There are only two times in life, either right now, or too late.*
    The best place to be is here, and the best time to be here is now!
15. *To desire nothing beyond what you have is surely happiness aboard a boat, it is frequently possible to achieve just that, that is why sailing is a way of life, one of the finest lives.*
    Travelling leaves you speechless then turns you into a storyteller.
16. *The world is a huge place. How will you know where you fit in unless you explore beyond your comfort zone?* (Ernest Shackleton)
17. *The hardest sailing is the one you make alone. That is the sail that makes you strong, confident, independent, and fearless.*
    I try to leave a little extra on the table during a deal, most times it is returned in appreciation.
18. *When asked, what is the biggest mistake one can make in life, the Buddha replied, the biggest mistake is you think you have time.*
    Man cannot discover new oceans, unless he has the courage to leave the shore.
19. *A great sailor isn't made from sailing on calm waters.*
    The best place to be is here and the best time to be here is now.
20. *Its normal pace, even with the threat of a gale. How long will it last, this peace I have found at sea? It is all of life that I contemplate—sun, clouds, time that passes and abides. Occasionally it is also that other world, foreign now, that I left centuries ago. The modern, artificial world where man has been turned into a money-making machine to satisfy false needs, false joys.* (Bernard Moitessier)
    An adventurer, a free-spirited person must never conform to other people's expectations. It is essential to live your dreams, to explore and to discover. Anything less would eventually lead to a life of regret, pursue the ultimate goal to never-die- wondering. [Alistair MacLeod]

www.ingramcontent.com/pod-product-compliance
Lightning Source LLC
Chambersburg PA
CBHW051422290426
44109CB00016B/1394